D1419971

WE CAN SPEAK FOR OURSELVES

HUMAN HORIZONS SERIES

WE CAN SPEAK FOR OURSELVES

Self-Advocacy by Mentally Handicapped People

PAUL WILLIAMS and BONNIE SHOULTZ

A CONDOR BOOK
SOUVENIR PRESS (E & A) LTD

1698980

Copyright © 1982 Paul Williams & Bonnie Shoultz

First published 1982 by Souvenir Press
(Educational & Academic) Ltd,
43 Great Russell Street, London WC1B 3PA
and simultaneously in Canada
Reissued 1991

All Rights Reserved. No part of this publication
may be reproduced, stored in a retrieval system,
or transmitted, in any form or by any means, electronic,
mechanical, photocopying, recording or otherwise without
the prior permission of the Copyright owner

ISBN 0 285 64938 8 casebound
ISBN 0 285 64939 6 paperback

Photoset in Monophoto Times New Roman by
Servis Filmsetting Ltd, Manchester and
printed in Great Britain by Ebenezer Baylis & Son Ltd,
The Trinity Press, Worcester, and London

You may say I'm a dreamer,
But I'm not the only one. . .

John Lennon
'Imagine'
(Northern Songs)

CONTENTS

ACKNOWLEDGEMENTS

We would both like to give special thanks to our families for tolerance while we were writing this book. Among the others to whom we owe much gratitude are:

In America
All the members of Project Two for their constant inspiration and friendship.

The individual members of Project Two who kindly contributed to Chapter One.

The mentally handicapped people in other parts of America who kindly contributed to Chapter Two.

People First International and their adviser Dennis Heath, for generous supply of information and support.

Jean Edwards of the Special Educational Department of Portland State University, Oregon, for sharing information collected for a book she is writing about the People First movement.

Jeff Woodyard, formerly of the Technical Assistance for Self-Advocacy project at the University of Kansas, for generous supply of materials and information.

The National Institute on Mental Retardation, Toronto, for permission to quote from *Normalisation* by Wolfensberger in Chapter Three.

People First International for kind permission to quote from their publications, especially in Chapter Four.

Annette Norsman and the Wisconsin Association for Retarded Citizens for permission to quote from the curriculum on self-advocacy in Chapter Five.

12

The Nebraska Advocacy Office for kind permission to reproduce the manual in Appendix Two.

Project Two and People First of Nebraska for kindly allowing us to reproduce the materials in Appendix Three.

The Kansas University Affiliated Facility for kind permission to make numerous quotes from their publications and to reproduce the materials in Appendix Four.

Shirley Dean of the Eastern Nebraska Community Office of Retardation, and Dave Powell, Director of the Nebraska Association for Retarded Citizens, for commenting on early drafts of chapters.

Staff of the Boystown Center for the Study of Youth Development, especially Stephen Greenspan for generous support and practical assistance, and Thomas Coles and Robert Dellinger for helpful advice.

In Britain
Alan Tyne of the Community and Mental Handicap Educational and Research Association who made the original suggestion for a British look . at American self-advocacy groups, which provided the inspiration for this book.

All the members of the Avro Adult Training Centre Students' Council, and Carol Scott, their adviser, and Mary Malinowski, the centre manager, for offering the opportunity to see self-advocacy in action in Britain.

The individual members of the Avro Students' Council who kindly contributed to Chapter Six.

David Russell, a student at Avro ATC, for kindly taking and supplying photographs.

Bronach Crawley of the Hester Adrian Research Centre, University of Manchester, for supplying information from her survey of ATC committees, and for help in identifying and contacting the committees mentioned in Chapter Six.

The managers of the centres, and the members and advisers of the trainee committees or students' councils, at Ditton Walk ATC, Cambridge; the Senior Training Centre, Mitcham;

Lisson Grove Social and Education Centre, City of Westminster, London; Perryfields ATC, Worcester; Conisbrough ATC, Yorkshire; and Crown Hill Workshops, Sheffield, for kindly supplying information about their work and written contributions for Chapter Six.

Helen Berent of Network for the Handicapped for useful information and guidance for Chapter Six.

The Association of Professions for the Mentally Handicapped for permission to quote from one of their publications in Chapter Six.

The National Society for Mentally Handicapped Children and Adults for permission to quote from *Tongue Tied* in Chapter Six, and from the STAMINA Papers in Appendix One.

Ann Shearer and the Campaign for Mentally Handicapped People for permission to quote from the 'Our Life' and 'Listen' conference reports in Chapter Six, and to reproduce materials in Appendix Five.

The Avro ATC Students' Council for permission to reproduce their Constitution in Appendix Five.

The staff of Castle Priory College for support and practical assistance.

Northern Songs Limited, for permission to quote the two lines from John Lennon's composition 'Imagine', which preface the book.

INTRODUCTION

A most exciting, impressive and politically powerful development has taken place in America in recent years. Groups of mentally handicapped people have been taught to organise their affairs, run meetings, take decisions and carry them through, with minimal help from non-handicapped people. The groups call this development 'self-advocacy'.

Typically, the founder-members of self-advocacy groups are mentally handicapped people with good social and communication skills, often people who have been in institutions. To a generous extent these people have identified with the problems and needs of all handicapped people, including those with much more severe handicaps, and have welcomed them into their groups.

A small number of non-handicapped people is involved in an initial process of teaching members of the group about their rights and how to claim them, and about running an organisation. After this initial stage, the involvement of non-handicapped people is reduced to the level of providing occasional advice and assistance to the group when requested.

Statewide and national conventions of self-advocacy groups have been held, giving a clear and powerful voice to mentally handicapped people themselves. An international self-advocacy movement of 'People First' groups is emerging.

Mentally handicapped people everywhere are beginning to have a voice of their own. In Britain there are examples of mentally handicapped people speaking for themselves, and of attempts to give mentally handicapped people a greater voice. Self-advocacy by mentally handicapped people is under way in Scandinavia, Canada and Australia.

This self-advocacy challenges traditional views of mental handicap. It addresses itself to the fundamental issue of our expectations of mentally handicapped people, who have historically been among the most devalued, neglected and

15

abused groups in society. The contemporary movements of deinstitutionalisation and normalisation seek to remedy this by enabling mentally handicapped people to play valued roles in society, to claim a valued status for themselves, and to be seen by others as valued people – in other words, to become true and equal citizens of their local community.

There is no better way to help a mentally handicapped person to become a true citizen than to give him the opportunity for self-advocacy. Self-advocacy means self-respect, respect by others, a new independence, assertiveness and courage. It involves seriousness, political purpose and an understanding of rights, responsibilities and the democratic process.

One remarkable example of a self-advocacy group is the group in Omaha, Nebraska, called 'Project Two'. The group was founded in 1975 by a mentally handicapped man, Ray Loomis, and now functions as a well-knit and highly motivated group of mentally handicapped people in and around the city, pursuing important issues of relevance to them with the help of a very small number of non-handicapped people who act as advisers only. Its membership is over 100 people.

They are people who have demonstrated: 'We Can Speak for Ourselves'. . . .

1 THE STORY OF PROJECT TWO

> If you think you are handicapped,
> you might as well stay indoors.
> If you think you are a person,
> come out and tell the world.

Raymond Loomis

The Background

Since 1968, Omaha, Nebraska, USA, has been recognised nationally and internationally for its community-based services to mentally handicapped people.

Before 1968, the families of virtually all of the state's mentally handicapped citizens had only two alternatives: their son or daughter either stayed at home with no services, or resided in the one state hospital for mentally handicapped people, known then as the Beatrice State Home. The State Home was charged with the responsibility of providing care to an ever-growing number of mentally handicapped people. By 1968, approximately 2,400 people lived at the Beatrice State Home, where the facilities were very old and overcrowded and the staffing levels were very low. A number of the buildings in use in 1968 had been condemned for years as unfit for human habitation. The kitchen was similarly condemned.

A study in 1968 showed that twice as much money per capita was spent on the large animals in the Kansas City Zoo as was spent on the human beings at Beatrice.

This study, prepared by a Citizens' Study Committee appointed by the Governor of Nebraska, had been requested by members of the Nebraska Association for Retarded Children. The study recommended both that conditions be measurably improved at the Beatrice State Home, and that a comprehensive system of services be provided in the state's communities so that people could remain at home or close to home. It proposed that the population of Beatrice be reduced to 850 people in six years (the population is now under 600).

While the Governor's Study Committee was preparing its recommendations, a similar committee made up of parents and professionals was working in Omaha. This committee wrote a plan for services to be developed at the local level and persuaded the Douglas County Board of Commissioners, who govern the county of which Omaha is a part, to provide funds to start the first services. The Douglas County Plan stated that mentally handicapped people should be perceived as human beings, citizens and potential contributors to their communities, rather than as objects of pity or burdens of charity.

The report argued that community-based services would enable mentally handicapped people to be perceived in a more positive light, and it demonstrated how the county could provide those services. The Douglas County Board approved the plan, and the first publicly funded services were opened in 1968 by the Greater Omaha Association for Retarded Children (GOARC). By 1970, other counties had joined with Douglas County to form the Eastern Nebraska Community Office of Retardation (ENCOR), an agency which took over the services begun by GOARC two years earlier.

Beginning in 1968, Beatrice State Home officials began to move as many residents as possible out of the institution. Many people were placed in employment in nursing homes and given as little as $5 a month plus room and board to care for elderly and sick people. Others were placed in badly run and neglectful boarding houses where they lived while holding a community job. Some were placed in nursing homes for elderly people, as patients, even though many of them were young adults. Few of the people placed in such situations had much support or casework assistance, as the social worker from Beatrice spent only one day per month in Omaha. As a result, many people were treated badly and exploited financially when they first came out of Beatrice.

Finally, Beatrice agreed to fund a liaison worker at GOARC to monitor the placement of these people. At GOARC (and later at ENCOR), this person located many of the people and helped them to find competitive jobs and more appropriate living situations where there was better supervision by the agency. Later, the inappropriate placements were ended through an agreement that every person brought out of Beatrice into Omaha must be placed through ENCOR. ENCOR then became the agency responsible for providing and arranging services for all the mentally handicapped people in the Eastern Nebraska region.

Since then, ENCOR has built up comprehensive community-based facilities of worldwide renown, including a pattern of residential services that uses solely ordinary housing.

Project Two's Beginnings

Few of the mentally handicapped people who came to Omaha from Beatrice realised that they were pioneers of a grand new movement called 'deinstitutionalisation'. Many had tried for years to get out of Beatrice, and for them their highest goal was to stay out, become independent and belong to some small part of the community. Many found the move frightening at first, but they courageously accepted the challenge. Most were also willing to use the supports offered to them by ENCOR and GOARC. They realised that they might need to be dependent for a while, as they worked towards achieving independence.

A growing realisation that the most natural and desirable human state is interdependence, rather than either dependence or independence, led one man to create an idea for a self-help group for people who had been in the institution. This man, Raymond Loomis, had this 'brainstorm' (as he called it) because he saw people struggling and having problems as they adjusted to life in the community.

Ray had his brainstorm in 1975, seven years after he left Beatrice. He had been in Beatrice from 1953 to 1968, a fifteen year period of institutionalisation which had included several attempts to escape and a prediction by the superintendent when he was released in 1968 that he wouldn't succeed for more than three days on the outside.

During his seven years outside, Ray had had many problems as well as successes, and because of his experiences he felt that people who were leaving the institution needed a group to belong to – a group whose focus was on helping its members to face problems. Although neither he nor any of the ENCOR or GOARC staff who helped him had ever heard of 'self-advocacy', Ray knew instinctively that the group must be self-directing. He saw that the members of the group who were not mentally handicapped should be supporters and helpers but not leaders. He knew and acted on this even though it was two years before the group even defined itself as a group for mentally handicapped people. In those early days it was seen as a group for everyone.

A Leader Develops

Ray worked hard to start Project Two. He asked GOARC to sponsor the group and provide meeting space. He asked others to inform as many mentally handicapped people as possible about the first meetings. He considered names for the group, finally choosing 'Project Two' because it sounded better than 'Rap Session' – his first choice – and because local initiative had got one innovative project going (ENCOR) and he wanted to start another. He thought about the purposes of the group and led discussions during the first three meetings on those purposes and on the individual and shared problems of the members. As he did all of these things, he learned how to be a leader.

Only three people came to the first meeting, but by the end of the year up to 40 were attending. In the first meetings, most of the group members thought the leaders were the three 'professionals' (Shirley Dean, Tom Miller and Bonnie Shoultz) who were present. Questions, for example, were often directed to one of the non-handicapped people rather than to Ray, because even those who were much older had always been led, directed and cared for by parents or professionals and therefore had rarely experienced self-direction, especially in a group setting. Whenever questions or statements were directed to a non-handicapped participant, that person would turn her eyes towards Ray for the answer, so that attention and eye contact would be shifted to him. Group members began to identify Ray as their leader and his voice as their own. A growing willingness to rely on their leader to speak for them, and to help them to speak on their own behalf, encouraged many to make an internal shift to a belief that they could shape their own destinies. Of course, this shift took place at different times for different individuals in the group.

Ray steadily uncovered and cultivated new leadership skills, both within himself and in other members of the group. At the end of three years, Ray had become a master at capturing and holding the attention of large audiences, engaging them through the use of humour, original sayings and brief but pithy explanations of ideas.

The Group Develops an Identity

Groups are formed in response to a need. Their first order of business is orientation – development of a purpose and a direction which will orient group members towards resolution of a problem or achievement of a goal.

The development of any group tends to follow a pattern. During a first stage, formal organisational structures are adopted and activities are held to forge a group identity. Action and evaluation characterise the second stage. Group members develop skills and learn how to act together to achieve their purposes. Leaders emerge from the ranks as responsibilities are assigned and carried out. Periodically, the group's actions are evaluated, at least by the leaders, and new directions may be proposed as a result of what is discovered in the evaluation. The third stage is one of mastery. Group process is understood, as are the necessary tasks, and the group functions smoothly. If crises arise, the group handles them without disintegrating. The group is able to achieve its goals, and the members have developed skills and confidence as a result of their membership.

Project Two developed through these stages, as do other groups. Because its members lacked group experience, each stage may have taken longer to pass through. The process, however, was essentially the same.

The first meetings were tentative. Goals and purposes of the group were discussed, as well as individual problems of members. While rights were not a major concern in these first meetings, social activities were important in several ways. The group first learned to vote when it became necessary to choose between suggested social activities. Voting was recognised as a way to arrive at decisions and to resolve differences of opinion. The social activities also built members' commitment to each other and to the group as a whole. These activities, which included a dance and a Christmas party, provided the group with tangible goals and gave members experience in choosing, planning and carrying out activities that were meaningful to all. The sense of accomplishment at the end of such an activity was obvious, especially because each activity drew new people to the group.

The non-handicapped members supported the group in each activity, helping members to learn to identify the steps involved in planning an event, helping them to learn to accept respons- ibility for carrying out the specified tasks, and ensuring as subtly as possible that the necessary jobs were done. Because the first activities were relatively simple, success was ensured and members' sense of mastery was complete. At the end of the year they felt prepared to organise a more complicated activity – an overnight camping trip.

The first year brought other changes as well. Midway through that year, Ray asked the group if they would like to elect officers. He realised that in suggesting this he risked not being chosen as group leader, but when the response was enthusiastically positive an election was arranged. In the event, Ray was elected President. The other new officers of Project Two were: Tom Houlihan, Vice-President; Ollie Rector, Treasurer; and Bonnie Shoultz, Secretary. Most self-advocacy groups have no non-handicapped officers. Project Two, however, defined the Secretary's position as one of keeping minutes of meetings, writing correspondence and carrying out directives given by the group members.

The election was an important step towards the development of a formal organisational structure for the group. The elected officers immediately began to grow into their new roles. Ollie Rector suggested that members could contribute to a 'kitty' each month and that a savings account be opened at the bank. Tom Houlihan began to look for ways to generate publicity for the group and to provide information to the public.

Continued Growth
Project Two's second year was a year for building skills and exploring ideas, especially ideas about self-advocacy. The group entered the 'action and evaluation' stage of group development. The year began with a plan to hold an overnight camping trip, and it ended with the resolution that Project Two would spread its ideas across the state and would host a statewide convention focusing on self-advocacy. The camping trip provided an opportunity for group members to develop many skills, and these skills were later used in planning the first convention.

An awareness of the concept of self-advocacy did not come, however, until the group had been meeting for nearly two years. During the early months of 1977 they learned about People First (the group first formed in Oregon – see Chapter Two) and decided that, as a group, they would learn to speak for themselves and learn about their rights. This decision – the spark that kindled the growth that followed – required a variety of new actions.

In May 1977, ENCOR held a public forum to launch its new planning process. Project Two members participated heavily, with many members standing before the microphone to tell ENCOR's planning committee that they wanted to stay in the community and they thought all people should have the chance to do the same. Several members spoke about specific service needs. When a group of parents whose children were still in the institution spoke against ENCOR and in favour of the institution, Project Two members reacted by contrasting their very negative experiences in Beatrice to the experiences they had had with ENCOR and with community living. It was the first time that mentally handicapped people in Nebraska had spoken out publicly for themselves and against institutionalisation of people with handicaps. It may also have been the first time that county officials, businessmen and others really listened to what mentally handicapped people had to say. Speaking out for themselves had become a reality.

The minutes of the meetings held during this second year show that Ray thought energetically and creatively about ways to shape the group. He introduced several innovations which strengthened group identity. For example, he learned to create an agenda for meetings and asked that the agenda be sent out with meeting notices. He suggested that, for a six-month period, the meetings be chaired by a rotating set of members. Three men and three women were selected to take turns planning and chairing meetings. Each person tried hard to fulfil the chairperson's role for the meeting he or she chaired. The effect of this was to show everyone that the group was not entirely dependent on Ray, and that many other people could develop skills that could enhance the group and help it to achieve any goals they might select.

Ray also led discussions on philosophical questions such as: 'What is Project Two?'; 'What is self-advocacy?'; 'What is a handicap?'; or 'What is the role of Shirley Dean, Tom Miller and Bonnie Shoultz?' From these discussions came some of the sayings that Project Two still uses today:

'Everyone has some kind of handicap, to tell the truth about it.'
'If you think you are handicapped, you might as well stay

indoors. **If you think you are a person, come on out and tell the world.'**

'**Self-advocacy is people speaking for themselves.'**

'**Project Two is people helping people.'**

And '**Bonnie, Shirley and Tom (the non-handicapped members) are bystanders. We make the decisions and they stand by to help us.'**

In June of 1977, Project Two saw the film *People First* for the first time. The film shows a statewide convention of mentally handicapped people, organised by People First of Oregon.* The following account is taken from the record of the meeting at which the film was viewed.

Elaine van Wie chaired the meeting and introduced the film. The film showed handicapped people setting up and conducting a conference. They said they spent about six months learning about how to set up a conference before they did so. They showed speakers, voting, and conference members dancing and eating meals together.

Tom Miller asked if people liked the film. Everyone was really enthusiastic.

Ray Loomis said he wanted to go statewide. He had written a letter to Dave Powell (Director of the Nebraska Association for Retarded Citizens) about this. He felt there was a real need for Project Two to be statewide. He asked the group to take time after work sometime and watch how people treat handicapped people in the community. He felt that many handicapped people are shoved aside and treated badly by other people – not by everybody, but by some people. He said that if we were all together, we could educate people better. He thought that we should do a statewide conference like the film showed.

Tom Houlihan: You need backing from people like your Congressmen to do a conference.

Ray Loomis: We don't need to ask for backing, we can do it ourselves. We could ask for their support.

A member: How would we pay for a conference?

Wesley Woodhead: We could raise money.

Rose Riederer: In Midtown 7 we thought about a car wash.

*See Chapter Two.

Ray Loomis: How about a carnival?

Ollie Rector: We could have a sideshow.

Tom Houlihan: You can't do a sideshow, it's not legal.

Ray Loomis: Yes you can do it, if it's clean and decent.

Tom Houlihan: How about if we go nationwide?

Ray Loomis: One step at a time. First we go statewide, and then if we do well we might go nationwide.

The next meeting brought the firm decision that Project Two would hold a statewide convention, as People First of Oregon had done. This determination emerged only after heated discussion, as some members took the pessimistic view that they could not possibly plan and carry out a convention. One person said: 'What would the Mayor say? What would the Governor of Nebraska say? They won't let us have a convention.' These ideas were finally rejected. Ray's stance during this discussion was one of patient faith in his group's abilities. As they discussed their fears, he calmly waited for them to realise that if they wanted it, they could do it. Finally, they voted unanimously in favour of having a statewide convention.

Since the camping trip was planned for August, that same July meeting also brought discussion and reports by each of the committees which had earlier been set up to plan and carry out the camping trip. There was a committee to purchase food, a cooking committee, a clean-up committee and a games committee. The officers of Project Two coordinated the activities of these committees, and Ollie Rector, Treasurer, made sure that each person who wanted to go had paid his or her share. Ollie was also responsible for paying the bills.

The camping trip, which was held at a nearby camp which had cabins and a dining hall and lodge, was a success. The cooking committee prepared the three meals, and the clean-up committee cleaned up afterwards. Another small group led games. This retreat provided the group with the experiences of planning, organising, coordinating and cooperating to pursue a goal. From that time on, there was a greatly increased confidence that they could do whatever they really wanted to do. A camping retreat had ushered Project Two into the 'mastery' stage of group development.

The First Convention

The idea of putting on a statewide convention was exciting, and frightening too, since no one – including the non-handicapped members – had ever planned a convention. Therefore it was necessary to do a great deal of discussing and planning. Who was the convention for? How should Project Two inform others about the convention? When and where would it be? How much would it cost, and how would it be funded? What would the convention do? Who would do everything that must be done?

First, because members felt they needed education and new skills, several meetings were devoted to topics which would help in convention planning and further development of leadership in more members. There were meetings featuring speakers on rights, on problem-solving processes, on team-work and cooperation, on relationships, and on how another state (Kansas) had planned its convention. Second, it was necessary to divide into committees to get the work done. There was a public speaking committee, a publicity committee, and an overall planning committee made up of the officers and the non-handicapped members.

The planning committee made several decisions, some of which have been used in every convention since that first one. First, the convention would be the first meeting of a statewide group to be called 'People First of Nebraska'. Second, the convention would be financially self-supporting, so that the costs would be paid by those who attended instead of by another funding source. It was agreed that if any extra funds were raised or money was left over, it would be used to assist people who otherwise could not afford to go. The advantage in this strategy is that independence has been fostered and maintained, and People First of Nebraska has not become dependent on outside funds. The disadvantages are that some people cannot afford to go, and that less can be done to prepare for the convention because there is no money to hire someone to support the group and organise the convention. For mentally handicapped people, however, it is marvellously liberating to complete a large undertaking without depending on outside sources of funds or staffing.

A third decision was that the most active outreach would be to other mentally handicapped people. Invitations would be extended to physically handicapped people with developmental disabilities such as cerebral palsy and epilepsy, but mentally handicapped people wanted to be in charge, at least for this first convention.

A fourth decision was that the convention would be run by mentally handicapped people, not professionals. The general sessions and the workshops or seminars would all be led by mentally handicapped people. They might invite a non-handicapped person to speak or to assist, but they would prepare and carry out these sessions themselves.

The committees began to meet separately. The public speaking committee included Ray Loomis and his wife Nancy, Ollie and Lowell Rector, and Robert Fox. They asked two ENCOR staff members to help them prepare and give speeches which would interest other mentally handicapped people in their convention. They began to prepare in earnest when they received an invitation to put on a workshop at the annual convention of the Nebraska Association for Retarded Citizens (the parents' voluntary organisation). They developed a routine, divided it up so each person had a part, and practised with tape recorders and in front of friends. They went to the ARC convention and did so well that they received invitations from the community-based programmes in twelve communities to give speeches there. They went to those twelve communities during the next three months (they were up to 300 miles away from Omaha) and recruited over 150 people to come to their own state convention. They told their audiences about Project Two and about self-advocacy, and they told them of their dream of having an organisation called People First of Nebraska.

The publicity committee developed ideas for posters and brochures to publicise Project Two and the state convention. They asked volunteers skilled in public relations to help them, as they lacked the skills necessary for producing these materials. Together they produced an attractive and simple brochure, which is still being used.

The coordinating committee was busy with organisational details, such as where and when the convention was to be, what the agenda would be, who would lead each workshop, what foods would be served, and what other amenities would be made available. They prepared and sent out registration forms which gave costs and a convention agenda. It was to be as much like any other convention as possible, even though the coordinators had only attended one other convention themselves – the convention of the Nebraska Association for Retarded Citizens.

As convention day approached and registrations began to return to the GOARC office, the coordinators called special meetings in which the workshop leaders practised leading group discussions and in which packets were prepared for each participant. The planners met even more frequently to go over the agenda and to prepare themselves to lead the convention.

Convention day finally arrived. Ray Loomis and Ollie Rector led the convention's general sessions. Their task was to explain the proceedings to the 160 people who were there from as far as 300 miles away, a distance covering half the state of Nebraska. Although the participants included many people who were severely handicapped, either physically or in their abilities to communicate, everyone was extremely interested and serious about the proceedings. After the guest speakers had finished, many participants rose to speak about their life experiences and their rights. Even after the group broke up into workshops, people were eager to speak out and did so as they dealt with the workshop topics.

By the end of that first day there was a great sense of sharing and anticipation, a feeling that remained through dinner and a dance which was held that evening to live music. During the dance, groups of people met privately to prepare resolutions for consideration the next morning. When they were finished they went back to the dance floor and enjoyed themselves.

The next morning was open for group discussion and almost all the participants were ready either to propose resolutions or just to listen. As Ray Loomis read some of the resolutions prepared the night before, Ollie Rector scanned the crowd for a reaction. Since many people seemed not to know how to respond, Ollie seized the microphone and said: 'You want that? If you do, raise your hand.' After that, Ray read and Ollie encouraged participation on each resolution. Soon people began to line up behind the microphones in the aisles and to propose resolutions of their own. By the time the morning was half over, 37 resolutions had been adopted (these are reproduced in Appendix Three). It was time to elect statewide officers.

The convention ended with a new set of resolutions, a group

of officers, and a determination to have a convention every year. Since then there have been two conventions, and each has used the framework established at the first. Each has been held on a weekend, starting at 1 p.m. one day and ending at 12 noon the next. Each has had general sessions and workshops, and since more people have come each year there have been more simultaneous workshops. In 1980, there were two workshop sessions in the afternoon with seven workshops being run during each block of time, almost all by mentally handicapped people. In 1980 too, the workshop leaders were from other cities besides Omaha, as there are now active groups in several other places. The agenda of the 1979 convention is reproduced in Appendix Three.

Each convention blends fun with work. There is a dance on Saturday evening, and there are also 'hospitality areas' where self-advocacy groups from several cities provide free soft drinks to conventioneers and tell them about their group and what it does. At each convention the participants assume responsibilities they may never have had in their own communities. For many it is the first time they have ever visited another city or stayed in a hotel by themselves. Although many have come with staff persons, they make it clear upon arrival that they are on their own; staff may provide assistance when needed (for example with medications) but are often asked not to intervene unless a serious problem occurs. Participants have their own hotel rooms, alone or with one or two roommates. The only difference between a People First convention and an ordinary one – according to the hotel managers – is that the People First participants tend to behave more properly; there is much less breakage and noise, they say, in a People First convention than in most other kinds of conventions.

The people who have accomplished all of the things described above are mildly, moderately and severely mentally handicapped. Most cannot read or write. Even more have not yet learned to follow a budget or live independently, although all are moving towards independence at their own speeds. It is true that non-handicapped advisers have been present to provide many kinds of supports, but the people in Project Two and the other self-advocacy groups in Nebraska have found that they are able to support each other and complement each other's skills and thus overcome each other's deficits. A person who reads can help a non-reader to follow an agenda; an able-bodied person can hold a page or a microphone for a person with cerebral palsy; a person who speaks can translate for a person who uses signs; and a person who is hard to understand can teach other members to listen more carefully. The support and teaching that they provide for each other has led to the continued growth and diversification of members' skills and understanding.

Survival

Tom Miller, the Executive Director of GOARC from 1975 to 1978, was one of the key non-handicapped members of Project Two. Ray contacted Tom to sponsor the group in 1975, and he attended almost every meeting for three years. Also, as the first full-time Beatrice liaison worker for the city, Tom had been the first counsellor for many of the members when they had come to Omaha from Beatrice. In 1978, Tom announced that he was leaving Omaha to travel around the world for a year or more. Project Two was strong enough by then to say 'farewell'; they had a calm certainty that the group would continue to function. This experience, as it happened, was important in establishing that the group could survive even if critical members were no longer present.

1979 started out to be a very good year for Ray Loomis. First, he was asked to serve on the GOARC Board of Directors. Then he was selected for the highest award given by GOARC, the Volunteer of the Year Award. In March, a local television station selected Ray as the winner of The Jefferson Award, an award given annually by the television station to people who demonstrate extraordinary volunteer leadership in the community. The nominees each year are Omahans of all kinds, from wealthy businessmen to the very poor like Ray. The local award winner is nominated by the station for a national award; Ray was later among the 16 national finalists for that award as well.

To announce the award, the station prepared a half-hour television programme on Ray. It showed him at home with his wife Nancy and son Billy, at work as a dishwasher for a local restaurant, and of course with Project Two. The reporter interviewed Ray's employer and many of his friends. Public response to the programme, which was shown twice during the month of March, was excellent. Ray and Project Two had significantly enhanced the image of mentally handicapped adults for a whole television viewing area.

Ray also spent that spring working with two other people to give a twelve-session course on self-advocacy (the course content was similar to the Wisconsin curriculum outlined in Chapter Five). This course culminated in a talk by a state legislator and a city councilwoman; the session was taped for the Jefferson Award programme.

That summer Ray received other honours, but his physical stamina slowly deteriorated. One day when he went to the restaurant, his employer told him to leave work and see a doctor. He was admitted that day to a hospital with congestive heart failure due to infection and fluid around the heart. After that had cleared up, Ray learned that he needed open-heart surgery to correct a damaged heart valve. He was in the hospital for two months before his surgery, and his wife Nancy had full responsibility for the first time for their apartment and their two-year-old son Billy. Nancy and Billy visited Ray every day, but Nancy became very apprehensive about Ray's illness and his impending surgery.

Ray's surgery was performed on a Tuesday. There were complications right after the surgery and he was sent back to the operating room for another three hours. He never regained consciousness, and his brain ceased to function on the Thursday.

Nancy, who was supported by family and friends, had felt all along that Ray would die. She understood the doctor well when he explained that Ray's brain had died and that his body, which was being maintained on machines, would cease to function in a matter of days. In spite of her grief, Nancy gave some of her first thoughts to Project Two. Since there was a meeting already scheduled for that Friday night, Nancy decided that that would be the best time to tell everyone that Ray was going to die. She was very concerned that members would not hear about it when they were alone or unsupported. Although several of her non-handicapped friends offered to do it for her, she insisted on handling it herself. She called people to ask them to come to the meeting in support of the members. She asked those she thought were strong – handicapped and non-handicapped alike – to come and support those who were less strong.

First, Nancy decided to tell a few people who would become

most emotional about Ray's condition. Then she would make her announcement to the group. Before the meeting she asked a few people to go into a back room. She explained the situation and asked them to be strong. Then she went out to the group. She announced: 'Ray had open-heart surgery this week. His brain isn't working and he's going to die. The doctor doesn't know exactly when. Ray wanted Project Two to keep on going, and I want that too.' The reaction was a shocked silence and then tears. People held each other and wept until they could calm down.

As people regained control, one member got up and said: 'We should close down Project Two. How can we keep going without Ray?' Nancy repeated very firmly that Project Two was going to go on, because Ray wanted it that way. Soon all of the members agreed that they could work together to keep Project Two going.

Ray died on Monday, 24 September 1979. His funeral was on 26 September. The large church was filled with people from all over Nebraska. Two eulogies were given at the service, the first by Edward Skarnulis, President of GOARC's Board of Directors and a former Director of ENCOR's residential services:

Knowing Ray Loomis was like being sure the sun would come up each morning. You could trust Ray when he said he'd do something. He loved to kid around and joke with people, and was a master at gently putting others in their proper place when they got a little too proud or a little too talkative. But behind the warmth of his laugh and the sparkle in his eye was a serious man who felt a sense of urgency. He knew that someone is sitting on a crowded institution ward somewhere waiting to come home. He knew that someone is staring at a TV set in an apartment, feeling lonely and desperately needing a friend to be with and to talk to.

Ray was a dreamer, but he didn't just hope for dreams to come true. Ray said that when he started Project Two he was scared, but that didn't make him back away. He used to say that he was a person just like anybody else, but that we all have to stand up for ourselves. Standing up for ourselves is going to be hard without Ray Loomis to lean on. Nancy and Billy will need all the courage they have, and all the encouragement we can give. All of the members of Project Two and all of us who worked with Ray on GOARC's Board are going to be missing an important part of our lives without him. But we owe Ray our best effort at standing up for ourselves and others and looking ahead to the future. We need to follow his footsteps, as people helping people.

The second eulogy was given by Tom Houlihan, the Vice-President of Project Two, a man with Down's syndrome: This is the story of a man who started the biggest project in the world, and he called it Project Two. His name is Ray Loomis. His dream was to close Beatrice State Home in Nebraska. Project Two people will keep their project going. To me, the world and Project Two, Ray has been a good friend. He also has a good wife, and son Billy. Everyone will miss Ray.

Ray's brothers and sister, who lived in another state, marvelled at the amount of love and respect that was shown for him. A local newspaper which had run a short article about Ray's death, received and printed several letters from the general public expressing their feelings that Ray had accomplished more in his life than most people who are not retarded.

The second People First convention had been scheduled for a weekend only ten days after Ray's funeral. It was attended by 220 people and, in spite of the fact that Project Two members hadn't had much time to organise it, it was a success. The videotape of the television programme about Ray was shown, and there were also many workshops and a guest speaker from Kansas. Nancy Loomis and Ollie Rector shared the duties of leading the convention on its first day. Chris Corso from Omaha and Jim Utter from McCook shared the duties on the second day. The guest speaker, a man whose severe cerebral palsy required him to communicate with an alphabet board operated by his toe, was very successful in capturing the attention of the large group. People First of Nebraska elected new statewide officers at this second convention. They vowed to carry on with Ray Loomis's dream.

The Advocacy Efforts Expand

That autumn of 1979, a newspaper report detailed a case of an alleged abuse of a ten-year-old boy at the Beatrice State

Developmental Center (the old State Home). The boy, who was from near Omaha, had been brought from Beatrice to an Omaha hospital by his mother. He had only been in the institution for five weeks when the injuries occurred. Many Project Two members became very angry at this news and went to the hospital to give their support to the boy's mother. They told her that the same thing had happened to them many times when they had been in Beatrice, or that they had witnessed beatings of other residents by ward attendants and other state employees.

After talking to the boy's mother, they explained the situation at a Project Two meeting. The group decided to do something about the alleged abuse. (The group's advisers, who were somewhat reluctant to become involved, agreed to support them as they proceeded.) At first, they wanted to hold a demonstration. They consulted with the director of the state Association for Retarded Citizens who told them that Nebraskans dislike demonstrations and do not listen to complaints made in this way. Instead, he suggested that they might hold a press conference to protest about abuse in the state institution and to launch a campaign to convince state legislators that all of the institution residents should be brought into the community. After visiting community services to see for themselves that everyone, no matter how handicapped, could live in the community, they wrote a statement to read to the press (this is reproduced in Appendix Three) and practised holding a press conference. Several television and radio stations attended, as did the local newspapers. The coverage was very good and reflected positively on group members.

After the press conference, the group asked Vard Johnson, a liberal state senator, to meet with them. They discussed their concerns with him and asked that he help them to close Beatrice and bring all of the residents back into the community. He stated emphatically that the institution would never be closed, because there was a need for it for the people who were 'worse off' than they were. The Project Two members, however, had visited community programmes serving profoundly mentally handicapped children and adults, and were prepared to argue on that point. The state senator then asked them how long it had been since any of them had seen the institution, as major changes had been made since they left.

When he found that no one in the group had been back since 1974, he asked them to accompany him on an unannounced tour. They accepted.

Many preparations were necessary before the tour. First, the group asked Dr John McGee, a nationally known veteran of evaluations of many institutions, to teach them how to inspect the institution. He spent several hours with them, explaining that although the institution had been changed, evaluators must look not at how new the buildings were, but at whether the people living there were receiving developmental program- mes and whether they were idle most of the time. Evaluators must look at whether residents were receiving humane treat- ment, and whether they were learning skills that would help them to be more independent.

Dr McGee explained that when one inspected a service, it was important to behave as professionally as possible. There should be no negative remarks about what was seen and no laughing and joking during the tour. Instead, the evaluators should make positive or neutral comments, ask questions, inhibit smoking and gum chewing, pay attention to the staff explaining the programmes, behave politely to direct-care staff, take notes or draw simple pictures of each unit visited, and dress as nicely as possible for the tour. He suggested that some members take tape recorders to record what they saw and to record interviews with residents. He advised that they talk to as many residents as they could.

The six-member committee which planned to conduct the inspection spent some time before the visit discussing which buildings they wished to see, and what they thought an ideal programme should be like. They decided that living units should look like homes, with normal furnishings such as would be found at home. When they had lived there, the Beatrice State Developmental Center had had several locked buildings and punishment wards. They wondered: Would the children be going to school? Would the adults be receiving vocational training? Were there still punishment wards? What was the policy on abuse? Why had the State Developmental Center decided that the boy had not been abused, when the boy's doctors in Omaha felt that he had?

Project Two rented a van for the hundred-mile trip. The institution had been notified that such a tour would occur, but had not been told when it might happen. Before the trip, several members grew very worried that if they went back to visit the institution they would not be allowed to leave. One man needed assurances by many people before he felt comfortable enough to take the trip.

There were ten people on the tour: six Project Two members, the state senator and his aide, Dr John McGee and one Project Two adviser (Bonnie Shoultz). One administrator was asked to escort the visitors throughout the institution, and to explain the various programmes that were observed. One Project Two member, Dave Menousek, stayed close to the adviser and dictated a running commentary about what he saw, so that she could write it down. Two others, Jack Conrad and Chris Corso, took tape recorders and recorded whatever they could. Vard Johnson and John McGee took side trips into wards not entered by the official giving the tour, and saw many people sitting and lying in idleness, often engaging in self-abusive and self-stimulatory behaviour to pass the time.

At the end of the day, the whole group met with the superintendent of Beatrice and two members of his staff. They asked to see the records of some of the people they had met that day, and they asked about the policy on alleged abuse: on how it is reported, investigated and resolved. They listened to the institution's side of the story on the young boy who had suffered injuries. Then they left for the long trip home.

The ride home gave everyone a chance to talk about what they had seen. Dave Menousek pointed out that nothing, not even the newest residences, looked like a home; that the furniture was hard and uncomfortable; that there were water pipes coming out of the walls; and that children's toys had been placed on many of the beds to impress the visitors. He recalled that in years past when visitors were expected, the toys would be brought out of the cupboard and placed on every resident's bed. Vard Johnson and John McGee discussed the meaning of what they had seen, with Dr McGee emphasising that the behaviour, demeanour and activity engaged in by the residents was not due to their retardation but to the years of institutional living and to the low expectations of them. Thus, even though each resident had a written record detailing the kinds of developmental programmes which would be provided to him or her each day, the same residents had been found sitting or wandering alone and in idleness.

At the end of the journey, the Project Two members asked Senator Johnson to join them on a similar tour of ENCOR facilities. He accepted, and this tour was undertaken in late December. Later, Senator Johnson was interviewed by a newspaper reporter who asked him why he had changed his mind. He described his experiences on both tours, especially citing the happy face of a severely retarded woman in a community programme. The resulting long article was one of the few pieces of positive publicity ENCOR had that year. The headline in the *Omaha World-Herald* proclaimed: 'Visits to Retarded Changed Senator's Attitude'.

Project Two Continues
Project Two held an election after the death of Ray Loomis. This election, held in November 1979, established Nancy Loomis as the new President. Nancy led the group during the time of the press conference and the tours of Beatrice and ENCOR. Because this was a very difficult time for Nancy, a group of six people emerged as co-leaders. This group became a steering committee which could be called together whenever there were decisions to be made or problems to be solved.

The group rested for a bit after the successes of their expanded advocacy efforts. They had not convinced the public or the legislature that the institution should be closed, but they had become firm in their determination to defend that stand. People First of Nebraska is the only group in the state which has publicly declared that the institution should be closed and that the right of each resident is to live in his or her own community, receiving services there to meet his or her own individual needs.

The steering committee was called upon to resolve one more crisis during Nancy's presidency. This crisis developed because GOARC, Project Two's sponsoring agency, underwent a great deal of turmoil after the departure of Tom Miller in 1978. While he was Executive Director, Project Two received clerical and other support from GOARC, but after he left that support was reduced. Project Two was still sponsored by GOARC, but GOARC had problems which almost resulted in a break between Project Two and GOARC in 1980. The Executive Director selected to replace Tom Miller was asked to resign only four months later. The position was vacant for many months while the volunteer Board of Directors ran the agency. Staff turnover was high during this time. A new Executive Director was appointed in mid-1979, but he had to replace staff, get to know the volunteers and the services, and set his own new directions. He and the Board of Directors began to ask questions about the relationship of Project Two to GOARC, questions which revolved especially around the issue of money. Project Two had money left over from the conventions it had sponsored and it had received donations which had come through GOARC. The members asked if they could deposit that money in the Project Two savings account and were told that it might belong to GOARC. The issue of where this money belonged became a crisis for Project Two. They felt that the new GOARC staff did not understand Project Two or its relationship to the Association, and they were concerned that the Board of Directors also lacked understanding. The Project Two steering committee met and drew up a proposal which explained their position on the money and which helped to clarify their relationship with GOARC. They then met with the Executive Committee of GOARC's Board of Directors and convinced them that the money should be deposited in their account.

This meeting was the culmination of a long and quiet process of self-advocacy within GOARC. In 1975, few mentally handicapped adults came independently to GOARC meetings, and many of the GOARC members disliked them being there, especially those who were former Beatrice residents. When Tom Miller became Executive Director, many of his mentally handicapped friends began attending meetings. At best, they were tolerated by many GOARC members. Many parents felt that mentally handicapped adults could not participate fully because they were 'too easily manipulated'. Gradually, as Project Two became strong and began to receive public recognition, the attitude seemed to change. But when Project Two successfully fought and won over an issue within GOARC, a new era of respect and equal treatment began for Project Two members.

The relationship with GOARC is now excellent. The new Executive Director, Dan Costello, attends every meeting and is very active as an adviser to the group. Project Two members freely attend GOARC meetings, and their participation is actively solicited when a meeting deals with an issue which concerns them. For example, a recent meeting was held over the effects on ENCOR of the budget cuts being proposed by the state legislature and the Reagan administration. Parents and others at the meetings now freely offer transport to members and engage mentally handicapped citizens in conversations. Some of the GOARC members have developed friendships with several of the Project Two members and attend parties, chat with them on the telephone, and do other things with and for them. Ollie Rector and Tom Houlihan are on the GOARC Board of Directors.

In 1980, Project Two decided to hold annual elections, with January as the month for elections to be held. In January 1981, Ollie Rector was elected as the new President, with Nancy Loomis as Vice-President, Linda Ault as Treasurer, and Harold Edwards as Sergeant-at-Arms (the person who keeps control at meetings – see Chapter Four).

Ollie Rector has led the group into strong efforts in two areas: social activities and advocacy training. Group members are learning to conduct training on rights, using a new training package developed by a project in Massachusetts. They plan to go through the training themselves and then take it into the sheltered workshops and residential facilities in ENCOR.

Thus the group continues. It plans next year to hold its annual convention in conjunction with the convention of the Nebraska Association for Retarded Citizens. It is felt that the experience of attending a People First convention will permanently affect Association members. In April 1981 Tom Houlihan, Ollie Rector and Tom Miller (now back from his travels) were the featured speakers at a convention in another state (South Dakota). With Tom and Ollie at the microphone, 400 parents and professionals listened, were deeply moved, and gave tumultuous applause. Afterwards, Ollie received letters of appreciation from, among others, the Executive Director of the Association for Retarded Citizens in South Dakota, and from the State Governor of South Dakota himself.

Project Two has taught all who have taken the time to listen that there is no limit to what people can do, except for the limitations imposed by restrictive attitudes and lack of confidence. The group now believes, and has convinced many others, that people with disabilities can gain the skills and understanding needed to do whatever they want to do.

The Voice of Project Two

The following contributions come from written accounts by Project Two members or interviews with them by Bonnie Shoultz. Bonnie has edited them to make their flow more coherent, but they remain the words of the members themselves.

To Better Ourselves in the World
by Ollie Rector

I'm 53 years old. I was born in Oklahoma but our family moved to Scottsbluff, Nebraska, when I was a child. I had lots of brothers and sisters. After we moved to Scottsbluff, my mother left my father and us, and I took care of my little brothers and sisters for a long time. I cooked, cleaned and did their laundry. Now I feel like I'm their mother too. Then the welfare people came and picked me up and took me to the institution. They said I wasn't able to take care of my little sisters and brothers.

I was there for seven years of my life. It was terrible. I just involved myself in my work, taking care of the babies in the nursery. I did what they asked me, but they didn't let me do any thinking for myself. They did all the thinking for me.

After seven years, I got out and went to work in a private home taking care of an old lady. I made $5 each week. Every Saturday I got paid. I would put $3 in the bank and spend $2 for myself. Then she passed away, and I was afraid I'd have to go back to the institution. But a bunch of people got together to help me so I wouldn't have to go back. I got another job in a nursing home. I had to get away from there, though, because the manager kept bothering me. I couldn't stay around that place because I had to get away from him. So I went back to the institution for a while. Then I got another job in a nursing home in Weeping Water, and I worked there about two years. I was responsible for three floors, taking care of the patients and cooking and cleaning. Some nights I was so darn tired I couldn't sleep because I was putting too many hours in. If I hadn't gotten out of there I would have had a nervous breakdown. So they sent me back to the institution.

Then I went down to Plattsmouth to work in another nursing home, taking care of patients. I made about $40 a month. I started putting that in the bank. Finally in 1964 they brought me to Omaha, and I worked in a nursing home here for six years. Tom Miller got me out of there. I worked in a couple of private homes, then another woman and I got an apartment by ourselves. We took care of the apartment, paid our rent and everything. I had a job in a hotel at the time.

When I was in the institution, they made all the decisions for me. I didn't know I had any rights. When I got out of the nursing home, Tom Miller told me: 'You've got rights!' and I've been speaking up for my rights ever since. I speak for my rights all the time now.

I started getting more independent after I got my own apartment. I got tired of the counsellors coming over to take care of my money and everything, so I said: 'Will you put it down on a piece of paper and see if I can do it?' Now I can write out 'one hundred' without even looking at the piece of paper. I take care of all my own bills by copying out the numbers on to my cheques.

Now I live in our own home. Me and my husband had it built for ourselves. We have lived here a year now, and we're trying to keep it going. We got married in December 1974. My husband is involved in self-advocacy too.

I got into self-advocacy in 1975. A guy by the name of Raymond Loomis got me involved in sticking up for ourselves and getting other people to listen to what we have to say. Raymond Loomis was a good friend. He died about two years ago.

I've been President of Project Two since January 1981. I find out what the people want, and I try to help them get it. I try to teach them to help themselves. I also do public speaking. I go to conferences and conventions and speak to the public about self-advocacy.

To me, self-advocacy means that I can speak out for myself and tell other people to speak out for themselves. It means to help them to speak out to better themselves in the world. Part of it is to get other people to listen to us, to see what we want. People shouldn't get everything they want, though. People shouldn't try to get too far ahead of other people. They should let other people help them, too.

Since I got involved in self-advocacy, I think I feel wonderful. I'm better at making decisions. Sometimes it's hard making decisions, seeing if it's all right with the other people and everything. You have to talk it over with other people before you make a decision, and see if it sounds all right to you and them. I'm better at helping other people now, too. People come to me and ask me questions and I answer them the best way I know how. I'm trying to teach other people to take responsibility for themselves.

My goals are to speak out for my people. I call the people with handicaps 'my people'. And to help my people to speak out for themselves. Sometimes people step on our toes, and we need to step on their toes too. I believe that all people have handicaps in their heads, in some way or another. I also believe that if people could meet us halfway, then this world would be better. Every person would help each other. They would trust each other, and listen, and help people to go down the road.

Going Worldwide
by Tom Houlihan

My name is Tom Houlihan. I am 38 years old – going on 40! I have had Down's syndrome since I was born. I lived with my parents in the community when I was growing up. At one time they were talking about putting me in an institution when I was little, but the family said no. Someone told me about that later on. I never want to be in an institution. I want to stay in the community.

My father died when I was in my teens, and I lived with my mother and brother after that. I lived with my mother in an apartment until she had to go into a nursing home a few years ago. She had become partially blind and she was getting sick all the time. She died just a few weeks ago, but before that I used to visit her a lot and I talked to her on the phone until she got too sick to understand me.

My family taught me some things about life and making decisions for myself. They worked hard to teach me the four R's: reading, 'riting, 'rithmetic, and romance!

Now I live with my roommate, Chris Corso. And I love my life. I had a lot of good education. I went to several schools when I was little. I went to the Opportunity Center (a school

run by parents) for a long time. Then I went to Goodwill
Industries for training. Then they put me out on a competitive
job at the car wash, and from the car wash I went to where I
work now, at the St Vincent de Paul Society. I've been there 14
years.

I got involved in self-advocacy when I got invited to come to
a meeting. I can't remember who got me involved. I liked
everything about the meeting. I wasn't getting out much then
because I was going home from work every day to take care of
my mother. I really liked the Project Two meeting, so I kept
coming to each one.

Weeks and months later we had our first election and I
couldn't believe what Shirley Dean said. She said: 'I nominate
Tom Houlihan for Vice-President,' and then I got elected. I
have held the positions of Vice-President and Treasurer. When I
was Treasurer I took care of the money in the 'kitty'.

I've done a little public speaking for Project Two. I had my
first chance at an ENCOR hearing. Of course, I was really
nervous that night. My left hand was shaky in holding that
microphone, and then all of a sudden my left leg started to
shake. I mentioned all my friends over the microphone that
night. I also did a lot of public speaking when I went to
England for the Campaign for Mentally Handicapped People.
I went in May 1980, with Bonnie Shoultz and Shirley Dean. I
wanted to stay there for ever. I think I left my heart in England.

To me, self-advocacy means learning to speak out for what
you believe in and having a good life. Since I got involved an
awful lot of good has happened inside of me. I've gotten better
at helping other people by listening to their problems, and I'm
better at listening to people to get advice from them. I'm also
better at speaking up for myself.

Being a leader can be hard. A leader has to have knowledge
of doing things on his own. He shouldn't get cocky. He should
be strong, and he should want to take part and fight for what he
believes in. Those things are true for anybody, not just for
leaders. Every self-advocate should think about those things.

I'd like to see Project Two and People First go nationwide
and then worldwide. I believe in peace between people – peace
between people who have different thoughts about life. I
believe we should try to make each other happy. I think People
First can help bring that peace.

Helping People is Powerful
by Chris Corso

I grew up in Denver, Colorado, in Cheyenne, Wyoming, and in Omaha. I lived with my parents until I was about twenty. I've been out on my own since then. It was a little harder to make decisions for myself when I was living with the folks. I've learned more about it since I've been out on my own.

I went to a few special schools. I went there because the public schools are harder. The private schools were a little bit easier for me and I learned quicker there.

When I moved out into my own apartment, it was really good. I felt self-confident. Now I live with Tom Houlihan, and that's tougher, living with someone else.

I first heard about Project Two from my adviser, when I got into ENCOR. I went to a few meetings. I was new at first and I didn't do much. Then I became more of a leader and I started to get higher and higher in it all the time. I started to learn about things and teach about things.

I have been a photographer for Project Two, and I was the Sergeant-at-Arms last year. My job was to make sure people paid attention and didn't make too much noise in the meetings. We have rules, and my job was to enforce them. I've also been a leader in People First of Nebraska. I was the President for Eastern Nebraska for People First. Another guy was President for Western Nebraska, and that's how we keep in touch with the whole state. I led the general sessions at our conventions.

It was a little scary at first, doing public speaking. Last year we heard about a woman's little boy in Beatrice. We talked with her about him, and she said he had two black eyes and his teeth were knocked out and he had large bumps on his head. The people in Beatrice said he was unsteady on his feet and he does things to himself, but that's hard to believe because he had never done it when he lived at home. Now he lives at home with her and she's taking good care of him and he's doing fine.

After it happened, all six of us leaders got together and talked to some people about Beatrice. We talked about it ourselves: should we close it down or should we keep it open? We would like to see it closed, and we've made that decision.

We had our press conference, the six of us, and I read the statement to the press. Then we answered questions. There were two newspapers, two television stations and some radio stations.

Later we toured Beatrice with the state senator. There was a lot of brand new stuff there, never used. We saw the swimming pool and all the other brand new things. There were some children there with real difficulties.

Self-advocacy is for your rights. It means you should speak up for yourself, do things for yourself, and speak up for the ones who can't speak for themselves, like we did when we had our press conference.

I'm more interested in other people since I got into Project Two. That's because I'm beginning to help them more. That's the way I feel that it should go on. I'm beginning to be relaxed towards more people. They help me out and I help them out. People helping people – that's what Project Two is. I believe helping people is powerful.

I want Project Two to be more efficient and stronger. And I hope the others will get out even more in the community, the way I have been. I'm going to become a reverend in my church soon, and I've become busy with other things too. I think if the others see me doing all those things, then they will feel like they can do them too.

A leader has to lead people into things. I suppose what I have to do as a leader is talk to people about Beatrice, and being on your own. I have to make them feel more at home. It feels terrific as a leader.

We Stick Up for Our Rights
by David Menousek

I'm 42 years old now. I was in Beatrice 30 years. I can't remember how old I was when I went in, but I've been out since 1974. It was like a state prison. It didn't look like a home; it looked like a church. They had the TV sets up on the shelf, and they had hard furniture. You couldn't go places. And the ward attendants would beat up on you every day. I got beat up a lot of times.

They watched you like a hawk. I did make some decisions, but not the kind you make at home. You could decide if you wanted to stand in the corner or push the kiddy-cart all day back and forth. You could decide if you wanted to work in the infirmary taking care of the kids or go to the curler factory and make curlers. I helped down in the diet kitchen, and I used to be a clothes boy, making up bath bundles on Monday and Tuesday. I made those kind of decisions.

I didn't feel I had rights at all. I did get to go to school. They don't call it first grade and second grade, but they teach you arithmetic, how to budget money – things like that. Then they transferred me to Rehab. You had to make your bed, be at breakfast bright and early, be on time at work, and do chores. Each one had to do chores in Rehab. My chores were to polish all the windows. You can't skip one, you have to get them all done – then you can go to breakfast. Sometimes you had to get up at four in the morning to get your chores done.

I left Beatrice because I didn't like it. My friend Bill Lewis from ENCOR helped me get out. First I moved to an ENCOR apartment. It looked like a home. My friend Bill helped me learn how to cook, make up the beds, do the laundry, go grocery shopping, go anyplace you wanted to go. Sometimes you'd go to the laundromat, and sometimes you'd go out to eat. You could go anywhere.

First I went to the Q Street workshop. Then I went to Lozier's (an ordinary factory where ENCOR has a supervised enclave). Then I got my first job, washing dishes at Coco's restaurant. I'm still there. I've been there four years.

After I moved out of ENCOR, I moved in with Bill Lewis. I was his roommate. When Bill moved to Blair, I moved in with another friend for a while. Then I bought my own house. I've been living here about two years. I take care of everything myself.

Project Two got me involved in self-advocacy. We have speakers, we have activities, and we have dances. We learn how to stick up for our rights. We talk about different things in our meetings. Sometimes we go to our convention. I'm just a member of Project Two, not an officer.

Self-advocacy means getting people out in the community. They need jobs, they need a home just like we do, and they need more activities like we have.

Project Two really helps me. We stick up for our rights. It helps us a lot. We all in Project Two help each other. We learn about more things in the community. I'll never forget to go to Project Two.

Everyone Should Have Their Rights
by Lowell Rector

I'm sweet sixteen right now! No, I'm really 52 years old now. I was born and raised in Weeping Water, Nebraska. I lived there with my parents until the police and the city got mad and said it would be better for me to live on the farm. Then after we lived on the farm my mom got sick and my dad got sick, and they couldn't do anything with me, and I couldn't do anything with them. My brother and sister were in Plattsmouth, and after I went to Plattsmouth the people there said: 'Put him in the Lincoln Regional Center and see if he can learn a job.'

They put all kinds of people in the Regional Center – all kinds, for all kinds of trouble. They even have people come over there out of the State Penitentiary. Well, I never took any medication; I was never under a doctor's care or anything. I didn't get any schooling; I just had to work all the time. I had to load boxes in the warehouse and load things on the trucks. Sometimes we would be working in the warehouse and the people would load up their cars with things. They would take them home and use them. I knew it was wrong, but they told us not to say anything. I always knew I wanted to get out of there.

After I was in the Regional Center for a while, they put me on a job in a nursing home in Plattsmouth. I stayed there about four or five years. That's where I met Ollie. She was a cook over there. Then she went to a place in Omaha. She was a janitor, a nurse and everything you can think of for that place.

I stayed there until the last minute, until they closed up. They had a chain over the door to keep people locked in. I had to take care of the patients. I had to work during the day-time, and at nights I had to stay awake – one eye open and one eye closed – and keep an eye on the patients and the medicine. I never went to bed at all one year, until they hired another guy to work at nights. Then I had to get up sometimes at night and help with the patients. I had to strap them down, put them in bed, and everything. Finally the Fire Department came over and said the place had to be closed down. It wasn't fit to live in any more. So after all the patients were sent away to another place in Omaha, they sent me there too. I stayed there until the last patient left.

I had a guardian for a while. He took care of all my money. He moved me to Omaha and got me into a boarding house. I got a job at a hospital and I stayed there for four to five years. One day, I walked off that job because I got mad. The supervisor told me I wasn't doing very well, and I just walked off. Later I got a letter from the hospital asking why I walked off, but after I told them the whole story they said they didn't blame me. I got a couple of other jobs and got fired, and finally I got the job I have now with Shared Services Laundry. I've been there six years.

About seven years ago, I got to know some people who used to be in Beatrice. One night they took me over to a friend's house, and guess who was there – Ollie! So I started going to see her every night, and we started talking about getting married. We went to my counsellor and her counsellor at ENCOR, and they said it was up to us if we wanted to get married. Then my guardian said I couldn't get married until I got discharged from the Regional Center and discharged from him. So I got discharged, and I married Ollie.

After we were married for a few years, I went down to GOARC one day and I saw Tom Miller. I told him we were looking for a house, and he said we should talk to John Clark (President of GOARC's Board, and an estate agent). We did. We looked at some houses, and we found out how much money we had to spend on a house. We didn't like the houses we saw, and John said we would be better off building a new house because it wouldn't cost so much to keep it up all the time. So we built a three-bedroom house. We moved in two years ago. We like it pretty good. Our yard hasn't been going too well, but we like the house a lot.

I got into Project Two after Raymond Loomis got together with Tom Miller to get Project Two started. Then we all got into it.

To me, self-advocacy is getting out, getting everything going, and getting things done. It's helping out other people. I like to help the handicapped who can't do as much for themselves. Now I'm better at speaking up for other people. If I see someone who is being mean to a handicapped person, I jump in and say: 'Hey! If you don't know how to treat him, leave him alone and find someone who does!' I believe everyone should have their rights, and they should get out and do it for themselves. If they can't do it for themselves, they can try to learn.

It's Not Easy To Be a Leader
by Nancy Loomis

I was put in Beatrice in 1957, when I was 17 years old. I got out in 1969, so I stayed there 12 years. I'm 40 years old now. Before that I was in a private school in Chicago. I got out of there after they said they couldn't teach me anything more. I used to live with my grandparents, but they had died in a car accident. My mother put me in Beatrice because there were too many boys after me. They said I was 'boy crazy', but it wasn't really me – it was them that were interested in me.

Beatrice was so-so. I met Ray there. I was only there a little while, and Ray was in punishment, and Jack Conrad told him: 'Hey, Ray, the new girl wants to see you. She likes you.' When Ray got out he looked for me, and that's how we met. He was my boyfriend the whole time. Of course they wouldn't let you hold hands or anything, unless you could hide from them.

They were letting a lot of the people out of Beatrice so it wouldn't be so overcrowded. They asked me if I wanted to get out, and I agreed. First I went to a boarding home in Omaha. I didn't get any more independent there, so Tom Miller helped me move into an apartment with some other women. He was my counsellor back then.

I got back with Ray in about 1970 when he moved to Omaha from Lincoln. We got married in 1974 after we lived together for a while. I was doing maid's work at Methodist Hospital. Later I did the same thing at University Hospital.

Billy was born in 1977. He's four years old now. Ray and I had already started Project Two. After Billy was born, Ray kept on working as a dishwasher and supporting his family.

Ray died about two years ago. He had to have open-heart surgery.

Since then Billy and I moved, and we rent our own house. I'm on my own now. We live on Ray's social security. I go every day to Metro Technical Community College to get my high school equivalency diploma. We have two teachers who can help us. We study on our own, and if we need any help we ask them. Billy is going to a pre-school programme in the mornings, and in the afternoon we both go to the Parent-Child Center where parents learn about how to solve problems.

Today was Billy's birthday. He had cake three times – once at pre-school, once at the Parent-Child Center, and tonight when we went to Positive Parenting (a discussion group for high-risk parents).

Ray got me involved in self-advocacy. I used to help him with the group. After he died I was elected President. Now I'm the Vice-President. I'm on the Public Speaking Committee and the Social Committee and the Planning Committee. But it's not easy to be a leader. A leader is supposed to make plans and get ideas about what's going to go on for the next few months.

I'd like to see Project Two grow. I'd like to see that we could do things for ourselves. To me, self-advocacy means that you know you can do things for yourself without being dependent on anybody else.

I believe there's some good people in the world. But how they treat you depends on how you act and how you are around other people. You've got to stand up for your rights. You've got to depend on yourself and help yourself before you can help anybody else.

2 THE NEW VOICE

A new voice can be heard in our movement. As yet it is hesitant, unsure, but it is steadily gaining in strength. It is the voice of those we once thought incapable of speaking, hence our battle cry used to be: 'We speak for them'. It is the voice of those once considered ineducable, who are now attending schools. It is the voice of those once deemed unemployable, indeed deemed 'incapable of sustained effort', who now bring a pay cheque for a full work week.

I have been privileged to attend some conferences managed largely by people with mental handicap themselves. Thus I was not surprised when I learned a few days ago that at a recent major policy meeting to discuss the future of the Canadian Association for the Mentally Retarded, no less than ten persons with mental handicap, one from each province, participated in the deliberations.

I am aware that many of our readers will comment: 'This may be possible for those who are only mildly handicapped, but surely for the majority this is just a fantasy, an impossible dream.' No more impossible than the dream that all persons with a mental handicap can go to school, can gain acceptance in the community, can learn to move about, can learn to make responsible choices.

Let us not argue how soon or how many of our young people will be able to express themselves. Let us instead ask ourselves: Are we ready to listen to their new voice?

Professor Gunnar Dybwad, President
of the International League of
Societies for the Mentally Handicapped
(from the ILSMH Newsletter, 1980)

The Start

The origins of self-advocacy by mentally handicapped people lie in Sweden. During the 1960s a network of leisure clubs for mentally handicapped people was established there. This was also the case in Britain, but unlike usual British practice at that time, a tradition grew in Sweden for the mentally handicapped people themselves to have control over their own clubs. It became common for the officers of the committees running the clubs to consist of mentally handicapped people themselves, assisted as necessary by non-handicapped people who gradually withdrew as the handicapped people developed more skills.

Courses were provided in Sweden in the 1960s to teach mentally handicapped people skills of decision-taking, committee work and voting, particularly to enable them to run their own social and leisure clubs. Officers and members of these clubs began to exchange visits with each other and to meet each other on short courses. Eventually, some regional conferences for mentally handicapped people were organised at which they exchanged views and ideas. Out of these regional meetings came the idea of a national conference of mentally handicapped people, and what is thought to be the first such conference in the world was held in 1968.

There were only twenty participants, and they met specifically to discuss leisure time activities, but the seed was sown for a more ambitious conference, and a second one was organised for May 1970. This took the form of a full-scale three-day conference attended by 50 elected representatives from all the counties in Sweden, and some guests from Denmark. The topics for discussion included leisure activities, residential living, vocational training and work. Groups of six to eight people met to discuss issues in these areas and report back to the whole conference. Non-handicapped helpers took notes and maintained some control over the timetable, but did not directly influence the outcome of the discussions.

News of this impressive national conference of mentally handicapped people themselves spread to other countries. In Britain, Ann Shearer, a journalist who in 1971 had founded a pressure group for improvement of services called the Campaign for Mentally Handicapped People (CMH), worked through CMH to set up the first national conference of British mentally handicapped people. This was held in July 1972 and was given the title 'Our Life'. Twenty-two mentally handicapped people attended from all over Britain, and fifteen non-handicapped people attended as helpers and discussion group leaders. Ann Shearer wrote a full conference report which was published by CMH. The cover showed some photographs of the proceedings, and many direct quotes from the mentally handicapped delegates were included in the report. This and subsequent conferences and other developments in Britain are discussed further in Chapter Six.

In 1973, a group of professionals in British Columbia in Canada decided to organise a conference for mentally handicapped people there, based on the Swedish and British models. This was billed as 'the first convention for the mentally handicapped in North America'. Invitations were extended to mentally handicapped people in western Canada and the north-western states of the USA, including Oregon.

In Oregon there was already a network of 'support groups' – groups of mentally handicapped people who had been discharged into the community from the main state institution, Fairview Hospital and Training Center, who continued to meet regularly with some of the social workers from Fairview. In 1973 over twenty such support groups were already being conducted by these social workers in the area around Salem, Oregon. Two staff members from Fairview went with three mentally handicapped people from the support groups to the British Columbia convention. They came back inspired with the idea of an organisation for mentally handicapped people that would organise conventions and be a voice for mentally handicapped people themselves.

A month after their return from British Columbia, the people who had attended called a special meeting of mentally handicapped people in the Salem area and some potential non-handicapped helpers. They described the event in British Columbia and sought and achieved agreement that Oregon could work towards holding its own statewide conference.

This was the beginning of the 'People First' movement in America.

The First American Convention
The idea of a convention was spread among the support groups and each group was asked to elect a representative to serve on a planning group. Officers were elected from this group and this committee began to spread the idea wider in the state and to plan the convention in earnest.

One of the social workers at Fairview, Dennis Heath (still an adviser to the self-advocacy movement in Oregon), sought the backing of the institution superintendent to begin a support group within the institution. A group of 25 residents met regularly to talk about their rights and their need for an organisation through which to express their views and problems. They decided to join with the support groups outside in the community to plan the convention.

Thus, a joint committee of institution residents and mentally handicapped people living in the community spent many months learning everything they could about how to organise a convention, and the detailed tasks that must be carried out beforehand. At one meeting, the group decided to vote on a name for their new organisation. Among others, the name 'People First' was put forward. The proposer of this name said: 'We are tired of being seen first as handicapped or retarded or disabled. We want to be seen as people first.' And this was the name that got the vote.

The convention was held at Otter Crest, Oregon, in October 1974. Its theme was 'We Have Something to Offer'. Although 200 people were expected, an incredible total of 560 people actually turned up. Despite some ensuing confusion, the conference was a great success. As Robert Perske, a well-known American writer on mental handicap, wrote in a later report to the US President: 'It was evident that these people had caught a contagious convention fever that continues to spread even today.'

All through the planning process for the convention, great care had been taken to ensure that the non-handicapped helpers did not become the leaders. The helpers and the handicapped people would learn how to develop the organisation together, with the helpers providing support and assisting with the development of ideas, but eventually trying to work themselves out of a job. Thus, the content of the convention was decided by mentally handicapped people themselves; they played a major part in all aspects of its planning and organisation; and the proceedings were directed and led by mentally handicapped people.

This first People First convention led to the firm establishment of the statewide organisation People First of Oregon, with officers elected at the convention. The organisation set out in the following year to establish support groups in all parts of the state, in institutions, in group homes, and among people living at home with their families or in their own apartments. They worked out a structure within which the support groups could work together to hold further statewide conventions and ensure the development of the People First movement.

The model for establishing and operating self-advocacy that has been devised and adopted by People First of Oregon is described in Chapter Four.

The Idea Spreads

The second People First of Oregon convention was held at Bend, Oregon, in the autumn of 1975, with 750 people in attendance. It was much better organised than the first, with workshop sessions covering topics such as 'How to start a People First chapter in your community', 'How to get people to meetings', 'How to hold elections' and 'How to raise money'.*

Since that time, conventions have been held annually in Oregon. The organisation found itself, partly through personal contact and partly through widespread viewing of the film, in the role of encouraging the development of self-advocacy groups throughout America, and even abroad. By 1978, statewide conventions along the lines of those begun by People First of Oregon had been held in California, Kansas, Washington state, Nebraska, and in the Canadian provinces of Ontario and Alberta. The People First of Oregon conventions began to attract many delegates from other states, and it was decided that the group would establish 'People First International', an organisation that would have a coordinating role in the development of the People First movement in America and elsewhere in the world.

Under the name of People First International, a two-day convention in Portland, Oregon, in 1980 was attended by over 1,000 people from all over the United States and Canada. The Governor of Oregon himself was a guest speaker. For 1981 a three-day international convention was planned for up to 2,500 delegates, timed to run over American Independence Day, 4 July. Workshops at these recent conventions have tackled issues such as 'Barriers to people in wheelchairs' and 'How to get more service from your service workers'.

The conventions have always been self-supporting, with costs being met from a $25 registration fee from each

*A film was made of this convention by James Stanfield Film Associates of California. It is called *People First* and is available for hire in Britain from Concord Films (address in Appendix Six).

participant. Many delegates have been proud to save this amount over many months from their small income.*

A Movement Grows

The concern of those who have been involved in self-advocacy has been to effect change, rather than to record their history for a wide audience, and for this reason the history of self-advocacy by mentally handicapped people is still emerging.

Although People First of Oregon had an influential role in the development of self-advocacy groups in America, it did not initiate all of them. As described in Chapter One, Project Two in Omaha existed for two years before they heard of People First of Oregon and saw the film. It is an extraordinary fact that during the 1970s a whole network of similar groups sprang up in America, many of them starting as independent local initiatives whose participants only later came to learn that they were part of a 'self-advocacy movement'. There are now at least 70 local or state groups that have a predominant membership of mentally handicapped people, and they all have a slightly different history.

Mentally handicapped Americans have been meeting in groups in some localities since as far back as the 1950s. Although some of these groups may always have engaged in activities which could now be identified as self-advocacy, this has gone unrecognised until recently. Most groups have in the past focused on social activities, and most have been run by professional staff members or non-handicapped volunteers rather than by the handicapped people themselves. Some groups, however, can be seen to have been evolving as self-advocacy groups for a long time.

One such group is the Mohawks and Squaws in Boston, Massachusetts, who have existed for at least twenty years. In common with other similar groups, they have developed a way of working that is virtually independent of any substantial help by non-handicapped people. About thirty members, led by a

*A book is being written about the development of People First International in Oregon. Its author is Jean Edwards and its title will be *We Are People First*. It will be available from the Special Education Department of Portland State University, address in Appendix Six.

small committee, have three types of meeting: one for social entertainment; one where the older and more able members teach social skills to the younger and less able members; and one where they discuss their rights and needs and decide on appropriate action to meet them. They are assisted in this by just one social worker, who helps them to write letters and to identify the right people to contact about particular issues.

Other more recently founded groups go by a variety of names: The Merry Macs and The Pioneers are two other groups in Massachusetts; CASH (Citizens Active for Self-Help) is a group in Montana; ACT (Advocating Change Together) is a group in Minneapolis, Minnesota.

Occasionally, groups have been started by mentally handicapped people in institutions such as the Syracuse Developmental Center in New York state (see Patricia Killius's contribution later in this chapter), where they may have met and pursued their interests in isolation from other self-advocacy groups, not even knowing the term 'self-advocacy' until several years after their formation.

Many states have started their own People First organisations. In some states an initial statewide convention has been planned by professionals who have then assumed the helper or adviser role to the people who attended. In other states a group of mentally handicapped people has planned the first convention themselves, with help as required. Either way, a convention has often been the impetus for the formation of statewide People First organisations. The mentally handicapped people who attend take the responsibility for organising the next convention and for trying to start local groups in their own communities. There is usually an election of a statewide Board of Directors or Planning Committee whose major task is the next convention.

Statewide groups that have adopted the name 'People First' are in operation in California, Colorado, Kansas, Nebraska, Oregon and Washington state. Ohio and Florida also have some local groups called 'People First'. Texas and Wisconsin have statewide conferences that they call simply 'self-advocacy conventions'. The self-advocacy groups in Massachusetts have conventions under the auspices of the state Association for Retarded Citizens, called 'Yes We CAN (Change Attitudes Now)' conventions.

Local action by these groups has been equally varied. People First of Dade County, Florida, have worked with the Quality Assurance Unit of the local Department of Health and Rehabilitative Services, to monitor the quality of community residential facilities. The Merry Macs of Lowell, Massachusetts, have members on a local Human Rights Committee. ACT of Minneapolis have been involved in changing the state Welfare Department's policy and rules concerning programmes in institutions, group homes and day services that involve aversive treatment or deprivation. People First of Colorado have lobbied the state legislature for a declaration of rights of handicapped people.

In several states, members of self-advocacy groups are on state government committees concerned with handicap, and a mentally handicapped person is now on the Board of Directors of the National Association for Retarded Citizens.

Strengthening the Movement
The work of all these disparate self-advocacy groups in America is still only loosely coordinated. However, two attempts have been made to organise the groups into a coherent movement, and already it is true that any new group is easily able to make contact with other groups and receive general information about self-advocacy, and is likely to identify itself with this national, and in the future international, movement.

As the first group to establish themselves as a strong, statewide organisation of mentally handicapped people – and coin the name 'People First' – People First of Oregon now fulfil a role, under their new title of People First International, of corresponding with groups, giving advice on the setting up of new groups, and pursuing their ideal of a well-coordinated international self-advocacy movement. Their address is given in Appendix Six.

People First International also publish *The People's Newsletter*, which includes offerings by groups and individuals from many states, giving information about other states' self-advocacy conventions and allowing self-advocacy groups to communicate with each other. Many of the groups previously mentioned in this chapter correspond regularly with People First International, whether or not they consider themselves to be part of a 'People First' movement.

In America, some important legislation and funding mechanisms have concerned what are referred to as 'developmental disabilities' – mental handicap, epilepsy, cerebral palsy and autism. People with these different handicaps thus have many common political interests. This sometimes acts as an encouragement for people with these different handicaps to join together in a local group, and thus it is that some groups have a mixed membership of people with mental and physical handicaps. In addition, many people foresaw a need for a coalition of self-advocacy groups concerned with these different handicaps, and became concerned to develop support for self-advocacy efforts by all people with these developmental disabilities.

In 1978 some federal (national government) money was made available to assist the development of self-advocacy among people with developmental disabilities. This money was given to a university-affiliated project called 'Technical Assistance for Self-Advocacy' (TASA), based at the University of Kansas. For three years, until its dissolution in 1981 due to lack of continued funding, the project produced literature, training materials and advice for self-advocacy groups.

The TASA project held a planning conference in Kansas City in March 1980 for leaders and advisers of self-advocacy groups from all over the country. Representatives from self-help groups of people with the disabilities of epilepsy and cerebral palsy, as well as those from self-advocacy groups of mentally handicapped people, were included. The delegates decided to form a new national coalition, uniting all people with developmental handicaps, to be called 'United Together'. Its goals were outlined as:

- Helping ourselves.
- Not letting other people do work for us that we can do.
- Serving on boards of directors and committees everywhere so we can better help handicapped people.
- Becoming a part of politics and working to change legislation that needs changing.
- Choosing our own helpers.
- Closing all institutions.
- Designing more community living situations.
- Getting more jobs for handicapped people.

- Getting equal pay for equal work.
- Encouraging others to help themselves.
- Keeping United Together together.
- Making United Together stronger by raising money.

The address of United Together is given in Appendix Six.

It was decided that a first task for the new coalition would be the organising of a national convention of self-advocacy groups concerned with developmental disabilities, to be held in Washington, DC in 1981. Its theme was to be 'Don't Count People – Let People Count'. Ten representatives from all over America were elected to work as a planning team for the convention. Because of the problem of getting together for this group, TASA provided some money for them to keep in touch regularly through 'teleconferences'. These involve the use of special telephone equipment enabling a number of people to communicate with each other over the telephone at the same time. Individual telephone conversations are brought together at a central point and can be heard by all participants. The ten people planning the 1981 United Together convention were able to communicate in this way every six weeks.

People First International and United Together thus represent the two attempts to coordinate the development of the self-advocacy movement in America. People First remains a loose network of groups whose membership is predominantly of mentally handicapped people. United Together is a national coalition of self-advocacy groups including those for people with epilepsy or cerebral palsy as well as those for mentally handicapped people.

Particular People First groups or groups belonging to United Together may well have members with a wide range of different handicaps. Many groups identify with both the People First movement and United Together. There is thus much overlap between the two. Neither has at present any substantial continuing source of financial support, and so each must stimulate future developments primarily by example, encouragement and whatever publicity can be achieved, supported almost entirely by voluntary effort and personal commitment. A cooperative partnership between United Together and the People First movement is likely to be the foundation for increasing the strength of the self-advocacy movement in future years.

Two other self-advocacy organisations which have primarily been concerned with physical handicap, but which are now opening their membership to mentally handicapped people and taking an increasing interest in their needs, are the American Coalition of Citizens with Disabilities, and the 'Centers for Independent Living' movement. The ACCD is involved in public education, monitoring legislation, and the development of training materials for groups. The CILs are centres where handicapped people themselves provide advisory and practical services to other handicapped people to enable them to live as independently as possible in the community. Addresses for information about the ACCD and about the CIL movement are given in Appendix Six.

Support for Self-Advocacy
In each state in America there are Developmental Disabilities Offices, carrying out, supporting and supervising the application of federal legislation on developmental disabilities. There is also a network across America of Advocacy Offices, developing and supporting advisory services to developmentally disabled people, sometimes including full citizen advocacy schemes (see Chapter Three). In nearly all areas of America there are also local Associations for Retarded Citizens – primarily parents' groups, but with an increasing involvement of mentally handicapped people themselves. In seeking funding or support in a particular area, a self-advocacy group might well look for help from these sources: the local Developmental Disabilities Office, Advocacy Office, or Association for Retarded Citizens. These agencies have often been instrumental in establishing self-advocacy groups.

As is typical of America, all sorts of written materials and other aids to assist the development of self-advocacy by individuals or groups are being produced. One example emanating from a state Advocacy Office is the manual on self-advocacy reproduced in Appendix Two, and an example prepared under the auspices of a state Association for Retarded Citizens is the curriculum on self-advocacy discussed in Chapter Five.

TASA had, between 1978 and 1981, some resources specifically to produce practical aids for the development of self-advocacy. Some examples of the information and advice produced by TASA are reproduced in Appendix Four.

One of the most useful items published by the project is a booklet called *How to Work with the System – and Win* by Barbara Noone Gibbons and Jacqueline Osborne. This describes in simple terms, with the use of cartoons: how to get people to change their minds, how to get people to understand your views, how to use a meeting to get your viewpoint across, how to prepare for a meeting, how to tackle objections, and so on. Typical of the advice given in the booklet is this:

Get a group of people together to go to the meeting with you. Be sure that everyone understands the problem and what you want to change. Remember: if they have four people at the meeting, you should have at least four people. Don't let them outnumber you.

At the time of its dissolution in 1981, TASA also had in draft form a *Self-Advocacy Workbook* written by Nancy Gardner. This has twelve chapters on:

- What is self-advocacy?
- Forming a group.
- Running a group.
- Working with an adviser.
- Working with a board of advisers.
- Writing a plan.
- Forming committees.
- Incorporation (legal registration as an organisation).
- Working with other groups.
- Publicity.
- Having a convention.
- Getting resources.

Each chapter has a simple, easy-to-follow format: an explanation of terminology, a story illustrating the point, questions and answers, and a checklist of actions to take after reading the chapter. The book is printed in large type.*

The National Institute on Mental Retardation in Canada has published a package called *Rights Now!* This is a set of tapes, slides and posters designed to teach handicapped people

*Kansas University Affiliated Facility, where TASA was located, is attempting to have the book commercially published, but at the time of writing it is regretfully out of print.

Other materials on self-advocacy produced by TASA may still be available from KUAF, address in Appendix Six.

about their rights. It can be used directly by handicapped people themselves, even if they cannot read, although there is a *Leader's Guide* for instructors leading training sessions; the materials can thus be used for teaching others or for self-instruction. The address of NIMR is given in Appendix Six.

The development and making available of such aids is a major step in ensuring that self-advocacy by mentally handicapped people can continue to be a reality in the future, and it is to be hoped that similar materials will continue to be developed and published.

Increased and better communication, a basic need of self-advocacy groups, also requires support and enabling structures. Helpers need to communicate with other helpers; groups need to hear from other groups; and groups and individuals need to communicate more – and more effectively – with the public, with decision-makers and with parents. There is still a great need for training materials on communication skills, and for official support for a network which will allow self-advocacy groups from around the world to share ideas and give encouragement to each other as they individually struggle with problems in their own communities.

Continued Growth

Meanwhile, the self-advocacy movement is spreading and growing strong. New groups are established monthly in America. Canada now has several People First organisations, and involvement of mentally handicapped people in the Canadian Association for the Mentally Retarded is extensive. At CAMR's annual conference in 1979, one hundred out of six hundred delegates were mentally handicapped people themselves, and many of them were featured as speakers.

In March 1981, Australia saw the birth of its first self-advocacy group, resulting from a conference for mentally handicapped people along the lines of the British 'Our Life' conference. Several such conferences were held in Australia during the 1970s. The new group functions in the state of Victoria and calls itself 'Force Ten – the Victorian Union of Intellectually Disadvantaged Citizens'. Force Ten has drawn up a manifesto of rights for residents in institutions and has sent a delegation of members to discuss this with the state Health Minister.

Self-advocacy by mentally handicapped people has been in America, and continues to be internationally, a revolutionary development contradicting deeply held views about the very nature of mental handicap.

Who Are the Self-Advocates?

A common response to the phenomenon of self-advocacy has been to suggest that it is only possible for an elite of relatively mildly handicapped people. As has been explained, some of the American groups include all people with 'developmental disabilities' (mental handicap, cerebral palsy, epilepsy and autism). Sometimes this has meant that people with primarily physical disabilities have been able to contribute their intellectual skills to the development of the self-advocacy movement. However, in the majority of groups the leaders are people firmly labelled mentally handicapped, and in some cases have a quite severe degree of mental handicap.

Self-advocacy does not develop on its own. Mentally handicapped people need time and strong support to develop skills of participating in the democratic processes of a group. The People First movement has shown that many severely handicapped people can do this. Some lend support to the group primarily by their presence. Others, including for example many people with Down's syndrome, have become committee members and officers of groups, and competent public speakers. In most of the groups, few members can read or write well; few are completely independent; many are under guardianship, do not have jobs, depend on social security benefits, or live in residential care. Many of them have been in institutions, some for many years. Some have severe communication problems.

The film *People First* and the photographs in this book give an impression of the degree of handicap of the participants in the self-advocacy movement at its present stage of development in America. Most of the members are typical of those one might find attending an Adult Training Centre in Britain. If their behaviour, demeanour and ability to participate are of a higher order than that which one usually encounters amongst a comparable group of mentally handicapped people elsewhere, this is precisely because of their involvement in the self-advocacy movement.

As Professor Dybwad says: 'Let us not argue how soon or how many of our young people will be able to express themselves; let us instead ask ourselves, are we ready to listen to their new voice?'

The New Voice in America
The following contributions come from written accounts by the members of self-advocacy groups themselves, or interviews with them by Bonnie Shoultz. Again, Bonnie has edited them to make their flow more coherent, but they remain the words of the contributors themselves.

I Like To Stretch Out Beyond Myself
by Joyce Lawson, The Pioneer Club, Massachusetts
I lived with my parents until I was about 22, and then I lived in a town called Gardner, Massachusetts. I lived in an apartment building for about two years. Then there was trouble in the building – some things happened that my parents didn't think were too appropriate, so I moved back with them for about a month and a half. And then in June of 1977 I moved to where I am presently living, in Greenfield. Greenfield is a medium-sized town west of Boston. I've lived here four years now, and am now 28 years old.

Now that I'm living here in Greenfield, things have changed for me. I do what I want, and I don't have to answer to anybody. I have a counsellor who helps me with my budget and other things, but I don't have to tell her where I am every single minute. Before, I felt like I didn't have any breathing space. My roommate and I live in an apartment programme run by the Association for Retarded Citizens.

I went up to fifth grade in normal elementary school, and then I started going to special classes because I couldn't keep up with the rest of the class and I kept falling back. When we moved to Massachusetts, I went to a special class in eighth and half of ninth grades, and then I went away to a training school for two years. From there, I worked, getting started on my first paying job. Then when I moved to Greenfield, they had a programme called CETA that was an adult educational programme. I went through that and I got my high school equivalency diploma in December of 1979.

I don't think I was labelled mentally handicapped until I was labelled 'mildly retarded' by the Vocational Rehabilitation Department of the Commonwealth of Massachusetts. But I'm a very quick learner, and I have a very good memory for everything.

For my first jobs, I worked as a maid in the private homes of elderly people. Now I'm in a programme where I get trained to work in a nursing home. In this programme the clients work for the employers, but the programme pays part of their salary until they have learned the job. That way you have someone over you to help you if you have any problems during work. At the end of the training programme the employer, if he thinks you have done a good job, hires you at the regular salary.

I used to volunteer my time as a teacher with retarded adults who lived in the Belchertown State Hospital. They would learn basic cooking skills, how to identify objects, and things like that.

I first learned about self-advocacy when I heard that retarded adults, namely people like myself, could become citizen advocates for other people. I have been an advocate now for about two years. My protégée is an eleven-year-old retarded child, and I see her often. The way I heard about it was that I once had an advocate that worked with me. Then when I found out that the best way to get involved with advocacy programmes is to advocate for yourself, I became really interested in becoming this little girl's advocate. I came to know her through a recreational programme that I used to work for.

There is a self-advocacy group here in Greenfield. We call ourselves the Pioneer Club. I'm a secretary in the club now, and I held the presidency for two years. When we started our club, we didn't know anything about self-advocacy. It was just to have something to do besides sitting around home. We were curious about the Mohawks and Squaws, the oldest self-advocacy group in Massachusetts. Three years ago we went down to observe one of their meetings. We were so impressed by it that we said: 'We want to do this, too.' The next thing I knew we had elected a chairperson, way before we had even thought of officers. Then we decided to have officers, and the chairperson ran an election. I was the first person to be elected as President, and eventually we elected the other officers. We had six officers for a while but now we just have four. At first we had two Presidents, but we didn't really feel we needed two because the Vice-President is supposed to handle the President's responsibilities if the President is sick. We also have two directors: a Public Relations and a Social Director. The Social Director is over the committees that get voted in to do certain things. The public relations man is supposed to make sure the community knows about our club. We've had mention of our club over the radio and in the newspaper. Many people have heard the public relations man talk about our club.

Massachusetts has had self-advocacy for 25 years, with the Mohawks and Squaws. To me, self-advocacy means that now people can advocate for themselves, doing things that they couldn't do before. You might say that it's being more of a person rather than something else. It's people learning to help themselves.

Since I got involved, I have found that I like to stretch out beyond myself. I like working with other people. If they have a problem, the members turn to me and talk to me. I tell them that if they have anything bothering them or any questions, I'll talk about it with them. I tell them not to be afraid to talk to me about it. A lot of people tell me I'm a real leader to them. I usually put myself last, behind other people. Since I became involved in self-advocacy, I feel that I'd really rather talk to a person who didn't understand it than a person who did understand it. I'd rather explain it to a new person.

It's made me feel good about other people, and about their feelings, and how they can react. What really makes me angry sometimes is when I have to listen to ignorant people saying that they feel sorry for these people or just saying: 'How can these poor people do this and that? How can they do things when they're so slow?' The minute I hear that it makes me so angry because we're no different from anyone else. I mean, we may learn slower but, in reality, we're just like anyone else. We're all born the same way, and I don't see why anybody would want to treat us any different. Sometimes they treat a handicapped person like a disease. They're almost afraid to approach them.

I think that if a person is able to show any kind of talent or anything, they should be given the chance to do it, rather than being discouraged. But I've found that that's happened many, many, many times where a lot of the slower people want to do something, and these other people, who think they know so much, kind of discourage it.

I've always wanted to have a high school diploma. But they told me a long time ago: 'No, you can't do it. It would be too hard for you.' It just made me furious. So I went ahead and did it. And here I am today, you know, I've got it.

Right now our goal is to have some conferences here, for our part of the state. We're trying to plan two regional conferences and one great big statewide conference.

I'm also on the statewide Consumer Advisory Board for the Massachusetts Association for Retarded Citizens. We haven't decided on a name yet for our statewide convention – that's something that all of us would work out together. I've heard that each state that has self-advocacy does it differently. Some of them call theirs 'People First'.

I hope that every other state that I met in Kansas, at the Coalition meeting, will become just as famous as Massachusetts. I hope that some day, somehow, we can all come together again and meet again. I made a lot of good friends at that meeting in Kansas. It was wonderful to meet so many people from across the country all involved in self-advocacy.

I Like Helping Other People
by Jana Elder, People First of Kansas

I'm 22 years old, and I've lived with my parents all my life. I live in Winfield, Kansas, and work at Cowley County Developmental Services, at Strother Field. In May 1978, I graduated from Winfield High School where I attended Special Education Classes half of the day and regular classes the other half.

I'm planning on moving to Arkansas City in July or August, when the housing is completed, with a girlfriend who did work in the workshop but now works in a restaurant. We're going to share the expenses of the apartment and all other costs. We will be living in the section for Independent Living. We'll get advice when needed, but otherwise be on our own.

I never knew anything about rights or self-advocacy until I went to the People First Convention in Kansas in 1978. I was elected State People First Secretary. This year I helped plan the State Convention in May in Arkansas City. It's a lot of work, arranging for the rooms, food, speakers, and everything. It was my first experience at doing anything like this and it was hard, but it all went well. We have a People First group at our workshop in which I'm active. We also have a local union that I am in charge of as to when we meet, etc. We discuss problems the clients have and if we can't handle it, we take it to the programme co-ordinator. We have different channels we can take. This has worked for us.

As an officer in People First of Kansas, I attended a National Issues and Planning Conference in Kansas City, Missouri, where I was elected as a Coalition Representative. There are ten of us who represent ten different regions of the country. We are called United Together, and incorporated as a not-for-profit organisation. We have a Coalition Telephone Conference monthly to plan and discuss reaching our goals. We are now planning a national convention, where disabled people from every state can meet and decide how to shape the future, in October 1981 at Hospitality House, Arlington, Virginia, in the Washington, DC area. I plan to go to the convention and see all the people again. I've really gotten to know people from all over the country and learn about their lives and their part of the country.

I worked in a restaurant as a dishwasher for several months. Then because of dental surgery I was replaced. Since then I have done janitorial work outside the workshop and now am assisting supervising at the workshop for the staff.

I can't really explain what self-advocacy means to me. I do know since I got involved I've made three public speakings, one at a City Commissioner's meeting. I attended a meeting where Senator Nancy Kasabaum spoke and I talked with her. I can write my own speeches but need help spelling. I'm more confident about things. I like helping other people even more. We help each other at the workshop.

I've met a lot of people through self-advocacy. The Coalition has especially brought some points out to me that I've never seen before. Like Jesse, one of the guys on the Coalition, who is in an institution. It really gets to me sometimes when I think about him. And I know I've learned a lot. He doesn't know why he's in there. I wish some day it would happen that a lot of these people would get out of institutions and into group homes. I was talking to Jesse, and that's one of the goals he wants to achieve.

I find that being a leader is not easy. I think everybody

should try to. I feel I've been lucky because I have parents and three brothers who love me and encourage me. Also Bill Vardy, Director at CCDS, gives me opportunities to use my talents and abilities.

I Always Knew What I Wanted
by Marvin Coile, People First of Dade County, Florida

I was born in New York City, but I've spent most of my life in Miami. I'm 34 years old, and I lived with my parents as I was growing up. I was never in an institution. I lived with both parents for 16 years, and with my mom for 14 years after that. I feel my parents helped me learn to make decisions on my own. When I was younger, I was treated equally with my brothers and my sisters. I moved out four years ago to get married, and we've lived in our apartment ever since. My wife didn't live in an institution either, but most of the people in our self-advocacy groups here – about 65 per cent – live in group homes. Most of those did live in an institution.

Right now, I'm the Consumer Coordinator with the state Association for Retarded Citizens. I am working together with several groups forming self-advocacy groups around the area. We are working on two in Miami, and my adviser, Nina Cohen, and I have gone on state visits in Florida. We have approximately eight self-advocacy groups going now. Most of them are in the community.

Before I did this I ran an elevator. And I worked at a place called Applefield, and I worked at North Dade Children's Center, with handicapped and retarded children.

I was in special education classes when I was growing up. What I mean is that I had three or four regular classes a day, and four hours of special education. I got up to approximately the ninth grade. Now I'm going part time to the Beverly Hoskins Vocational School in Miami. I'm trying to get a high school equivalency diploma. I never had any vocational training.

I always knew what I wanted. I felt all the time that the handicapped and retarded citizen had a right to be treated as an equal. I became a member of the Board of Directors of the local Association for Retarded Citizens. The Director had heard about People First, and he told me about it, and the rest is all history. I helped to found People First of Dade County, and we had our second anniversary in March of 1981. I will also be President of People First of Florida, when we finish getting formed. We had elections last May and I was elected President then. Both groups will be trying to show the public that handicapped and retarded citizens can be treated like normal persons, and deserve the same rights as everybody else. We have had a small convention in Orlando and we plan a larger state convention. In Orlando, there were about 80 of us, and we set a format for what we wanted to do for the future. We are having a small convention of 25 people in April, and we're having a large one next year.

I do a lot of public speaking and public relations. In fact, this morning I picked up two proclamations naming this Sunday 'People First Sunday'. The mayors of Miami and Dade County issued those.

I am also on the Board of Directors for the Florida Association for Retarded Citizens. When I accepted my paid position as Consumer Coordinator, I had to give up my position on the Dade County ARC Board.

To me, self-advocacy is feeling good about yourself. It's proving to the world that you can get out in the community. It's proving to the community that you can hold on to a steady job. Of course, along with self-advocacy there are a lot of responsibilities. Some of those are things like getting up in the morning, getting to work on time, getting along with your neighbours – things like that. I feel that every person can live as independently as possible, and that is their right.

When I first got involved in self-advocacy, I knew what I wanted but I couldn't express myself. Then I learned to speak out. It just gives me a good feeling when my brothers and my sisters, as I call them – the handicapped people of Dade County – learn to speak up and say: 'We want this, and we need that.' It's just made me more of a person. It's also really helped my wife out, because she had some real emotional problems when she was young, and now she's really come out of her shell.

Self-advocacy has helped me help other people, and it's helped me to take responsibility. I don't claim to be the best person in the world – nobody is – but when I make a mistake I want to be told about it. Then I'll try not to do the same thing again. Although a lot of times I'll do the same thing again!

Self-advocacy has also caused my family, my brothers and

sisters, to see me with new respect. They'll call me and say: 'I saw you on TV today.' They always say: 'I always knew this would happen to you!' They say they knew ten years ago that this would happen.

We are hoping that the groups we are working with will form client governments. In one institution that I'm working at, in Semiem, Miami, I'm hoping that these people will get out in the community. I'm working with a client government there, with eight or ten clients there. They are all really whizzes. Our other goals would be to have People First chapters in every county in Florida. We're on a five-year grant, and if that's approved we'll create ten new chapters. People First of Florida will be formed, but we will only have eight or ten chapters at the start. Actually, I think People First of Florida would continue even if we didn't have any funding. Our consumers really want that.

I'd like to say this about being a consumer leader: start with small things. Maybe the first thing a leader could do is just get to know his Board of Directors, and get to know the members well. That's an accomplishment right there. When we started People First in Dade County, we thought we'd change the world in one year. Then, when the end of the year rolled around, we hadn't even started yet. We were discouraged until it was brought to our attention that we had applied for a grant and gotten it. That made us feel good. In other words, don't expect to change the world in one year. It's hard work, but it can be a lot of fun, and it doesn't all have to be work. Once in a while you can have a party to raise funds.

We have people running for offices who, two years ago, would have never thought of running. It just makes you feel good, seeing people coming out of their shells and all that. I don't claim to be the best leader in the world, but I believe in myself, and I feel that if a leader believes in himself he's got half the battle won. The other half of the battle is to win what he wants and to expect also to accept defeat and responsibilities.

I Would Give My Life for People First
by Larry Rice, People First of California

I was in a lot of institutions, in New York, Chicago, and California. I had a very upset life, and I kept running away by going into institutions. I ran away from my own personal problems. The reason I ran away was because I kept wanting to take my life all the time. I was in hospitals for mentally handicapped people and people with problems.

I'm 39 now. I lived with my parents until I was about eight. Then they put me in Sonoma State Hospital for 15 years. I didn't stay there for 15 years straight in a row, but I went in and out. When I got out, I'd be in a Family Care home. Seemed like every three years I would go back to the hospital, then I would stay in there for a while, and then I would go back in the community. This is the longest I've stayed out of the hospital, because I left in 1962 and I've been out ever since then. I did go back to other hospitals, trying to commit myself, but they wouldn't let me. So they made me stay out, which I'm glad they're doing now, because it's so simple to go and get away from your problems instead of working your problems out. When I was a teenager, I kept not listening to people much, 'cause I had so many problems in my whole life that I didn't know who to believe.

I even went to Florida for two years when I lost my government job in 1975. I did the same thing again, running away from my problems. I thought I would stay there and live there, but it didn't help my problems at all. I just took my ticket and took a one-way trip.

I'm not doing that kind of thing anymore, because People First here has helped me to face my problems, and to live with my problems, and to live with other people. I would give my life for People First.

I was in special education, but I didn't really stay with it, because I was very stubborn and had my own thoughts and wouldn't listen. I wish I did go to school and listen. But I've learned a lot since I've been with People First.

I worked in food service in the Air Force for five years, and I worked in janitorial service in a naval hospital. And I had problems in both jobs, and they didn't work out too well, so they decided to put me on disability pension. I went to Florida when I was on disability. I came back to California in 1977, and I lived in Fairfax then.

I got involved in self-advocacy in 1978. It started with my roommate – he was involved. But it was really the Support Center that helped me the most. That's who I work for now. The Support Center is a self-advocacy organisation. It started with a girl who was in home placement, and she needed some support, so that's how the Support Center got involved with People First. I got involved about two months later, because I was still kind of shy and didn't want to listen to people. I had to find out for my own self. They told me: 'If *you* don't get any help with people, then you're not helping yourself or helping other people.'

I was the Vice-President of People First of California most of the first three years. Then I was the President, but it flew by so fast. I was only the President a month and a half! Then People First of California hired me to be Project Coordinator, so I had to give up my presidency. We had our first Board meeting on 8 March.

My job now is with the Support Center. My title is Assistant Trainer, and I assist Kathy in everything she asks me to do, and I go to meetings and give speeches. Now I'm the Project Coordinator for People First of California. I'm the head one, but I have a co-worker in the evenings. My job is to get the south and north ends of California together as one big family, and I'm also supposed to do legislating. Sometimes I meet with legislators and talk about politics. If there's an issue we don't like, we might go up to the legislature and fight about it and talk about it. I have a Speaker's Bureau together. It's made of handicapped people who speak for themselves and others. We held a convention this last year.

Self-advocacy means a lot to me, 100 per cent. It helps me in standing up for my own life, and helping others. It helps me in renting my own apartment, and standing up to professionals and telling them what we want.

Before I got involved, I was very suicidal and very shy, and I never did trust people. I was *very* unhappy all the time. I still have my personal problems, but since I have met People First, my life has changed by a 90-degree angle. I've learned to help others. I've always wanted to be a teacher. I've taught people to speak for themselves. I taught them to use their own judgement on things, and I've taught them to speak their feelings, not let it stay in. And I've done role-playing with them. In fact, I'm working with a guy now in my own home. He lets everybody take advantage of him, and I'm teaching him not to let people do that. Even I try to use him too much. Then I ask him to help me. I tell him to say: 'No, I don't want you to be telling me what to do!' I'm working on that with him now.

You know what I found out? It's consumers helping consumers. You see, a lot of you people go to school to learn this. But we have the true experience, because we know what they are and what they feel. It's really true. Even the teacher I worked under at Sonoma State Hospital in 1959 said that people opened up a lot more when I took over once in a while.

I'm better at taking responsibility now. I have a little bit of scaredness yet. It's only been three years now. It's still kind of new. And what makes me so mad is when programmes don't allow you enough time. They should allow you at least five years for funding. It took me about three years. Now I feel if we had at least five years, we'd really be able to handle the programme on our own from then on.

Our next goal is to work with parents, to get them to understand us, and for us to understand them. I'm giving a talk to a parents' group at Sonoma State Hospital soon. Our other goal is to get the two halves of California together by the end of the year.

I believe that our rights are very important, just as important as anybody else's rights. I believe we should be treated equal, have good jobs, and let people *see* us. I believe it's happening. People are beginning to look at us and see us as people.

I have two other goals. I'd like to get an Independent Living project going, to let people live on their own. For so many years, people have been in these Family Care homes, and in living projects, with advisers being over them all the time. They don't have the freedom to speak and feel what's on their minds. I also want to be a teacher. The teacher I worked with at Sonoma State Hospital tells me I was born a teacher. Some day I hope to do that, too.

Who the Hell Do You Think I Am?
by Bernard Carabello, One-to-One Foundation, New York

I was placed in Willowbrook when I was three years old, and I was there 18 years. I am 31 years old now. They placed me there because they thought I was mentally retarded. I have cerebral palsy. I couldn't communicate at all when I was placed there.

Willowbrook was overcrowded. I rotated from building to building, and every building was not the same. In some buildings, they had 70 to 80 severely retarded people on one ward with two or three people to take care of them. Other buildings would be a little better. You were placed according to your age and sex and what they thought was your functioning level.

We just got custodial care there. I did learn to walk in 'Rehabilitation'. Not everyone got rehabilitation. I don't know how I was chosen, but I was one of the lucky ones. They taught me to talk, too. The first thing I learned was how to curse.

They made all the decisions for us. We didn't know anything about our rights. Finally I met a doctor named Mike Wilkins. He got fired from Willowbrook because he organised a panel group. We became good friends while he worked there. He started in 1969, and I thought he was crazy because he put his hands on the patients to examine them. No other doctor ever did that before, because they thought they might catch some kind of disease. He's the one who got Geraldo Rivera to do an exposé on Willowbrook on ABC (a national television network). I met Geraldo Rivera through him. The exposé was done in the beginning of 1972. I was on a ward for severely and profoundly retarded persons at the time. I helped them with the exposé, and they put me on the air.

I left Willowbrook on 16 February 1972. Actually, I left before that, and when I refused to go back, my mother signed me out indefinitely. I saw Dr Wilkins every week after that, until he moved to Kansas City, Missouri.

When I left Willowbrook, I stayed with my mother for a while. I got an apartment with a roommate, and stayed there for a year until I got my own. Ever since then I've been on my own. For a while it was really difficult to make my own decisions, because I was so used to people making all my decisions for me.

I have very little education. In Willowbrook, we went to school for three hours a day and worked another two to three hours a day. I was a janitor, but they didn't use the word 'janitor'. They used the word 'work-boy'. They paid you $5 a month, but they called that 'store cards' – you didn't get cash, you got store cards. If you ran away, or if you had sexual relations with anybody, they locked you in seclusion. You only had a mattress on the floor, and one window in the room. Do you know what the biggest crime was? It was sex and homosexuality. They beat the hell out of you; they put a stick to your head.

After I got out, I was going through an identity crisis. I got SSI (a federal disability pension) and Aid to the Disabled for a while. I used to work at One-to-One Foundation (a private organisation founded by Geraldo Rivera to change public attitudes towards group homes and towards persons with handicaps) as a volunteer. I wouldn't call it all work – I used to goof around a lot. I was lazy until 1978, when I got my first job – I didn't know what I wanted to do. At the time of the exposé on Willowbrook, with me being on TV, I had stars in my eyes. After it's all over, you begin to realise who you are.

I got my first job with Protection and Advocacy Systems for Developmental Disabilities. It's a federally funded programme run by the state. They were interested in self-advocacy. I knew nothing from nothing – didn't know the word, didn't know what the hell it meant. I said I would take the job. I was desperate at the time. I was scared. Every day I would quit my job because I didn't want to do it. But as I got into it I liked it more and more. At first, I didn't understand what I was supposed to do, and I didn't have the back-up support I wanted. I had a volunteer, but that was not enough. I needed someone to tell me what to do for a while. I only stayed there about seven months. Then I resigned because they were not meeting all their obligations. They were not giving services to the people that needed them. I was not going to be a part of that, and I told HEW (the Health, Education and Welfare Department of the federal government) and other officials. I got fired by the administrator, and I was rehired by the Board of Directors. But I quit that same week. Two years later HEW took the grant away.

I was unemployed for two months. Then I took a job with the National Association for Retarded Citizens. I worked there a year and got laid off because of cutbacks.

Then I went to One-to-One Foundation. I actually started with One-to-One when the organisation started nine years ago. I'm on their Board of Directors. I don't get paid by them. It's a crazy relationship, but the state's crazy anyway.

My job now is paid for by the State Office of Mental Retardation and Developmental Disabilities. But I work in One-to-One's offices, because I refuse to work in the institution. I'm a borrowed staff. I do self-advocacy for One-to-One. I work just in New York City right now, because I'm having a hard time with a lack of funds. I work mostly with mentally retarded people because they've been singled out all their lives.

We had a statewide conference at Columbia University. About 110 people came. We had a local one at New York University. Only about 50 people came, because New York City is so wide. It's hard for people to get transportation.

I'm trying to set up a Speakers' Bureau – not for me to give speeches, but for other people who are retarded. I want them to learn to speak in front of groups and to legislators.

To me, self-advocacy means being yourself; fighting for your rights; doing things for yourself; respecting yourself and other people; taking responsibility for your actions; and knowing what your rights are.

When I got involved, I began to recognise who I am, and how important I am to other people. And I never saw that before, up until now. Other people respect me, respect my opinion. A lot of things happened to me since I got involved. My whole personality changed around.

I'm much better at helping others. I talk to people. I got SSI for someone who really needed it. I got a home for someone else. That makes me feel really good.

I try not to treat people 'special'. They don't need that. I have people come to me and talk down to me, as if I'm a child or hard-of-hearing: 'How *are* you?' 'You're a *good* boy!' I had a woman give me a dollar and tell me to go buy myself some ice cream. I said: 'You need it more than I do.' She said: 'Thank you.' Sometimes I'll jokingly say: 'Hey, you've got to do this for me – I'm handicapped!' It makes a point. One time a salesman knocked on the door, and he saw me and said: 'Is anybody home?' I said: 'Who the hell do you think *I* am?'

Another time I had to go to make a speech early in the morning. I took the subway. I was standing up, and there were two women there, one sitting down. The one who was standing said: 'Oh, give the poor kid your seat. He's sick.' I said: 'I was okay when I left the house this morning. I didn't have a fever.'

Public education is very important. But you've got to do it with humour, too, to get the point across. You can't take everything so seriously.

My goal for the New York groups is to pull them all together with a state convention. Other than that, I want the groups to set the goals. I don't want to be the one making the decisions. They have to do it. They have to tell me what they want. I cannot tell them what they want.

I don't consider myself a leader. I don't want to lead anybody. I consider myself a follower. I want to be a part of the people. Being a leader is important to some of the people I work with, because they've never been a leader of anything before. It makes them feel important, and that's important to me, that they feel that way. I think the most important thing to me is people respecting themselves, so they can win the respect of other people.

These next four years are going to be hard, educating the legislators who are so conservative. But if the self-advocacy movement can give the people the sense of importance within themselves, then they can't lose – even if they have their funds cut, and even if they don't win politically.

I Can Do Something for You
by Patricia Killius, Resident Government Group,
Syracuse Developmental Center, New York

I'm 30 years old. I was born here in the Syracuse area. I was born blind, and I also have cerebral palsy. I also had seizures until I was 16 years old, when I grew out of them. My family still lives here in this area. My mother is a registered nurse. I lived at home until I was 12. Then I lived in Craig Developmental Center, which is much bigger than this place. I came here to the Syracuse Developmental Center on 28 December 1973, my 23rd birthday. I was one of the founders of this Resident Government Group.

Syracuse Development Center is for people with mental retardation. Many of us here were in Craig before. They're trying to get us into the community. I don't know how many people live here, but I know there are 20 on a unit and there are quite a few units.

I went to the New York Institute for the Blind for four years, but I couldn't learn braille because of my palsy. I don't have fine finger coordination, and you need that to do braille.

They tried once to get me into a home in the community, but it didn't work out for me. But there is a worksite, a sheltered workshop near here, and I go there every day, eight hours a day.

I have to do special work at work, because I have a dexterity problem. Sometimes I don't get paid much. But I like the work. I like the supervisors. I like the people. Right now I'm putting rubber mats into bags. I started working there just two or three years ago.

I went to Craig in the first place because my mother was in a very bad accident. I got sick also, and started having really bad seizures, and my mother couldn't handle it. I still have a lot of contact with my mother. I don't see her as often as I'd like, but I do talk to her on the phone a lot.

I'm learning to make decisions, being the Vice-President of the Resident Government Group. A lot of times the decisions don't come easy, but they're coming. It's a really, really hard process.

A few weeks ago I was interviewed by a Syracuse newspaper reporter. I said: 'All our rights are being violated.' She asked me a specific question: 'Do you believe what people are doing for you is right? For example, getting you out in the community?' I told her: 'I believe they're trying, but not hard enough.' When you go through an interview, and get promised a home, and the next thing you know you get turned down, because either you're too bright for them – that's what happened in my case – or for some other reason, it's hard to take. Now I'm waiting for a second home to be built, but it's going to take a while for them to do it. I'm willing to take the risk. I think the Resident Government Group has shown me what I can do while I'm taking the risk of waiting.

The Resident Government Group has been in existence eight years. I helped to found it. We have meetings once a week; people come from the units to talk over problems that are facing them, and also how they can cope with it.

We write letters to people if there's an emergency, to let the people at the Center know we mean business. We had a problem with a chemical called PCB, which is a very bad chemical, a cancer agent. They did a test for it in an office building in Binghamton (a neighbouring town) and said it was here also. They evacuated the office building, but they did nothing for the people here. I was responsible for writing a letter saying: 'If you can do this for the people in Binghamton, why can't you do anything for the people here?' Only staff people knew about it, and not residents. There was very poor communication there. No one who worked here and knew about it passed it on to the residents. We were exposed to it. The day it came out in the paper, one of the people who works here stepped on some of it and it was spread through the halls. I wrote to the Director, saying: 'Will you *please* tell me what is going on? We are in a danger zone here! Whether you like it or not, there is a problem.' I'm still waiting for answers to my letters.

I'm one of the four officers in the group. The only reason the staff are there is to advise us. They're not to run the meeting in any way. When I write a letter, the President or the Secretary takes it down for me.

We're trying to get other teams involved. The institution is organised into teams; the teams are made up of a number of units, and there are 20 people to a unit. Each team has a letter (like Team A, Team B, etc.) and a leader who runs the team. My team is Team B – Adult Service. Because of our Resident Group, we've gotten things done like you wouldn't believe. We got stoves hooked up for our use, and ours was the first unit to get a stove. We got the first refrigerator. Last week we had a bake sale to raise money. This was a big accomplishment.

We're using the money from the bake sale for our own letterhead paper. Right now, when we send a letter, the reply comes to other people's mailboxes, because we didn't have our own mailbox or our own stationery. Now we'll get our own replies. Once we organised a dinner dance in the community at a restaurant. The first year, we organised to vote in elections – that was a big deal, learning how to do that, getting assistance, etc.

We don't have many rights in here. We do have the right to organise, and to speak up. But you can't go anywhere without telling someone where you're going to go; you can't set up things without having other people know about it; you're always being watched, especially if you're in a place where people don't want you to be. The infringement comes in especially with our right to privacy. That's why I like the transportation I take to work – at least I know I'm not being watched on my way to work. It's bad, especially for someone who is able to take care of herself.

I'm especially concerned about continuing the work I'm doing when I go out into the community. When a lot of people go into the community, they go into these workshops, and it's not fair for them. They don't get paid the same amount. They don't have the transportation that they should have for the community. They don't have the same services in the community that were given to them here. For example, I get physical therapy here three times a week. If I go into the community, I'd like to continue getting it. If I don't, then I can't move or do anything for myself. My muscles get really, really stiff. I have to have that physical therapy. So I'm concerned about my rights in the community as well.

The community has to accept us. We're handicapped, but we have needs like everyone else. Some of our needs are special, but they have to be accepted. We're not asking for your blood – we're just asking to be treated as you'd want to be treated, if you were in our position.

Self-advocacy means that you can do what you want for yourself. It means you can represent yourself in several groups and tell them how you feel about yourself, without being afraid of saying it. I'd never have known I'd be saying this after eight years. It wasn't easy to do, either. We've just gotten to the point where we're getting really good at talking and writing letters. We're being really honest with ourselves.

I feel more secure within myself. I feel better about myself. I feel more open than I used to be. All this has happened because of self-advocacy!

My goals are that if I go into the community, someone can help continue the job I did, to take over where I left off and never let Resident Government die. I think that's the most important thing – we need a government like this, and I'm hoping we can spread it all over the state. We're unique, we're the only institution that has it.

Gen Sepanek, the President, and I, have been really good friends for eight years. We've been through a lot together. After we started Resident Government, people came and went. Lots of people left the institution, and the Resident Government Group started going downhill. People were leaving, people didn't care, but we kept it up. Now we have a four-unit system. We got three other units to join us, and we're going to help Team C and Team D to start a Resident Government Group, also.

It's good being a leader. It's really helped me a lot. I know more about myself and other people. I've always cared for people, but not in the respect that I do now. Years ago I could care for people, and say: 'Okay, I like you. I wish I could do something for you.' But nothing would be done. Now it's: 'I *can* do something for you. I can tell people how you feel, because I've been that way myself, and I feel the same way you do.'

Everybody Is an Important Person
by Judy Cunio, People First International, Oregon

I am 29 years old. I was in Fairview for six years. I was 22 when I got out. I was there part of the time when Valerie was in there. Then she left, and then I did. People First got going after both of us were out.

In Fairview, I didn't feel I had any rights. I had no say in what happened to me. They made all the decisions. They did everything for me. Nobody ever asked me what I wanted to do. They just said: 'No, we're going to do it this way and we know what is best for you.'

I left there because I never really belonged there. My handicap is cerebral palsy. I am not mentally retarded. I went there because there was no other place to get help, and I needed several operations. Fairview was the only way I could get help.

I had lived with my parents before I went there. Then after I was there, my mom didn't really want me to get out. I had to talk with her for about two years. I told her I had to try. It has worked out okay. She saw that I could work at the office, and she's been happy about it ever since.

I lived in a group home for about a year. Then I lived in a private home for about two years. I've been living by myself for about three years. I worked for Goodwill Industries for a year, and as an aide in a group home for a year, and also as a co-office worker for People First.

I have been the Secretary and the Treasurer of People First. Now I'm a Board member. I got involved seven years ago. I heard what they were trying to do and I thought: 'Yes, it sounds really good.' So I joined them and I've been involved ever since.

I do a lot of public speaking in Oregon. I have been to Idaho, California, Missouri, and quite a few other places.

To me, self-advocacy means that everybody is an important

person. Everybody has something to offer. Everybody has the right to be their own person, and to feel good, that: 'Hey, I am okay!' You don't have to be ashamed of who you are. No matter who you are, you have yourself. And people should say: 'Hey, I want to hear what you have to say. I do care about you.'

Before, I really felt bad about me. I felt that I was weird. I felt that I was no good to anybody. Now I feel: 'Hey, I'm okay.' Now I try to be there if other people need me. I say: 'You don't have to feel sorry for yourself. Get up and do something about it. You have that right!'

As a leader, I would like to tell people what they can do. It's hard work. You have to use energy. You really have to get out and work. You have to learn what other people are like. I used to be very worried about what everybody thought about me. I don't care now because I feel that if you do what you are able to do, you shouldn't worry about what people think of you. Just do it.

We Can Be a Valuable Person
by Valerie Schaaf, People First International, Oregon

I've been the first President of People First, and the second Treasurer. Now I'm President of the Board of Directors. I've been President of the Board since 1977. The Board covers the whole state.

I've done public speaking all over Oregon and in many states in the United States. So far I haven't been asked to go to a foreign country. I'm waiting for that.

To be a leader, you should just get out and stand up for your rights. It's hard because you have a lot of people who have different opinions, and you have to be able to take all those and decide between two sides. It is hard at times to say: 'No, you're wrong.' You've got to be able to try to balance the beam between the sides. It's been a learning experience for me.

I'm 31 years old. I lived with my parents until I was 16, and then I went to Fairview. I was there six years. I got out shortly before my 22nd birthday. Fairview is an institution that helps mentally retarded people to achieve living situations. They teach some how to cook. Some get schooling. If they don't know how to dress, they teach them to dress and take care of their personal hygiene.

I was in a special school from seventh through ninth grades.

At Fairview I finished my high school education. I also have my GED (high school equivalency diploma) and I got that in the shortest time of any handicapped person in Oregon. They're thinking of putting my name down in the *Book of World Records*. But I'm not sure I want it! I've also gone to Chemeketa State College. I've gone to school in any way you can!

I learned most about how to make my own decisions while I lived at home with my parents. At Fairview, everything was done for me. I felt I had no rights. Whenever I was pushed around or abused by another resident or by an aide, it was kept quiet. Whenever you wanted to report something, they wouldn't believe that an aide or anybody else had done something to you. It wouldn't leave marks of any sort, so you couldn't prove it.

I left Fairview because I felt I was able to do things in the community. I didn't feel that Fairview was for me any longer. I left on 19 January 1972. I went to a group home. That was pretty good, but not something that I really liked. I was in two private group homes, in fact. I felt I'd be better off on my own. I've been living on my own since 1975. I live all by myself in Salem, Oregon. Living on my own is great. I've gotten to where I can make decisions about anything.

I've had quite a few different jobs since I got out. I've worked in sheltered workshops, but I didn't find that too amusing, because you couldn't make enough to live on from that. I was in one workshop for a year and in another for a year and a half. But jobs haven't been too good with me. It's hard getting a job and hard getting the community to see that you could do a job, or how good a worker you are. I've been a dishwasher in a restaurant, a housekeeper, a maid, a psychiatric aide in Fairview, and a co-office worker with People First.

I got started with the Oregon Youth ARC (Association for Retarded Citizens). That inspired me to be also with the ARC at that time. I was with the ARC even before People First came about. People First came about after Canada had their convention for the handicapped in 1973. Some of our people who lived in the community went up to take part in that. They found that most of the convention was run by the professionals, and the handicapped could not speak for themselves very much. They weren't given enough time to.

So we thought we'd have a convention run by the handicapped themselves, without the professionals doing anything. Except that they'd be kept in the background, and make sure that everything was going under good control. I ran the first two conventions by myself. For the first convention, we only expected about 200 people, and we had over 500. It was a real shock. We had to overcrowd the little motel. We had to overcrowd the rooms just to get everybody settled down. We had people from the community and from the institution.

People First of Oregon has had small conventions and big conventions. We have regional workshops, chapter meetings, and fund-raisers. We talk to legislators. We plan to get involved in the budget cuts proposed by the Reagan administration. We also once called for an investigation of the superintendent in Fairview. We wanted to have more freedom in having choices, and making our own decisions. That's being done now, and people can get out now when they are ready. That's been one of our biggest accomplishments.

We've also helped to get legislation passed. We got a bill of rights for the handicapped through the legislature: that's the freedom to vote, the freedom to marry, and all the other rights.

There are so many things going on that it's hard to keep up with it. Thank goodness the ARC handles most of it, and we just help them.

Our goals for the group are to accomplish the unaccomplished and to help other handicapped persons in Oregon and throughout the United States to feel that we can be a valuable person. Not everyone in the community may realise how valuable the handicapped person can be. We're also trying to get more people out in jobs.

To me, self-advocacy means helping other handicapped people learn what you have learned. It means to help them accomplish more than they've ever dreamed of accomplishing. It's helped me to grow and handle my handicap as though it was nothing to be afraid of or worry about. I've been able to live as though I don't have a handicap at all.

There are lots of people with handicaps in this world who are looking for help. This is one of the biggest things I think I can do in life, helping them.

3   THE FOUNDATIONS AND NATURE OF SELF-ADVOCACY

There's a story about three baseball umpires standing behind home plate before the start of a game. They were discussing their individual methods of calling balls and strikes. 'I calls 'em as they *are*,' said the first umpire, an idealist. The second umpire, a realist, said: 'Well I calls 'em as I *sees* 'em.' The third umpire, a pragmatist, shook his head in disagreement and said: 'They ain't *nothing* till I calls 'em.'

The key for developmentally disabled individuals is to be in the position where they are 'calling 'em'. The rightness or wrongness of their decisions is not nearly so important as having the opportunity to make the decisions.

> From 'Self-Advocacy – A Basic Right'
> by Barbara Welter, John Hanna and
> Randy Kitch, Kansas University
> Affiliated Facility, 1978

What Is Self-Advocacy?

In a book entitled *A Multi-Component Advocacy and Protection Schema*, published by the Canadian Association for the Mentally Retarded in 1977, Professor Wolf Wolfensberger of Syracuse University, New York, a leading proponent of the concept of advocacy, cautions us against what he calls 'Kraft cheese advocacy'. On American television, Kraft cheese adverts try to persuade viewers that cheese goes with everything. Likewise there is a temptation to think that anything that happens to mentally handicapped people is a form of advocacy. As Wolfensberger suggests, no doubt there are people who are locked up in institutions under the name 'institutional advocacy'.

The term 'advocacy' cannot usefully be applied to everything. In particular, 'self-advocacy' cannot refer to everything a mentally handicapped person does or says, individually or with others.

Advocacy means speaking or acting on behalf of oneself or others, or on behalf of a particular issue. Self-advocacy by mentally handicapped people means that individually or in groups (preferably both), they speak or act on behalf of themselves, or on behalf of other mentally handicapped people, or on behalf of issues that affect mentally handicapped people.

There are other important components identified by Wolfensberger. True advocacy involves fervour and depth of feeling, vigour and vehemence, doing much more than is done routinely or would be found routinely acceptable. It also involves cost, in time, stress, money, sacrifice of sleep, leisure or pleasure, the incurring of resentment or hostility from others, being ridiculed or considered foolish, being rejected or hurt, or putting one's job or security at risk.

Advocacy is thus a very serious business. It can be allied with enjoyment, entertainment and fun, but it does not itself consist of enjoyment, entertainment and fun.

Self-advocacy by mentally handicapped people has two aspects. The first involves handicapped people pursuing their own interests, being aware of their rights and taking responsibility for tackling infringements of those rights. The second involves joining with others to pursue the interests of the group and of mentally handicapped people in general. Both require to be done with vigour, and both are likely to incur costs, but within a self-advocacy group the effort and costs are shared in a way that enables issues to be pursued more powerfully with the support of others and with the rewards that come from helping others.

Lengthy teaching and preparation of mentally handicapped people for true self-advocacy is required. Individual people must learn to respect themselves and to be self-confident, and to recognise their rights and needs, the most appropriate ways of meeting them, and the most effective channels for seeking help in doing so.

The process of learning self-respect and confidence, and of learning to advocate on one's own behalf, leads, with guidance, to an appreciation of the need to respect other mentally handicapped people and to speak and act on their behalf as well as one's own. Knowledge of one's own rights and needs develops into knowledge of the rights and needs of all mentally handicapped people. Knowledge of ways of pursuing one's own rights and needs, and effectively seeking help for oneself, develops into an awareness of ways of jointly pursuing common rights and needs and seeking help for mentally handicapped people in general through group action.

Incidental skills then have to be learned: of functioning in an organisation, perhaps culminating in membership of a committee entailing controlling meetings, following through group decisions, handling finance, etc.

A fully functioning self-advocacy group is thus a group of mentally handicapped people who are aware individually of their rights and needs and are motivated to pursue these, but are equally concerned to work with other mentally handicapped people to pursue common interests and the interests of mentally handicapped people everywhere. In practice, such a group is likely to welcome all mentally handicapped people into its ranks, and thus will be in a continuously developing state with members at different levels of awareness of their rights and needs and at different levels of involvement in the group's organisation and activities.

In our present state of knowledge about how to teach mentally handicapped people we are not able to teach this knowledge and these skills to all mentally handicapped people. However, the experience of the American self-advocacy groups shows that many mentally handicapped people can be taught the knowledge and skills required to run a group effectively on their own, with minimal direct help from non-handicapped people. People whom we call 'more severely handicapped', because at present we lack ways of teaching them, can take an active part in the group at whatever level they are capable of at a particular time. The most grossly or profoundly handicapped people may, with help as required, attend meetings and lend support by their presence.

The Foundations of Self-Advocacy in America
As we have seen, self-advocacy by mentally handicapped people in America grew partly out of the notion of conferences for mentally handicapped people, the history of which can be traced back to Sweden in the 1960s, and partly from the independent development of local self-advocacy groups in many parts of the United States in the 1970s. America seems to have been a fertile place for this development, and several trends seem to have contributed to this.

First, as in other countries, there has been a strong parents' movement in America – the Associations for Retarded Citizens. This movement began after the Second World War and grew strong in the 1950s. In America at that time – even more so than in other Western countries – there were few alternatives for a mentally handicapped person other than living in his family home with no services at all, or being admitted to a large isolated institution. The parents' movement fought to achieve recognition by professionals and by government that mentally handicapped people could learn and develop and should therefore be provided with appropriate services. In recent years the ARCs have tended to put their weight behind getting as many people as possible out of institutions and into community settings, and avoiding admissions to institutions through the provision of comprehensive community-based services. The ARCs have also tended to adopt the philosophy and principles of normalisation in their pursuit of adequate services – involving helping mentally handicapped people to have a valued role and status in their community. A natural corollary of this has been the gradual welcoming of mentally handicapped people themselves into active membership of the ARCs, and a concern to develop their skills of entering into decision-taking processes.

The ARCs themselves operate in a climate of widespread acceptance of the importance of consumer representation in service planning and management, and consumer monitoring of services. This has tended to be seen in America not just as an expedient, but as a fundamental right of consumers. An excellent example of such involvement is the role of the parents' group in Omaha in drawing up the Douglas County Plan which led to the establishment of ENCOR in the late 1960s (see Chapter One).

There is too a general acceptance of the notion that politics works through the action of 'pressure groups' or 'special interest groups'. Many political decisions are influenced by groups of people with a special interest who get together to provide information to politicians and civil servants, to demonstrate that there is a unified body of concerned citizens with an informed viewpoint, and to counteract tendencies for resources and interest to be diverted away from their special cause. Special interest groups of this kind are pervasive on the American scene, and they provide models of political action and influence which self-advocacy groups can learn to emulate.

One of the biggest and politically strongest special interest movements in the United States has been the civil rights movement. Its importance, its power and its effectiveness have strengthened in many Americans the respect for the rights of citizens that is enshrined in the Constitution, giving strength and support to other minority groups. The civil rights movement also originated and developed strategies which can be studied and adopted by self-advocacy groups. The continuing relative deprivation of black people in some parts of America, and prejudice towards them, also gives other groups a realistic view of how difficult their task may be.

Allied to the development of special interest groups has been the growth of the self-help movement, in which people with the same problems meet to help each other. Examples include groups for widows, groups for heart attack survivors, or groups for parents who have lost a child. The work of these groups has led to a general recognition of the importance and effectiveness of self-help, and the movement has provided a model for self-advocacy groups of mentally handicapped people to follow. Some of the self-help groups have, of course, been formed by physically handicapped people, for example the Centres for Independent Living mentioned in Chapter Two.

More specific developments that have provided the foundations for the growth of self-advocacy by mentally handicapped people in America have been deinstitutionalisation, the articulation and application of the philosophy of normalisation, and the growth of the concept and practice of advocacy.

Tens of thousands of mentally handicapped people have come out of institutions in America in the last decade. Some of these people have simply been transferred to equally inappropriate nursing homes or large hostels, but many have become the clients of newly developed community services and are living in well-integrated community settings. In many local areas in America there is thus likely to be a number of former institution residents who have common problems of adjustment in the community, and perhaps a common interest in the closure of institutions and the further development of community-based facilities. The potential nucleus of a self-advocacy group thus exists, and some of the people are likely to have some basic communication and leadership skills that will get a group off the ground. Though possibly less motivated to start a group on their own, mentally handicapped people who have always lived in the community are of course also potential members.

The philosophy and principles of normalisation have been extremely influential in determining the thinking behind many services and approaches to mentally handicapped people in America in recent years. Normalisation starts from the premise that a major handicap of disabled people is their devaluation in society, and it seeks to remedy this by enabling mentally handicapped people as far as possible to have experiences that are generally valued in society (like living in a homely environment) and to achieve a public status that is valued (like being a home owner). An integral part of normalisation is that people with mental handicap should have a say in their lives and should be given the opportunity to learn useful and self-enhancing skills. The self-advocacy group is a natural vehicle through which this can be done. In America, organising into a self-help group, and pursuing needs politically through a special interest group, are valued activities of many citizens, and hence in themselves give mentally handicapped people the valued experiences and status that normalisation seeks to achieve.

Finally there has been the development of the concept of advocacy, and frameworks for its realisation.

The General Principles of Advocacy

As defined earlier, advocacy is speaking or acting on behalf of oneself or another person or an issue, with self-sacrificing vigour and vehemence. Wolfensberger's concept of *advocacy* was not so much that of self-advocacy as that of advocacy on behalf of handicapped or disadvantaged people by others – a practice that he called 'citizen advocacy'. In such a scheme, a competent, non-handicapped 'citizen advocate' is allocated to each handicapped person, to befriend him and to help him to achieve the meeting of his needs and the protection of his rights, as far as that help is required. Such advocates would be recruited, matched to individual protégés, trained and supervised by independent advocacy agencies.

Wolfensberger argues that it is essential for advocates, and advocacy schemes, to have minimal conflict of interest. Thus, an advocacy agency should not be tied, financially or organisationally, to a service-providing agency, and individual advocates must be unpaid volunteers who are not involved in other service provision. Advocacy, as long as it is done with the self-sacrificing vigour that treats the interests of the protégé as if they were one's own, can include any action from simple friendship and occasional contact to guardianship of a handicapped person or adoption of a handicapped child, or living and sharing one's whole life with a handicapped person.

In America and Canada many citizen advocacy schemes have been established, run usually by independent Advocacy Offices or by local Associations for Retarded Citizens. Thus in many areas advocacy is established as a concept, and supports for it exist.

Wolfensberger's view is that *self-advocacy* – although it is itself a special case of the application of the general principles of advocacy – needs to be underpinned by strong advocacy on behalf of mentally handicapped people by others. He says: 'A severely limited person learns self-advocacy best within the demanding shelter, protection, love and friendship of a citizen advocacy relationship, because these processes are especially apt to bring the person towards growth and independence.'

However, advocacy can take place without a formal advocacy scheme, and many self-advocacy groups have been fortunate to find the support of non-handicapped individuals who have practised the principles of advocacy on behalf of handicapped people without the formal back-up of a citizen advocacy scheme. Such is the case with Project Two in Omaha, for example. Additionally, many believe that a form of genuine advocacy is possible by people employed in service provision, if they fully recognise the conflicts of interest that are inevitably involved.

A major consideration for a self-advocacy group may be the avoidance of conflict of interest in its helpers and advisers. The problem is apparent if one considers an instructor or manager within an Adult Training Centre acting as the initiator and helper in the establishment of a self-advocacy group amongst the trainees or students at the centre. There will be obvious limitations to the extent to which the instructor or manager can encourage concern and protest about the centre, its operation, its management, the type of work available, payment to trainees, relationships with parents, and so on, without facing serious and probably irresolvable conflicts of interest.

The non-handicapped people who are helpers or facilitators of self-advocacy groups should ideally not be involved in service provision. In practice, however, especially initially and in the absence of a local citizen advocacy scheme, the helpers are likely to be interested and concerned members of staff of service facilities. In this situation, it is important that they be aware of the potential conflict of interest, and be open about its possible influence on the group's activities and development. There are likely to be occasions when the person's role in the group conflicts with her role in the agency she works for, and the group itself is likely to be hampered by concern over the adviser's position if the group pursues certain issues or takes certain actions.

The ideal is that a partnership develop between the mentally handicapped people in a self-advocacy group and one or a small number of non-handicapped helpers whose conflict of interest is minimal and who are thus free to treat the interests of the group members as if they were their own. Individual members of the group might be supported by other individual citizen advocates, and if so the self-advocacy group can complement and strengthen a system of citizen advocacy as well as *vice versa*.

The Importance of Self-Advocacy

With established frameworks for other individuals or groups to advocate on behalf of mentally handicapped people, it might be thought that there was little need for mentally handicapped people to form their own self-advocacy groups. Indeed, this is the position of many parents' groups who believe that they already speak and act effectively on behalf of mentally handicapped people.

However, one problem with advocacy by other people is that there are likely to be assumptions by those people about what the needs are, which may not always reflect the views of the mentally handicapped people themselves. Now that handicapped citizens are increasingly articulating themselves what their needs are, significant discrepancies are surfacing. Far from wanting protection from the hurly-burly of everyday life, for example, mentally handicapped people have made clear that they want to be an integral part of community life, with all the problems and worries that it brings. Rather than seeking life-long security through the provision of specially supported environments – a common demand of parents – mentally handicapped people themselves have tended to want to seek this security through relationships and a satisfactory income, just as the rest of us do.

Only mentally handicapped people themselves can speak from the real experience of their daily lives, and of the attitudes and behaviour of others towards them. Only they know what they are talking about from personal experience. Bengt Nirje sums this up in the following passage from 'The Right to Self-Determination', a chapter in *Normalisation* by Wolf Wolfensberger, published by the National Institute on Mental Retardation, Toronto, in 1972:

There is more to the issue of self-determination than pedagogic and therapeutic benefits. And this is the realistic content of what is being said. That is what counts, in the same way as it does for others. The persons affected most intimately – the mentally retarded themselves – have added the voices of their real experiences. They are, in their daily lives, dealing with behaviours and attitudes of those who are delaying their adjustment as adults; and as they have a need to identify themselves as adults, these real frustrations have to be expressed and recognised.

Also, retarded adults are not only talking out of this kind of real experience, but are able to describe in detail conditions of life with which they are familiar and in which they have deep-going concerns and interests. Their experiences have not only a personal experience base, but are also shared by many others whom they know. They can express not only their own concerns, but those of their retarded friends who are less capable, and perhaps even incapable, of expressing themselves. They know what they are talking about, and they know that they are describing the realities of their existence. They realise as well that they have or should have the right to express those concerns. They are acting as citizens with the same right to be respected as others.

Where and how far the self-determining developments

with retarded adults will lead, only local enterprise and initiatives will completely reveal. But when mentally retarded adults express their right to self-determination in public and in action, and thus gain and experience due citizen respect, they also have something to teach – not only to other and obviously more capable minority groups, but also to society in general. They teach something about the deeper importance of democratic opportunities, the respect due to everyone in a democratic society – and that otherwise, democracy is not complete.

It is an important part of normalisation – or the revaluing of devalued people – that handicapped people should be given maximum opportunity to take decisions for themselves. Teaching individual mentally handicapped people to do this is a vital part of any normalisation programme, and it is a fundamental step in enabling mentally handicapped people to advocate for their own rights and needs. Having the opportunity to make decisions *is* even more important than the rightness or wrongness of those decisions. Such decision-taking for individual mentally handicapped people may take the form, depending on their ability at a particular time, of simply choosing what clothes to wear, or of participating in voting procedures on a planning committee.

Being a member of a group enables a person to develop these decision-making skills in the context of sensitive, informed advice and assistance in making decisions that are helpful to one's own development and to the interests of others. For example, a self-advocacy group can widen each member's knowledge and experience of the range of helpful choices that are available, in living arrangements, in dress and behaviour, in leisure activities, in work, in relationships, and in personal assertiveness and contribution to society.

There is no other way of achieving all this than by fostering and nourishing self-advocacy by mentally handicapped people themselves. And, as Nirje also points out in his chapter, this has to be done with real respect for the right to self-determination of mentally handicapped people. Self-advocacy must be taken seriously as an expression of the genuine adult citizenship of mentally handicapped people. It therefore in itself often requires a considerable shift in attitude by parents' associations and by service personnel. Some of the perceptions of mentally handicapped people that need to be fostered or overcome are discussed in Chapter Four.

The Components of Self-Advocacy

Although the initial emphasis in teaching people self-advocacy is on sensitising individuals to their own needs and rights and ways of pursuing them, the focus of a self-advocacy group is on mentally handicapped people advocating on behalf of each other and on behalf of mentally handicapped people in general. Wolfensberger identifies two distinct types of action or activity that can constitute this advocacy on behalf of others: instrumental action and expressive action.

Instrumental action involves helping others in the solving of practical and material problems, for example by advising and assisting with day-to-day problems, decision-taking, transport, shopping; by representing the interests of the person in relation to agencies and the law; ensuring inclusion in appropriate services for training, work, education; and in administering property and income.

Expressive action involves meeting the needs of others for communication, relationship, warmth, love and support, for example by providing emotional support during stress and crisis; maintaining sympathetic communication and interaction; bringing friendship and fellowship to lonely or abandoned people; sharing emotionally significant activities, trips or events; exchanging meaningful tokens (cards, gifts, visits, meals) on special occasions such as birthdays or Christmas.

Instrumental and expressive actions are combined through such activities as sharing one's home with another handicapped person or in offering practical friendship to another person.

Expressive action can be undertaken through an organised concern for the emotional needs of members and for the needs of members and of other mentally handicapped people for support and communication. A socially important part (though only a part, and maybe a small part) of meeting the expressive needs of members is likely to be the organising of entertainments, parties, discos and other fun events.

Some of the instrumental actions that can be undertaken

extremely effectively by a self-advocacy group are the teaching of social skills to members (as is done by the Boston Mohawks and Squaws), and the representation of the interests of mentally handicapped people on local committees and in local community affairs. A politically important part of meeting the instrumental needs of members is likely to be the involvement of the group in discussions with particular services about the needs of clients and the policy of the service, and in discussions with community agencies to ensure rightful inclusion of mentally handicapped people: this part of the group's work may be the most demanding in effort and cost to members.

Most important is the function of a self-advocacy group in offering practical friendship to members. The advantages of a self-advocacy group in doing this come from the understanding of members about the needs for instrumental and expressive supports and the best ways of providing them. The friendship is not born out of security, but out of the realisation that oneself and other mentally handicapped people are in grave danger of devaluation, neglect and oppression, and out of the sharing of the effort and costs of self-advocacy.

With this concept of friendship in relation to self-advocacy in mind, it is instructive to read the book *Tongue Tied*, the autobiography of Joseph Deacon, written with the help of three friends, published by the National Society for Mentally Handicapped Children and Adults, London, in 1974. (This book is discussed further in Chapter Six.)

Some of the possible strategies of action that can be adopted by self-advocacy groups can be divided into three categories: those concerned with supporting and providing practical help and friendship to members; those concerned with pursuing rights and needs on an everyday basis; and 'heavy' actions that may be required when really important issues need to be pursued against strong opposition or lack of interest. The remainder of this chapter discusses some of these strategies that groups might adopt. It should be remembered throughout that these are *group* actions, that can be supported by even the most severely handicapped person by his membership of the group and presence at meetings or events, especially if helped by his own non-handicapped advocate; and they are actions that can benefit all members from the most disabled to the most able. Of course, many of the strategies can be, and often will best be, pursued jointly in cooperation with other groups.

Actions to Help Individual Members

Visiting
Small groups of members of a self-advocacy group can undertake to visit individual members in their homes or in other settings to offer support, information, advice or friendship. Especially helpful can be the visiting of mentally handicapped people who are lonely or isolated, have few friends, live in institutional or unsatisfactory conditions, have no job, or have few leisure opportunities.

Arranging Transport
One of the major restrictions on the lifestyle and opportunities available to handicapped people is the lack of adequate transport facilities to enable them to get about in their community. As well as pressing for improvements in public transport facilities for handicapped people, a self-advocacy group can explore ways of providing suitable and flexible transport for individual members through, for example, recruitment of volunteer drivers, or raising money to hire transport.

Financial Assistance
A self-advocacy group might seek grants or other sources of finance that could be used to assist individual members in financial need. At the time of the illness and eventual death of their founder, Ray Loomis, Project Two in Omaha organised several events to raise money for his family at a time of severe emotional and financial strain.

Social Education
A helpful service to members very successfully operated by some self-advocacy groups – for example the Boston Mohawks and Squaws – is for the more experienced and skilful members to take new or inexperienced members into community settings to teach them the skills of, for example, handling money, opening a bank account, riding a bus or train, ordering food in a restaurant, shopping, using community leisure facilities,

enrolling for evening classes, or going to church. This is an excellent way in which a self-advocacy group can offer practical support and friendship to its more severely handicapped members.

Social Events

Not all the work of a self-advocacy group needs to be deadly serious. Parties, discos, picnics and other social events are good ways of bringing people together and sharing in fun and enjoyment. They enhance group cohesion as well as providing pleasure for members. Often these events give opportunities to all members to contribute, by bringing food or drink or assisting in the arrangements.

Contacting Professionals

Sometimes a group can help individual members to make contact with professionals who can help them in their particular circumstances. To this end it is useful for a self-advocacy group to have a list of professional people who are known to be friendly and helpful. This list can include lawyers, policemen, doctors, bank managers, postmasters, clergymen, social workers, social security officials, officials of health, employment, housing and education departments, politicians, and leaders of voluntary organisations.

Arranging Legal Advocacy

Particularly important might be assisting members to achieve good legal advice or representation when, for example, they are seeking to establish eligibility for financial, housing or other services, or are appearing before tribunals or appeal bodies, or are seeking to enter into important contracts.

Involvement in Community Life

In order to increase the extent to which mentally handicapped people are seen in the local community as valued citizens participating constructively in community life, and to ensure that individual members feel fully involved in their local community, a self-advocacy group can support and encourage its members in making maximum use of community facilities and opportunities for community involvement. Such activities can include: using local shops, pubs and eating places; belonging to local clubs; using the local library; voting in elections; attending public meetings; expressing a view on local issues; supporting local schools, churches or voluntary groups; forming a wide network of good relationships; being good neighbours; and helping local people in need, especially through friendship with them.

Special Achievements

A group can give special support and encouragement to any members who wish to try to achieve things that would be an impressive accomplishment for a handicapped person and could be a model for others to follow or gain inspiration from. Examples might include taking challenging educational courses, pursuing difficult leisure-time activities, making strong personal commitments to helping others, purchasing one's own house, or attempting to become self-employed or to run a small business. (All these things are actual achievements of some members of self-advocacy groups in America.)

Actions to Pursue Rights and Needs

Communication

Publicity, keeping in the public eye, and getting one's message across as often and as effectively as possible, are at the heart of successful self-advocacy by a group. Strong efforts at communication help to educate the public and serve as a symbol that self-advocacy is an influential reality. Communication can include preparation and distribution of written materials, such as booklets, pamphlets, brochures, information sheets, newsletters or resource guides. It includes arranging meetings, seminars, workshops, debates and slide or film shows. It can involve the use of photographs, audiotapes, films or videotapes. The media can be used, through press conferences, articles for newspapers, magazines or journals, appearances on television and radio programmes, public service announcements on television or radio or in newspapers, and press releases. The telephone can be used to contact particular people or to run general phoning campaigns. Advertisements and posters can be used.

Letter-Writing

A constant flow of letters from the self-advocacy group, raising issues or responding to situations, can serve to keep people aware of the group's existence as well as being an important part of the process of pursuing aims. Letters can be to seek information, literature, advice, practical help or financial aid, or they can be in response to requests for information, literature, advice or help. Unsolicited letters can be sent offering information, advice or help, or expressing a viewpoint. Letters of support and encouragement can be sent to individuals, families or other groups. Letters of invitation, or of complaint, can be sent to politicians, planners, providers or managers of services, and to the press. They can be open letters, with copies widely distributed; or copies of individual correspondence can be distributed to interested people. Letters can solicit opportunities for participation. They can be sent in cooperation with other groups, with joint signatures.

Attending Public Meetings

Whenever a public meeting is being held, members can attend and, where appropriate, express a personal view, or if possible an agreed view of the self-advocacy group. This is particularly useful in question and answer forums involving planners or politicians, as it brings the needs of mentally handicapped people to their attention and to the notice of the audience. Where a public meeting is being held on an issue of particular direct relevance to mentally handicapped people, for example a meeting to discuss a proposal to establish a group home in a neighbourhood, an organised party of members can attend to support each other in putting forward the group's position and counteracting inaccurate statements that may be made about mentally handicapped people. There is a need to plan ahead exactly what will be said at such meetings, and how to make valid, relevant points.

Running Fact-Finding Forums

On important issues that affect mentally handicapped people, the group itself can run a public meeting to discover and disseminate facts. Such issues might include what is being done to change or close down inadequate or inappropriate services; the establishment of new community services; improving transport available to handicapped people; improving access to public buildings; deciding which candidates to support in local or national elections; improving the pay of low-paid workers; examining the implications of existing or proposed legislation; and so on.

Education

Activities with a primarily educational focus can be held for members, for parents, for professionals, for the general public. Members can contribute to courses or educational events organised by other people, or the group can organise its own. These might include seminars, workshops, teach-ins, conferences. Here are just a few examples:

- a course of regular evening sessions for members to increase their self-advocacy and leadership skills;
- a seminar with invited speakers on the legal rights of handicapped people;
- an all-day exhibition and teach-in on the work of the group, open to the public;
- a workshop for parents on the future for their children;
- a joint conference with another group of disadvantaged people to discover common problems and ways of giving mutual support.

Of course, education is itself likely to be a major aim of the self-advocacy group, and will be pursued through other strategies too.

Demystifying

This refers to translating complex, jargon-filled expressions of information from official sources or from professionals, into statements and language that can be understood more easily by ordinary people and by group members and their families. Research findings, government reports, legislation, rules and regulations, diagnostic terms, case reports and test results, and general professional terminology or jargon can all be the subject of this extremely valuable process. In particular, this strategy serves to counteract any tendency of professionals to use jargon and complexity to intimidate and control consumers, instead of making strong efforts to assist communication of ideas, results or opinions.

Monitoring Services

An important way in which a self-advocacy group can get its ideas across and bring about the changes it would like to see is by drawing up its own criteria for evaluating the quantity, quality, appropriateness and availability of services, and itself applying these criteria to the local services used by members. Evaluation can be based on quite simple but pertinent questions, like David Menousek's: 'Does it look like a home?' when Project Two visited the institution (see Chapter One). There are manuals and tools available to help groups to assess services. A British example is the National Society for Mentally Handicapped Children and Adults' STAMINA papers (see Chapter Five and Appendix One). The most comprehensive and effective evaluative tool is PASS – Program Analysis of Service Systems – involving a searching examination by a team of people to discover to what extent a service conforms to the principles of normalisation and aids the revaluation of de-valued people.* Self-advocacy groups would need major assistance in applying PASS, but there is no reason why they could not commission evaluations, receive them and demand action on the results. In America and Canada there are already some examples of mentally handicapped people themselves taking part in PASS evaluation teams.

Visiting Services with Politicians

As described in Chapter One, a strategy that has been used very successfully by Project Two in Omaha is to arrange for a prominent politician to visit a service accompanied by members of the self-advocacy group who have had past experience of the service. Members of Project Two who had been in Beatrice State Institution arranged with a state senator to visit Beatrice with him. Being a senator he could not be refused permission to visit any part of the institution, and being accompanied by previous residents he could be well advised on what parts to visit. He returned much better informed, and pledged his support to Project Two in their fight to achieve community services. Of course, such visits can also very fruitfully be arranged to services that are considered good

*Information about PASS can be obtained from the Training Institute for Human Service Planning at the University of Syracuse, New York, or from the Community and Mental Handicap Educational and Research Association in London (detailed addresses in Appendix Six).

models, as Project Two also did when they visited ENCOR's services with the senator.

Involvement in Model Programmes

Generally it is not a good idea for any voluntary organisation or advocacy group to get involved in long-term direct service provision; it leads to inevitable conflict of interest that makes true advocacy impossible. It may be, however, that a group has an opportunity to become involved in a demonstration project designed to provide an example of a superior or model service. At the present stage of development of self-advocacy groups they are unlikely to become involved in providing major educational, training, work, residential or professional therapy or counselling services for mentally handicapped people (the group would of course employ properly professionally qualified and competent people to do this, just like any other organisation). In the future, however, such an opportunity might possibly arise. As long as the group does not fall into the trap of involvement in ordinary service provision, a very useful strategy in pursuing the group's aims might be to become associated with establishing a demonstration model of good practice: involvement would only last through the demonstration period – it would not be long-term.

Petitions

Drawing up a petition on a particular issue with as many signatures as possible, and presenting it – preferably with publicity – to politicians, planners or decision-takers can be an influential means of seeking change. In Britain in the late 1970s, the Campaign for Mentally Handicapped People drew up two petitions that many mentally handicapped people themselves signed. The first was to the publishers of a textbook of psychiatry that portrayed mentally handicapped people in a very derogatory, misleading and unhelpful way. The outcome was that the publishers agreed to amend the offending chapter in a reprint of the book. The second petition was to the producers of a television series intended for mentally handicapped people, protesting at the withdrawal of a programme on cycling (the only programme in the original series that accorded mentally handicapped people any degree of dignity of risk). This petition was not successful in having the programme restored to the series. Petitions thus do not always work in producing change, but they do serve to demonstrate strength of feeling about particular issues.

Negotiation

Straightforward negotiation through meetings, exchange of letters and discussion, can often achieve results and should always be tried before more confrontive strategies are adopted. Effective strategies for meetings can be developed, using such materials as the booklet *How to Work with the System – and Win* (see Chapter Two and Appendix Four).

Visiting People

There is nothing like face-to-face contact. Appointments can be made to visit people whom it would be useful to contact, in their offices or homes, to seek information, advice or support, or to discuss or challenge their views or actions. Of course, such people can also be invited to meet members of the group in one of the members' homes or at some other place, but a personal visit may often be the best way to gain a meeting.

Invitations to Social Events

If outside people are invited to the group's social events, this provides an opportunity for informally explaining the group's aims, making friendly, relaxed contact with potential allies, and generally fostering good relationships.

Group Community Presence

A group can keep the local community aware of its existence in a very positive way, by carrying on group activities in community settings. The group might hold its meetings in a community hall; it might have occasional celebrations in local restaurants, conferences in local hotels, exhibitions in local schools, dances in local dance-halls; it might organise clean-up campaigns to remove litter from streets or parks; and it might become involved in the campaigns or voluntary effort of other groups, for example in health education or nature conservation.

'Heavy' Actions

Symbolic Acts

When a policy or practice or need requires exposure, one powerful way of focusing attention on the issue may be to carry out a symbolic, unusual or unexpected action. An example would be to refuse an award because of an aspect of the nature, policy or funding of the award-giving body. Such a strategy needs to be used only rarely, and with caution.

Demonstrations

Demonstrations are a form of public expression or 'community presence' that have been used by the women's suffrage movement, the civil rights struggle and other human rights movements. They serve to publicise issues and they are a relatively easy, effective, short-term action that can have the added effect of creating a sense of group purpose and accomplishment. Demonstrations, and the demands made through them, often serve as effective community education tools; people do not expect traditionally powerless groups such as mentally handicapped people to make demands. Because of their power, demonstrations should generally also be employed sparingly, and with caution. Some of the different forms that demonstrations can take are: marches, vigils, sit-ins, phone-ins, overloading administrative systems, sing-ins, leafleting and picketing. It will normally be essential that the support of other groups be sought and achieved before embarking on demonstrations, so that any action finally taken is the joint action of several groups in cooperation.

Boycotts

Allied to the strategy of demonstrating, this strategy includes such actions as refusing to use or pay for services, non-cooperation, strikes, working to rule, etc. There are two problems with this strategy for self-advocacy groups: first, the boycott has to be extremely well organised and everyone concerned has to abide by it for it to be successful; second, one must be a valued customer, consumer or employee – that is, there is no point in boycotting a service that does not particularly want you as a client. At a time when many services, especially integrated community services, have only just been

won for mentally handicapped people, the group may have to
be aware of this second factor. As with symbolic acts and
demonstrations, boycotts should be used only rarely and with
caution. Nevertheless, it is true that boycotts have proved
effective tools for other groups in lobbying for change, and
there is no reason why this should not be so for self-advocacy
groups. Again, cooperation with other groups in joint action
should always be sought.

Legal Action

Use of the law has been a favourite strategy of many social
change movements in America – less so, but still to some
extent, in Britain. Since a primary concern of self-advocacy
groups is the establishment and protection of rights for
handicapped people, including legal rights, a group needs to
have access to legal advice when required, and it may be that in
certain circumstances it would be appropriate and necessary
for a group to take legal action in the courts to establish or
protect the rights of individual members or of mentally
handicapped people in general. Once more, cooperation with
other groups in doing this is strongly advisable.

4 DEVELOPING AND SUPPORTING A SELF-ADVOCACY GROUP

In this movement the power belongs to the People First members. The professional who is involved with the movement must learn to be comfortable in accepting a secondary role. If there is glory to the movement, it belongs to the People.

People First International, Oregon

A Model for the Development of Self-Advocacy

People First International have the following model for the establishment and growth of self-advocacy, based on their experience in Oregon:

Stage One   – An initial impetus leads to the formation of a Steering Group to sell the idea and to encourage Support Groups.

Stage Two   – Support Groups meet to gain experience, helpers are coordinated, and members receive training in self-advocacy.

Stage Three   – The Steering Group becomes representative and brings the Support Groups together in a Self-Advocacy Group.

Stage Four   – The Support Groups continue, the Self-Advocacy Group meets regularly and a Committee is elected.

Stage Five   – A Regional Self-Advocacy Organisation is founded, a Regional Convention is held, and a Regional 'Core Group' is elected.

Stage One

There is an initial impetus that inspires enthusiasm for beginning a self-advocacy effort. (For People First in Oregon this was the attendance of a group of people at a conference for mentally handicapped people in Canada.) A meeting is held to which mentally handicapped people and potential helpers are invited. At the meeting, the idea of a self-advocacy group is explained, and support is sought for establishing a local self-advocacy group.

A steering group of interested people is set up. The steering group must not be dominated by non-handicapped people; and it must always be remembered that when the self-advocacy group is established, voting membership will be open only to handicapped people. Non-handicapped associates will remain in the role of non-voting helpers whose aim is to leave the group if and when they are no longer needed.

Through personal contact, visits, letters, distribution of information, the steering group encourages the setting up of 'support groups'. These are groups of handicapped people in training centres, colleges, hostels, group homes, hospitals, clubs – wherever mentally handicapped people congregate – who meet together regularly. At least one non-handicapped person acts as helper to each group. The support groups meet at specific regular times, usually once a week.

Stage Two

Over a long period – two years is typical before a wider, fully functioning self-advocacy group can be formed – the support groups gain experience of how meetings work, the sort of fruitful group discussions that can be held, how to involve every member, and the rules that need to be established to enable meetings to run effectively. In all this, the role of the helper is a crucial but delicate one of modelling and encouraging relevant skills and behaviours without over-controlling or dominating the proceedings or imposing his or her own views.

The helpers from the support groups can meet together to support each other, to exchange experiences and ideas and to discuss and resolve problems. Usually, one particular helper will take a leading role in organising these exchanges.

The steering group works with helpers and with local agencies (for example a Further Education college) to establish training in self-advocacy (see Chapter Five). Support groups can nominate individuals to attend such a course, or a group can attempt its own course for some or all of its members. Teaching includes how to behave at a meeting, how to vote, and the purpose of voting procedures and other rules of order.

Stage Three

Support groups can nominate handicapped members (or pairs

of handicapped person and helper) to serve on the steering group. Members of the steering group work especially hard to develop skills of self-advocacy and leadership, through attending courses, gaining as much experience as possible, and helping each other. The steering group prepares for the meeting together of the local support groups, and other interested handicapped people, in a wider self-advocacy group.

An inaugural meeting is planned which is run by those handicapped members of the steering group who have developed the skills of running meetings. Time, place and agenda are fixed well in advance and the meeting is extensively advertised. It should be made clear that the meeting is primarily for handicapped people themselves, not for staff. Only handicapped people will be eligible for voting membership or nomination for election as officers. (If it is considered useful to have non-handicapped helpers on the committee, this can be done through co-option.) Nominations are sought from the support groups or from individuals for officers of the new self-advocacy group.

At the meeting, the self-advocacy group is inaugurated and voting takes place for officers. The meeting is run according to rules of order:

- the meeting is called to order (with a gavel) by the person chosen by the steering group to act as chairperson;
- a roll call of people present is taken and a written list compiled;
- apologies for absence are noted;
- minutes are kept by the person nominated by the steering group to act as secretary;
- proposals for financing the group are put forward by the person nominated to act as treasurer, and may be the subject of a vote;
- a formal motion for inauguration of the self-advocacy group is put forward, seconded and voted on;
- nominations for the officers are read out and voting takes place;
- the newly elected officers take their places;
- thanks are recorded for the preliminary work of the steering group;
- date, time and place of the next meeting are decided;
- any other business is taken;
- the meeting is formally closed by the chairman.

Stage Four

Regular (weekly) meetings of the support groups continue. They are generally informal and their main aim is to give the handicapped people concerned an opportunity to take part in a supportive group, to discuss issues or views or problems that are important to themselves or other members, and to develop some of the skills of self-advocacy and taking part in meetings.

Meetings of the new self-advocacy group should take place regularly, though less frequently than the support groups – usually monthly. They are always formal, with the committee of officers running the meeting. An agenda and rules of order are always followed. Helpers attend the meetings but do not vote; they can make suggestions or offer advice and help, but without becoming dominating or coercive. The formal meetings are usually followed by a relaxed, informal social get-together.

The committee of officers will meet in between meetings to follow up the business of the previous meeting and to prepare for the next. Helpers will assist by invitation, as required. Usually, considerable advice and assistance of helpers will be required in organising elections and in planning major meetings or events. Annual elections take place for the officers at a general meeting of the self-advocacy group.

Stage Five

When there are two or more self-advocacy groups functioning, they can meet together to pursue the aim of a regional self-advocacy movement. In America this would usually cover a state; in Britain the region might cover two or three counties. (In practice, single groups have sometimes organised regional meetings or conferences on their own, in order to stimulate the founding of other self-advocacy groups in the region.)

Representatives of the local groups in the region meet on a Saturday once every two months, to facilitate exchange of information and support between groups, to plan annual regional conventions, to encourage and support new local groups, to enhance further the leadership skills of the representatives, and to form and maintain links with other regional groups. These meetings, depending on their function, can be open to anyone, or just to those people concerned with the task in hand, for example organising a convention. They are held in different local areas around the region. Again, helpers assist only by invitation, as required, though in practice the advice and assistance needed is likely to be considerable in the organising of major events and the seeking of financial aid.

Every year there is a regional gathering open to all members of local self-advocacy groups. This is called a convention. It is properly organised as a residential conference, lasting over several days. The magnitude of the planning task for such an event is indicated by the fact that conventions in America have attracted up to a thousand handicapped people. Planning has to be under way at least six months in advance.

At the conventions, regional officers of the self-advocacy movement are elected, for two years. These handicapped people, with invited or co-opted non-handicapped helpers, form a 'core group' who adopt an ongoing responsibility for encouraging and supporting self-advocacy throughout the region, in whatever ways they can. They produce information about the regional organisation; they make its existence known to appropriate professionals or agencies; they arrange general publicity for the organisation throughout the region; they seek regional financial aid; and they liaise with other regional self-advocacy organisations. They may be called in by other regions to assist in getting self-advocacy started there.

When such a 'core group' is established of highly motivated people committed to self-advocacy, this is a powerful catalyst for the further development of a whole self-advocacy movement in a particular country.

The Final Aim

The self-advocacy movement becomes a cooperative venture between non-handicapped helpers and mentally handicapped people, in which the mentally handicapped people are in the vast majority, and have the power. It works towards the ideal of a worldwide movement based on the following principles:

- The needs of mentally handicapped people everywhere for dignity, respect and a voice of their own are the same.
- Mentally handicapped people want to be perceived by others as people who have something to offer and skills to share, rather than only as persons with handicaps and limitations.
- Mentally handicapped people can speak for themselves

through a self-advocacy organisation.

- Voting membership of such a self-advocacy organisation should be open to all mentally handicapped people and only voting members should be eligible for election to be officers.
- The organisation aims to allow mentally handicapped people to learn to speak for themselves, listen to others, make decisions, solve problems, and ultimately develop leadership skills.
- The self-advocacy movement can neutralise barriers that stand in the way of mentally handicapped people advocating for themselves.
- Everyone should be able to participate to the best of her or his ability; for some this may remain, even with the full support of the self-advocacy movement, at the level of simply being present at meetings; others may become able to represent the self-advocacy movement on local, regional or even national decision-making bodies.
- The self-advocacy movement develops through the advice and assistance of dedicated, sensitive helpers who are particularly aware of the limits to their role, in providing the modelling and support for the development of self-advocacy and leadership skills among mentally handicapped people themselves.
- The members themselves – that is, mentally handicapped people – should remain in control of the content of meetings and should make the major contribution to the discussions; helpers should suggest and advise, but never coerce.

Starting a New Group

Mentally handicapped people should be involved in starting a new 'support group' or self-advocacy group. Instead of non-handicapped people embarking on trying to set up a group, therefore, discussions should always take place with mentally handicapped people themselves so that they can be the people who plan the setting up of a group, with help as required. In the People First model, it is envisaged that there will be some sort of initial impetus that will inspire some mentally handicapped people with the idea of self-advocacy, such as attending a conference for mentally handicapped people. The idea of establishing a group should come from the mentally handicapped people themselves, and the group must be seen by the mentally handicapped people as *their* project, not someone else's.

Basing Self-Advocacy on Existing Groups

We have seen in Chapter Two that there were already some 'support groups' in existence in Oregon before the initial impetus to begin a self-advocacy movement occurred. It may well be the case in other areas that existing groups can become the basis for a self-advocacy organisation. (This is certainly so in Britain, as is discussed in Chapter Six.)

There are two main kinds of groups that may be already in existence, which have potential for developing into fully fledged self-advocacy groups. The first are groups based in particular services, for example committees in Adult Training Centres, groups of hostel or hospital residents, or student groups in colleges. It is usually the case that a major role is played in these groups by staff of those services. We will call these groups 'service-related'. The second type are groups that function independently of any direct service, for example clubs (like the network of Gateway Clubs in Britain), or groups fostered by local parents' associations, or groups like Project Two that start from a local initiative of one person. These we will call 'independent' groups.

Service-related groups form an excellent basis for the development of a self-advocacy movement. They correspond to the 'support groups' in the People First International model of development of self-advocacy.

Independent groups, however, have the potential to bring together service-related groups into a wider organisation which is free from the inevitable conflicts of interest that abound in service-related groups that have strong service-staff involvement.

This, then, is one possible way in which self-advocacy can develop – through independent groups, such as social clubs sponsored by parents' organisations, bringing together members or representatives of service-related groups, such as committees in Adult Training Centres, from a particular area. The way could then be open for these independent groups to follow the stages in the People First model, eventually forming a regional and perhaps a national organisation.

However, one problem with many existing 'independent' groups – for example most of the British Gateway Clubs – is that they have been initiated and developed, and are largely controlled, by non-handicapped people, albeit volunteers rather than professionals. It is vitally important that mentally handicapped people themselves be involved in the initiative to set up a self-advocacy group, and this is difficult if an existing group is seen as the 'brainchild' of a parents' association, for example.

An alternative way for service-related groups to come together in a self-advocacy movement is for them to form their own independent alliance or coalition. In many ways this would be ideal. Such an organisation could seek *support* from bodies like parents' associations, but would be in the position of themselves taking the initiative, rather than acting on someone else's idea. Existing 'independent' groups could of course also join, or take a part in initiating, such a coalition or alliance.

As with starting a group from scratch, the initiative to change the orientation of any existing group towards self-advocacy should be taken by the mentally handicapped members themselves, perhaps as a result of some initial impetus that inspires them with the idea.

Being a Helper
If you wish to advise or help a self-advocacy group you must give serious thought to your role. How can you give support without leading? Do you have a potential conflict of interest because of your job or other volunteer activities? Have you clarified your values and commitment?

An adviser to a self-advocacy group is a person who makes a commitment to provide a special kind of assistance to the group. Usually but not always it is someone who volunteers the time. Your major responsibility as an adviser is to help mentally handicapped people to move into a position where they are full participants in the processes that affect their lives, helping them to acquire the skills and attitudes necessary to act as effective advocates for themselves and for others. Thus, your role is significantly different from that of the traditional volunteer.

You should be aware that a new group may need your strong

and active assistance for several years. You should not give too much help to a group, but also you should not think that a group will be able quickly to function on its own without *any* help. Self-advocacy groups of mentally handicapped people are likely always to need someone to whom they can turn for sensitive advice and practical help.

Although an ideal goal might be for the group to develop to the point where the adviser is not needed, few groups actually exist without advisers. On the other hand, there are advisers who have continued to support a group for six, nine, even for fourteen years. The group members may never be able to meet certain of their needs, such as transport to and from meetings and speaking engagements, or assistance with letter-writing. Advisers can provide support in these concrete areas, even after the need for the more active support required at the beginning has lessened. Certainly in the early years – and it will be years rather than weeks or months – there is likely to be a major need for help, teaching, advice and support.

On the other hand, there is a danger of swamping a group with unnecessary help or intervention. Advisers and helpers have an extremely delicate judgement to make as to when intervention is required and when it is best to take a back seat. Both too much help and too little help are bad. Don't be afraid to use your own best judgements on this, as long as you constantly question whether those judgements are right.

Involving All the Members
A self-advocacy group needs to define its membership and organise its activities around the whole membership, not just a small committee. The whole membership can be involved in the election of a committee, and then two types of meeting can take place – meetings of the membership, led by the committee, and separate meetings of the committee alone.

One of the problems of committees is how to keep in touch with the membership. One solution, adopted by several of the British committees in Adult Training Centres (see Chapter Six), is for individual committee members to relate to a group of ordinary members before and after committee meetings. However, we believe that it is very important in addition to have regular meetings of *all* members who wish to come, run by the committee.

For a long time such meetings are likely to be chaotic, but

sensitive support to individual members and to the
iority of the committee, order can be maintained and
business conducted. If one looks carefully at the convention
proceedings shown in the *People First* film, one can observe a
certain amount of disorder there; but it is tolerated, and the
fact is acknowledged and respected that everyone contributes
by his presence. It is vitally important to tolerate this disorder
until effective solutions can be found – disorder should not be
used as a reason for saying 'self-advocacy cannot work for
severely handicapped people'. Solutions are likely to lie in the
direction of having formal rules for meetings that people are
expected, to the limits of their ability and of the help that we
can give them, to observe. It may be years before these meetings
of the general membership of a self-advocacy group assume a
satisfactorily orderly and dignified form.

They are, however, vitally important, because without them
many mentally handicapped people are likely to be left out of
the process of participating in the self-advocacy movement and
supporting that movement by their presence. All mentally
handicapped people should have this opportunity, if they wish,
to become involved in self-advocacy. Self-advocacy is for every
person, *not* just for an 'elite'. Involvement in one annual
election is not likely to be sufficient – regular general membership meetings are necessary as well.

Membership of a group, and even of a committee, by people
who cannot communicate very well, should be encouraged.
Such people *do* contribute by their presence and they will, with
help, slowly learn skills of participating.

Fostering Awareness of Self-Advocacy and Rights
In the course of describing the development of Project Two in
Chapter One, we outlined three stages in the evolution of a
group: forging a group identity, action and evaluation, and
mastery. Awareness of the nature of true self-advocacy, and a
concern for rights, may develop only slowly through the first
two stages of a group's growth. For some time at the beginning
of a group's existence, the members may not have a very clear
idea of what the group exists for or precisely what the nature of
the group is, apart from a loose notion of 'speaking for
ourselves'. As an adviser, you may have the role of introducing
or clarifying concepts of rights or of self-advocacy to a group.

Whether this should be done, and the stage at which it should be done, are matters of sensitive judgement for you.

Here is an example, taken from the record of a Project Two meeting in 1977, two years after the founding of the group, which shows the two advisers, Tom Miller and Bonnie Shoultz, introducing the concepts of self-advocacy and rights to the group. Note also the support that members give to each other for their achievements – an important function of a self-advocacy group. Twenty-four members were present at this meeting, plus the two advisers.

Tom Miller introduced a discussion on self-advocacy. He asked if anyone knew what it is? He said advocacy is speaking out. Self-advocacy is speaking out for yourself. He asked if members ever have problems and what kind of problems they have?

Ray Loomis: I have sex problems.

Debbie Becks: I had a problem. I talked to Carl Sullivan about it.

Tom Miller: What kinds of things can you do if you have a problem?

Nancy Loomis: Don't do anything.

Tom Miller: That's one thing you can do, not do anything. What else can you do?

Ollie Rector: You can talk to friends.

Tom Miller: So you can talk to people if you have problems. Like if you don't have a job. Could you talk to someone else, like at ENCOR, and have them get you a job while you sit at home?

Members: No.

Ollie Rector: You can go out and look for your own job.

Tom Miller: What if the bus company said that no handicapped people could ride the bus? Could handicapped people get together and try and change that?

Members: Yes.

Tom Miller: Yes. Sometimes when you have a problem it's easier to work with other people on it. Like if handicapped people picketed the bus company, do you think they would get that changed?

Members: Yes.

Tom Miller: Getting people together to speak out on their own needs is advocacy. What did Ray do when he wanted to start this group? He came to GOARC and we worked on it together.

Tom Houlihan: If you need help, my employer says you go to one person. You go to God.

Tom Miller: Yes, a lot of people pray about their problems. Midtown Seven members, who helps you?

Wesley Woodhead: We try to help ourselves.

Bill Lancaster: I got my job myself.

Tom Miller: Who do you go to when you have problems on your job?

Bill Lancaster: I talk to people at ENCOR.

Bonnie Shoultz: Sometimes people don't know what their rights are, and then you need to talk to other people to help you find out what they are.

Rose Riederer: If you have a job, and say you stay with it a long time and you have money, you can drive a car if you have a licence.

Bonnie Shoultz: Yes, that's an example of a right that people have – if you have a licence you can drive.

Member: In meetings like this, sometimes people don't like to speak out in a group. It's really good if people can talk in a group because everybody has important ideas and if you don't speak out, we all miss what your ideas are.

Ollie Rector: I'm going to be on a board (ENCOR's five-year planning committee) and I'm going to say what I and my husband need. A lady who talked to me about it said she thinks I'd be a good person to talk about other people's needs too.

Lowell Rector: Can you get a car? Most of us here don't have one, and you have to get a job that's on a bus line. When I didn't have a job I went to ENCOR and to the employment office and they said I had to get a job on the bus line, so I did. That really limits where you can get jobs.

Ray Loomis: I have an idea. Why don't we have the TV cameraman come to one of our meetings and have us talk on TV?

Nancy Loomis: He's the brains in the family!

Ollie Rector: I have another idea. I'm going to have a woman come to my house every Monday to teach me to read and write – and then watch out!

Member: You can do a lot even if you can't read and write, if you stick to your guns.

Another member: What if you don't have a gun?

Tom Miller: Ollie lost fifty pounds in weight because she stuck to her guns.

Members: applause.

Paul Adams: Maureen, my girlfriend, she's from Beatrice, and she was there a long time. She was from Douglas County, so when she came back she came back to the Douglas County community. First she lived in a core residence and now she's going to move to an apartment with two other people. She goes to Benson Industrial Training Centre and someday she wants to have a job.

Members: applause.

Member: I've been wondering about someone else and how he's doing. I know he's had a really difficult time and I was wondering how he's doing now. Paul – that's you.

Paul Adams: I've been out of work for a year. I quit my job at University Hospital, then I came back into the ENCOR programme. Now I'm at the workstation and I go to work everyday and I get along with the people there and I do everything that I'm told on my job.

Members: applause.

Debbie Becks: I'm moving out of the hostel. This is my last week there and I'm moving into an apartment with two other girls.

Members: applause.

Rose Riederer: I've been in my own apartment with Residential follow-along and I haven't had any problems. I cook my own meals and handle my own money and my own socialisation.

Members: applause.

Adoption of a Statement of Purpose

As will be seen from their contributions at the end of Chapter One, Project Two members are now extremely well aware of the purpose of their group, and of the importance of the concept of rights. A growing awareness of rights is a key factor in the development of self-advocacy groups.

A statement of purpose is important for a group, and in order to draw this up it is useful for the group to adopt a list of rights that are to be pursued. It is good if a group can itself think through what rights its members consider important, rather than simply adopt someone else's list. Learning about rights is discussed further in Chapter Five, and in Appendix One we reproduce some items that may generate ideas for the incorporation of particular rights into a statement of purpose of a group. An example of how a British group – the Avro Adult Training Centre Students' Council – has done this can be found in Appendix Five.

The adoption of rights that are taken to apply to all mentally handicapped people, regardless of degree of handicap, is a good way for a group to become sensitive to the needs of severely handicapped people and to see that all mentally handicapped people can benefit from the self-advocacy movement.

The Adviser's Influence
There is one member of Project Two who is often very negative about himself and about society. He has often interjected his views during group discussions, saying: 'You can't do that when you can't read and write,' or 'The Governor won't pay any attention to what you say.' He expresses opinions based on restrictive ideas which must have been imparted to him many years ago – ideas which his own life experiences should have dispelled but did not. In the past, he could almost be counted on to make some attempt to quell enthusiasm or to interfere with group plans.

This member is valuable to Project Two for several reasons. He expresses doubts which many of the members may once have held about themselves, and by so doing he forces them to encounter those doubts and to argue them away. He makes them aware of the irrationality of many of society's attitudes about mentally handicapped people, and this awareness reinforces their determination to counter those attitudes. Getting angry at him has strengthened their resolve. He is now more aware that these opinions are not acceptable to the group, so he expresses them less often.

One of this man's recent arguments was that the advisers to Project Two were going to resign from the group, and then the group would fold up. One adviser received many worried telephone calls about this rumour, which was based on the fact that she had accepted a new job and was therefore leaving

ENCOR. In his mind, that meant that she would also leave Project Two. The rumour was aired at the next meeting, and it was dispelled in two ways: assurances were given that it was not true; and the question of Project Two's existence without the advisers was raised. The strongest members insisted that the group would continue to function without the people who were advising them at any particular time, and that if they needed help they would ask someone else to give it. Once again, the man's negativism worked to the group's advantage, as they were forced to confront another of their fears.

This story illustrates some of the most important aspects of the role of the adviser to a self-advocacy group. First, it demonstrates that the adviser is extremely important to the group. At the beginning, you may be admired and followed just because you are not mentally handicapped. Later, the relationship may grow to include a mutual love and a great deal of trust, both of which increase as the group experiences the growth which you have encouraged and supported.

Second, the role of the adviser in a group is to encourage and support, not to lead. Consequently, you must always be aware of your influence on the group, and you must be conscientious about not using that power except when necessary. In the case of the negative Project Two member, the advisers have rarely entered into the group's arguments with him. They have worked with him individually, pointing out the contradictions and fallacies in his thinking and helping him to see the positive side of his experiences. The group, however, has had a greater effect on his behaviour, and has benefited from the discussions his views have stimulated. The advisers did participate in discussing the rumour about themselves; but as they did so, they helped the group to see, once again, that it could function on its own.

Values
In 1980, Tom Houlihan had become so comfortable about travelling, public speaking and engaging in social interactions, that he gladly accepted an invitation by the Campaign for Mentally Handicapped People to travel to England with two of the advisers to Project Two, Shirley Dean and Bonnie Shoultz. In England he travelled on trains and on the Underground, sometimes on his own; he stayed in five different homes in

Oxfordshire, London, Essex, Kent and Sheffield; and he met with individuals, toured services, and gave talks to groups of parents and professionals. He impressed everyone he met – even strangers on the train who often talked to him or assisted him.

Only two years before, Tom had been extremely nervous about speaking in public or travelling and staying in strange places without a member of his family. How did Tom change so much in two years? No one gave him any systematic training on how to travel, although they travelled with him occasionally. No one even spent much time discussing appropriate and inappropriate behaviour in new settings, except casually. Tom changed because both he and the advisers took it for granted that he could and would learn to conduct himself with ease. His difficulties were never attributed to his mental handicap (he has Down's syndrome), but were seen instead as due to his lack of experience. The advisers' roles in this change were to act as models, to support Tom, and to be willing to step back and let the change take place.

This points out that one of the first things an adviser must do is to examine and define his or her own values. Unless you believe that people are people, regardless of their abilities or disabilities, and that they can do what they really want to do, you will impose limitations on them. Unless you are willing to give support, to step back and let things happen, and to refrain from using your influence to manipulate or control the group, the group will not grow as it could. Unless you are sensitive to and able to meet the group's need for help at crucial times, however, the group may make serious mistakes which would damage its self-confidence, or it may just stand still, making no progress at all.

To achieve the right balance between doing too much and doing too little, you must think through your values and attitudes towards people with mental handicap. No one should assume that since his intentions are good he need not examine the assumptions underlying his behaviour. You should know the history of how people with disabilities have been devalued, neglected and oppressed in the past, and you should be aware of how devaluation and oppression still operate in the present. You should be aware of the history of the abuses of rights of disabled people. With this awareness, you can put yourself in

Ray Loomis, founder of Project Two, with his son Billy.

Above: Susan Detty and
Paul Adams.

Left: Shirley Dean, adviser
to Project Two, with Dave
Menousek.

Below: Ollie Rector with
her daughter Nancy.

The committee at a meeting of Project Two; Alan Salmon, a guest from Britain, is second from the left.

Elected officers of Project Two, 1980: Nancy Loomis, President; Ollie Rector, Vice-President; Chris Corso, Sergeant-at-Arms; Tom Houlihan, Treasurer.

Below left: Dave Menousek was the first mentally handicapped person in Omaha to own his own house.

Below right: Nancy Loomis in her flat, with a certificate of award from the Greater Omaha Association for Retarded Citizens.

People First of Nebraska—1979 Convention

Pat Miller.

Officers elected at the convention.

Dave Menousek.

Larry Swan addressing a workshop.

Harold Edwards.

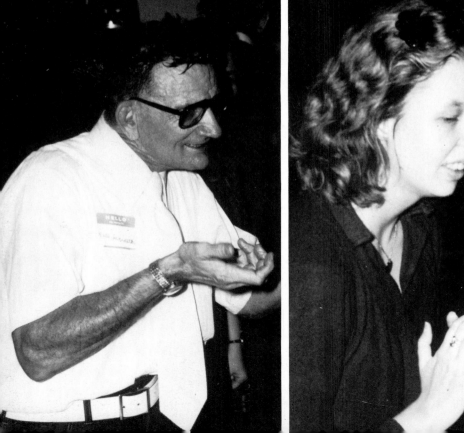

Top left: Shirley Dean
(helper), George Sanders and
Ollie Rector leading a
workshop session.

Far Left: Bill Lancaster.
Left: Susan Detty.

Above and right:
Other participants.

Jim Utter and Chris Corso, convention leaders, assisted by Bonnie Shoultz.

Andy Pollard, a member of the President's Committee on Mental Retardation, was guest speaker. The PCMR paid his fare from California. He is shown here with Ollie and Lowell Rector.

280 people attended the convention from all over the state of Nebraska.

Members of Project Two conduct a workshop session on rights.

Members of 'Advocacy First' of Lincoln, Nebraska, conduct a workshop session on leisure activities.

Posters displayed
at the convention.

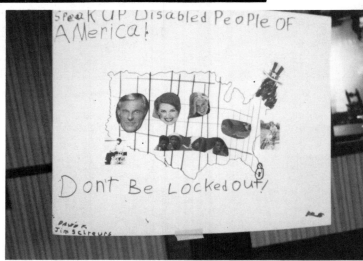

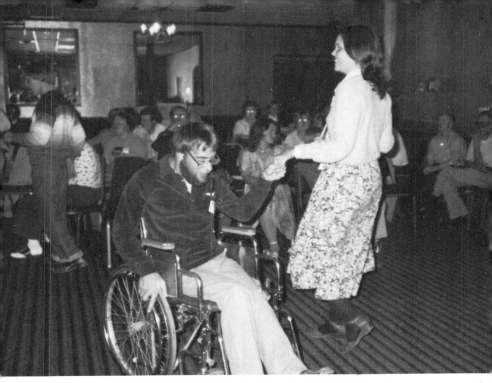

Above: Friends relax at the convention dance.

Below left: The group have their own shirts for publicity.

Below right: Jana Elder, People First of Kansas, contributor to Chapter Two.

Self-Advocacy in Britain—The Avro Adult Training Centre Students' Council

The secretary reviews the agenda for a weekly meeting.

Carol Scott, adviser to the group, goes through the minutes of the last meeting.

A proposal is made . . .

. . . An
alternative is
suggested . . .

. . . The
alternative is
supported . . .

. . . A vote is
taken . . .

. . . Defeat is conceded.

Representatives of the Council arriving at the studios of ATV to be interviewed for the 'Link' programme, June 1981.

Hugh Townsend
and David Ward.

Nat Gold and
Christine Lingley.

Above left: Barry Woodwood.

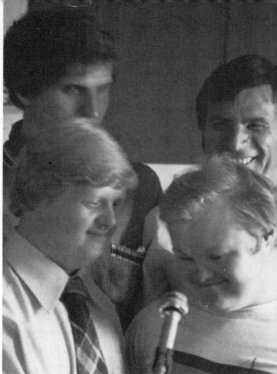

Above right: John Mynott and Peter Cullis (Hugh Townsend and Barry Woodwood look on).

Below right: Julie Danvers and Hugh Townsend.

Below left: David Ward.

the place of a person who may rarely have been treated as a valuable, contributing adult human being. You will come to understand how the person may lack self-respect, skills and confidence. This knowledge will help you to see how your behaviour as an adviser and role model can influence the development of the group, even if you never directly impose your personal views when particular decisions are made.

A central message of self-advocacy is that people respond to our expectations of them. Because in general our expectations of mentally handicapped people are so poor, you as adviser to a group must have expectations that, while remaining realistic, are powerfully high.

Personal Change

The process of reviewing one's own values involves personal change for an adviser. You will find that you learn as much about yourself and develop as many new skills as any member of the group.

Our own personal attitude has to be right before we can assist a group to tackle injustices arising outside. There is a strong but pertinent quotation by Burton Blatt, a long-time campaigner on behalf of mentally handicapped people in America:

> If I blame an evil world, a stupid system, blind leaders, or man's obvious imperfections, I may be right. But if it means I do not have to change, I contribute to the evil. You and I are all that is needed to change the world. Our necessary confrontation is not social. It is personal. The battle is not against society but with oneself.

Here is a comparison of the personal perceptions that determine our expectations of mentally handicapped people and our behaviour towards them, that we need to foster or overcome in order to help them to speak for themselves:

Perceptions of Mentally Handicapped People to Foster	*Perceptions of Mentally Handicapped People to Overcome*
• Adult.	• Child-like.
• Valuable, serious people who can act responsibly.	• Trivial, foolish people who need to be entertained all the time.

- Capable of self-confidence and courage.
- Weak, ineffectual.

- Capable of contributing to self-advocacy at the highest level that we can successfully help each individual to reach.
- Incapable of taking part in self-advocacy.

- Capable of learning skills of paying attention, cooperating with others, and taking decisions.
- Lacking the skills to be involved.

- Having important things to say that are worth listening to.
- Not having any worthwhile views.

- Capable of acting unselfishly for the benefit of others.
- Selfish, incapable of understanding the needs of others.

- Behaviour and skills a reflection of the expectations of others.
- Behaviour and skills a reflection of inherent 'mental handicap'.

- Having much to give.
- Presenting many problems.

- Capable of having a voice of their own.
- Needing us to speak for them.

The self-advocacy movement requires some drastic rethinking of attitudes and perceptions by us all. That is where the excitement and challenge of self-advocacy lies.

Using Your Influence to Support Growth

The following are some steps you may take to help a group and its members to develop strength and self-confidence. Because you are important to them, the group can easily become dependent on you, believing that you are the source of their success. These steps, which are based on values and a belief that every person can grow and learn, will encourage the group and its individual members to grow towards independence and autonomy.

Assist the Members to Deal with Labels That May Have Been Imposed on Them.

Labels become part of a person's self-concept. Adults who

have lived for years with a label such as 'mentally handicapped' may need help in facing and understanding the label, and in seeing themselves as people who can transcend the limitations which the label has placed on them.

Accentuate Positive Qualities and Achievements.

The group will probably deal sufficiently harshly with members' individual weaknesses. As adviser, you can encourage growth by communicating your genuine pleasure in the strengths and growth of the group and of individual members. Even when problems or conflicts arise, an emphasis on the positive aspects of the problem can assist the group to resolve it.

Encourage a Sense of Mastery and Control.

People who believe that they can influence events and control fate achieve far more than those who feel that they are controlled by others. The self-confidence that develops in the members who have gained this sense of control will spread to others and will encourage the development of a feeling of autonomy.

Believe That the Group Will Succeed in Meeting Its Goals.

Research has shown that individuals are much more likely to succeed when the expectations of people who are important to them are high. The same is true for a group. If you expect the group to learn to work together within a structure which will allow them to carry out their chosen tasks, they will.

Treat Each Person with Respect and Dignity.

All people, including those who are mentally handicapped, are quick to discern signs that they are viewed as children, or as sick, or as anything less than an equal person. They are quick to notice even subtle signs of ridicule or disparagement. On the other hand, people are also aware when they are treated as though they are valued for themselves. A climate of respect and dignity can be enhanced by you as adviser, through real, active listening, through your belief that the group and its goals are important, and through your caring and support.

Listen to Yourself as You Communicate with the Group.

Are you speaking too loud or as if you were with small

children? Do you take the time to explain things in language the members can understand? Do you give too much praise, more than you would give to a person who is not mentally handicapped? Do you brush aside people's expressions of concern or displeasure? Can you have fun with the members and allow yourself to learn from them? You should periodically monitor your behaviour towards the group and be willing to change it if it seems as though your behaviour reflects negative attitudes. If there are two or more advisers, you can decide non-defensively to evaluate each other's behaviour and provide feedback to each other.

Issues Pursued by the Group
At an appropriate stage in the development of a group, though this may only be after some years of slow progress, it will need to begin paying attention to serious issues of relevance to any fully fledged self-advocacy effort. An adviser's work with a group should include the long-term aim of tackling these serious issues. Examples of these issues are:
- labelling practices;
- the lack of dignity and respect accorded to handicapped people by others;
- the treating of people inappropriately to their actual age;
- the placing of people in institutions (hospitals or hostels);
- the lack of availability of adequate housing;
- exploitation: social, financial, or at work;
- poverty;
- brutality and ill-treatment of handicapped people;
- lack of educational opportunities;
- overprotectiveness by staff or families;
- denial of freedom or rights.

There is no escaping the ultimately political nature of self-advocacy. The above are all political issues, concerned with the place of mentally handicapped people in society. There is a need for change in society's system of values towards handicapped people, and this is the overall aim of self-advocacy by mentally handicapped people.

Again, advisers have to ask themselves honestly whether they subscribe to society's existing values, or to the new values on which a new deal for handicapped people depends.

Potential Conflicts of Interest

Although ideally an adviser should be free from any potential conflict of interest (see Chapter Three), in reality many advisers are people who work in agencies which provide services to mentally handicapped people. There may even be advantages in this, if your work has helped you to form values which will support the group. Such beliefs might guide you if a conflict of interest were to arise, and could protect the group against undue influence resulting from that conflict of interest.

The disadvantages, however, are more evident. First, if the group wishes to complain about or attempt to change the service agency of which you are a part, you may have divided loyalties. Second, the group may be afraid of criticising the service agency for fear of hurting your feelings or making you angry, or causing you trouble in your job. Third, if you are used to playing a professional role in relation to mentally handicapped people – for example as a teacher or social worker – it may be difficult for you to relinquish your professional role when you are with the group. This is likely to be a particular problem with service-related groups, as defined earlier, where you may be expected by your employing agency to be applying your professional skills in your work with the group. The relationship between an adviser and the group needs to be a very much more equal one than is usually the case in professional-client relationships, and this may conflict with your employers' expectations of the extent and nature of your interventions.

Advisers or potential advisers to self-advocacy groups should be aware of the problems associated with potential conflicts of interest. These problems, however, should not necessarily inhibit you from becoming an adviser, especially if you are the only person who is willing to make that sort of commitment to the group. If an adviser with a potential conflict of interest can work with his or her supervisors so that they may achieve an understanding of his or her role as an adviser, the conflict of interest problem may be alleviated.

The Development of Citizen Advocacy

As explained in Chapter Three, a very useful (some think essential) support for self-advocacy is the existence of 'citizen advocacy' – the linking up of valued non-handicapped people (advocates) with handicapped people (protégés), ideally with independent support and supervision, so that the advocate can represent the interests of his protégé as if they were his own. Although citizen advocacy can take place without formal organisation, the existence of supports and structures to assist the process of citizen advocacy can be invaluable in assisting self-advocacy too. As an adviser to a self-advocacy group, you can support and encourage any local efforts being made to establish a citizen advocacy scheme, and any individual examples of good advocacy on behalf of group members. People who are interested in impartial citizen advocacy are a good source of independent advisers to a self-advocacy group.

Important Concrete Assistance

There are many concrete details which are extremely important to the success of a self-advocacy group. The adviser can help the group to deal with these areas.

First, the group should, at a fairly early stage in its existence, adopt rules and procedures for meetings. These will include: regular meetings at times fixed well in advance; a committee; officers; agendas, circulated before meetings; minutes, with copies circulated; motions put, seconded and voted on; elections; a constitution; a statement of purpose; rules of membership; and rules of behaviour and procedure in meetings.

It is important that there should be a regular time and place for meetings. If the group is made up of people from a large area, a central location which members can get to, perhaps by public transport, should be sought. Project Two, for example, has had three different meeting places. Each transition has caused a decrease in attendance until people have learned how to get to the new place. The present meeting place, a public library building, has restrictions on its use that are also proving to be detrimental. These restrictions, which include no smoking and no food or drink, limit the group's ability to take a break during meetings. The meeting place, even the arrangement of chairs, is important also. A room that is too large or too formal may inhibit communication and prevent closeness from developing among the members. On the other hand, the room should be large enough to accommodate as many members as may potentially wish to attend group meetings in the future.

It is just as important to have a regular meeting time. Some groups meet weekly. Project Two meets on the third Friday of every month, and they hold a social activity each month as well. In addition, committee meetings or special meetings are held during most months. These meetings usually involve a smaller number of people, although they also need the support of at least one adviser.

Advisers can also assist by providing transport to those who need it. Project Two expects people to get to meetings on their own, but the meetings end late at night when public transport is either unsafe or non-existent, so advisers drive members to their homes. This may mean two or three trips for each adviser. In addition, individual members are often asked to attend other meetings in the community or to give talks to community groups, and they may need transport to meet these requests. Ways of meeting the transport needs of potential members should be addressed when a group is first formed.

Concrete assistance can also be offered by the adviser when needs for funds, materials or services (such as typing) arise. Group members may wish to send meeting notices by mail, to produce brochures or posters, to have agendas typed, or to raise funds for a specific use. You can assist the group in locating services or materials or in deciding on methods of raising funds. Decisions on some of these areas should be made as early as possible in the group's existence, in order that group members can spend their time on more important issues and in learning crucial skills.

Another important detail is the group's name. You can help the group to generate ideas for possible names and can assist the members to become sensitive to the image the name will suggest to the public. The name should suggest a positive or at least a neutral image. Names which suggest inferiority, child-ishness or deviancy should be avoided. Group members may need assistance in seeing the image that a given name projects.

Early Tolerance
In the early stages of a group's development, an adviser needs to be tolerant of performance that does not match up to the ideal, and to be confident that such problems can be resolved by patient work with the group on developing appropriate procedures or skills. You should not worry too much about:
  • Domination of the group by one or a few vociferous

people. If you concentrate on encouraging the use of formal committee procedures and democratic processes, you can cultivate the possible leadership qualities of the most eager and vocal people while formal opportunities are created for involvement of others.

- Long silences. In our experience, many mentally handicapped people are quite tolerant of silences; it is professionals or volunteers who often feel they must rush in to fill every gap in conversation.
- Trivial or inward-looking items on the agenda. People will need practice in the procedures of formal meetings and it is best that they get this initially by discussing topics that are of immediate interest. However, the group should be encouraged to move on, as time passes, to more serious issues and more general issues that affect handicapped people other than themselves.

Assistance with Problem-Solving
It is possible that one of the most difficult challenges facing the self-advocacy group and its adviser will be the mastery of problem-solving techniques. Every decision, from selection of officers to decisions about goals, requires the group to solve a problem. Project Two, for example, made its first decisions rather awkwardly. Usually, a problem would be noted and a member would offer a possible solution, a solution which would be seized upon by the group as if it were the only possible alternative. The advisers might then, before the group had made a final decision, ask if people could think of other alternatives. Other alternatives would usually be suggested, some by advisers; a discussion of these alternatives would be held, and finally the vote would be taken. Members also needed to learn to vote for only one alternative.

You should assist the group in recognising that the best way to solve a problem is to look at several alternatives. You may assist in the generation and evaluation of these alternatives, but the group must decide, usually by taking a vote. Most groups make good decisions if they are helped to see and evaluate several alternatives. If a bad decision is made, later reflection on the other possible alternatives will help them to learn from their mistakes.

One of the reasons that elections are important to a group is that the election teaches group decision-making skills. The election process is, essentially, a problem-solving process which follows several rules which can be applied to other types of decision-making. The election process enables the group to solve a very important problem, the problem which exists when the group has no structure. It allows the group to decide upon its leaders, and it allows the group to see, in the form of those who are nominated, the process of generation of alternatives. Voting for one candidate teaches the group members that usually only one alternative can be implemented. The count of the vote and announcement of the winner teaches the group that, even when there is conflict or disagreement, voting is an excellent way to come to a positive resolution. The losers and their supporters must learn how to handle and accept defeat. The entire group learns to give its support to the alternative which was chosen by the greatest number.

Assistance with Voting
Midway through its first year, Project Two decided to elect officers. Many people were not sure what the officers' roles would be, nor had most of them ever been present at an election of officers. Because many people had never seen candidates being nominated, they seemed to think that nominating a candidate for an office meant that that person would have the position. Many people knew about voting, but did not understand that voting meant making a choice between a number of candidates for an office. When asked to vote on a particular office, many members would either vote several times or, if not allowed to do that, would vote for the first candidate whose name was announced. Careful teaching about the process of voting therefore had to be done.

Groups may need to experiment with different ways of voting. It is difficult for anyone to hold several different alternatives in his mind at once while he evaluates each one and selects the best. Most of us use the written word to help us remember what we are doing. It is especially difficult for a mentally handicapped person, who may be unable to read and write, to remember all of the options long enough to evaluate each one.

Project Two has tried voting by secret ballot with the advisers assisting each individual to vote. This method takes too long to be used very often. They have tried writing the alternatives (or the candidates' names) on a blackboard or on a large pad of paper for members to refer to. (For those who cannot read, this may at least serve as a visible reminder that several alternatives exist.) For the 1981 election, they tried something new: they brought shoe-boxes to the meeting when they were to elect new officers. The candidates who were nominated came to the front of the room and stood before a shoe-box. Each member was given one slip of paper at the beginning of each round of voting, and he or she then deposited this 'ballot' in the box in front of the candidate he or she preferred. This method worked very well. Because it forced members to choose only one candidate, people were deterred from voting many times or from voting for the first candidate on the list.

A variant on this method would be to place drawings or photographs representing the alternatives on the front of the boxes. Members could then cast secret ballots if the boxes were placed behind a screen or in another room. An adviser could act as an election judge to ensure that voting was done properly.

Carrying Out Decisions

Because they may have little experience in making decisions, many mentally handicapped adults may not know how to carry out a decision or to reach a goal. You can help the group to isolate the action steps involved in acting on a decision and to assign responsibility for each step. At first, you may need to do almost all of the work involved in carrying out a decision, involving the designated members but not leaving the entire step to them.

A recent instance will service to illustrate. The adviser to a new group was experiencing frustration because, she said, the group 'just sits around and talks about their rights, but never does anything'. Further discussion with the adviser revealed that the group had decided that they had community responsibilities as well as rights, and had decided to get involved in a community health campaign. They had not, however, done anything concrete to get involved. In this case, the adviser was probably helping too little. She should have felt free to assess the skills and needs of individual members, so that she could help the group to decide on tasks and assign responsibility. She might have to go with a delegation of group members to explain the group's wishes to the health campaign's leaders. She might also have to provide many other kinds of concrete support to help to ensure that the decision is carried out successfully.

As adviser, you should also help the group to evaluate what it has done, and should provide specific feedback to members who have assumed responsibility for any part of a task. This evaluation will prepare them for the next task they undertake, and it will help members to be realistic about their accomplishments. Many members may find fault with their actions and need positive support. The evaluation can also help people to learn how to learn from their mistakes without condemning themselves.

Methods Adopted by Groups
It is as well to be aware that there is a vast range of methods that a group can use in pursuing its purposes. We have listed some of these in Chapter Three. It is best if the range of strategies that are to be considered usable or acceptable is determined by the group itself, with necessary non-directive counselling, advice and teaching as required. In particular, it should be left to the group, ultimately, to decide whether it wishes to adopt any strong, confrontive tactics, or not. An important component of the skills required for self-advocacy is self-assertiveness, and a self-advocacy group as a whole may feel that it has to be an assertive group. But assertiveness can be pursued through negotiation and knowing the skills of getting things done through meetings. Some groups may wish to be more militant; some groups may wish to remain more introverted in their approach. We should not push groups into being acquiescent, because it is important for traditionally weak people to develop some effective means of exerting influence – that is what self-advocacy is all about. However, neither should we push people into excessive militancy, especially if this is likely to damage their chances of successful integration into ordinary life. As Quentin Crisp once said: 'I will not be nudged into a quarrel with the human race. Now that we've finally met, I love it.'

Of course, certain strategies are likely to be more suited to particular circumstances, times, places or cultures than to others. What is appropriate in America may not be in Britain, for example.

Supporting Leadership
Groups cannot function without effective leadership. It is likely that leaders will emerge as the group begins to meet and deal with problems. Once leaders have been selected, the adviser can assist by supporting them as they develop leadership skills. Often, group members are not accustomed to paying attention during meetings or to following rules. There may be a great deal of private discussion, and individuals may talk out of turn and interrupt each other. A good leader must know how to discourage this activity while at the same time he or she encourages self-expression by group members. You, as adviser, can assist first of all by encouraging members to look to their leaders for answers to questions and for control over the group. The natural tendency of many members will be to direct most of their conversation to you. You must discourage this and lend a great deal of support to the leader.

The leader of a self-advocacy group in another city once asked Project Two for assistance with problems she was having during meetings. The meetings were unpleasant because members talked and interrupted each other. The leader repeatedly tried to bring order, usually by getting angry and shouting at the group, but this never provided more than a temporary resolution to the problem.

Project Two had dealt with the same problems in a variety of ways, depending on the leader at the time the problem arose. One solution was for the leader to use a gavel to call for order. Another solution was for the group to elect a sergeant-at-arms to circulate and maintain order quietly. The leader who came to Project Two for advice also needed hints on how to maintain a cool but firm demeanour. She needed to learn to remind the group of the rules without losing her temper.

Another way in which an adviser can help is by teaching a leader the skills necessary for running a group. This might mean practising parliamentary procedure, assisting the leader to learn to develop agendas and run meetings according to an agenda, and assistance with ways of handling particular problems that might arise.

Leaders should be more proficient in using problem-solving techniques than other group members. Therefore, you can help the leader to learn decision-making skills. The leader can also be encouraged to help the group to generate alternatives as it faces a problem.

You can help the leader to distinguish between decision-making and carrying out decisions. Once a decision is made, you can help the leader learn to make lists of steps to take and can help him to assign responsibility for each step.

You must communicate your respect for and belief in the leaders' abilities to lead the group. Leaders soon discover that leadership is both rewarding and difficult, and that the leader must find ways of balancing the interests and opinions of all the group members.

Dealing with Conflict
Conflicts arise in most groups, with self-advocacy groups no exception. A group like Project Two, for example, has meetings which are open to anyone. The group has expelled one person for an indefinite period of time for his behaviour, but usually people are given the chance to attend meetings, even if it is known that they have private grudges against one another which could erupt in a quarrel. Therefore, conflicts may occur between individuals, or they may arise in regard to issues that are addressed during meetings. A story will serve to illustrate how the adviser can help the group to deal with conflict.

Ray Loomis was a big man with a reputation for great strength. When he conducted meetings, people did not fight. One month, however, he could not be there. A physical fight broke out between two members, and the advisers had to be very firm with both of them (both were much larger and stronger than the two female advisers), telling them that they could not return to the meeting that night. Many members were frightened, however, and thought they might stop attending meetings. When Ray heard about what had happened, he and the adviser worked together to resolve the problem. They sent out a notice which stated that the group would spend the next meeting discussing ways of preventing such an occurrence. Ray made certain that the two who had fought would attend.

At the meeting, Ray asked the group to propose some rules

for meetings. The man who had started the fight at the last meeting raised his hand and suggested: 'No fighting!' The other rules also dealt with immediate problems the group was having. The members learned that they could resolve conflicts and feel more secure if they worked together to develop a framework of rules within which to operate. Now in any conflict, the rules can be quoted to bring people to order. The likely timescale of the development of a self-advocacy group is illustrated by the fact that this meeting to devise these rules was held in 1979, some four years after Project Two was started. These are the 'Rules for Working Together' that the meeting decided on:

- No fighting.
- We are all supposed to be brothers and sisters; let's act like it.
- Do unto others as you would have them do unto you.
- Pay attention in meetings.
- No arguments during meetings.
- Make up and be friends if you argue.
- Act like gentlemen and ladies.

Not every leader is as skilled as Ray Loomis at resolving conflicts. The adviser can help the leaders to deal with disagreements that arise over issues as well as those which come about between individuals. An issue which affects people personally is more likely to result in a heated argument, and that may occasionally be healthy for the group. If an argument seems to be getting more heated and to be going nowhere, you may wish to intervene very directly. You can point out things the members may have overlooked; you may suggest that a vote be taken; or you may suggest that people think about it until the next meeting, or work on the issue in smaller groups between meetings.

Contact with Other Groups

A major factor in the development of a self-advocacy move-ment is the getting together and keeping in contact of different groups. Our strong advice to any self-advocacy group, there-fore, is to get into contact with other groups and visit each other or hold joint meetings. The group might well, as an extension of this, initiate some of the later stages in the People First International model of development of self-advocacy –

i.e. the forming of a regional self-advocacy organisation and the holding of regional conventions. Correspondence could very usefully be initiated and maintained with People First International and with United Together (addresses in Appendix Six). Groups may also find it useful to make and maintain contact with other self-help groups of disabled people in their locality, to share experiences, to learn from them, and to explore possibilities of joint events or action on issues.

Further Guidance for Advisers

TASA, the Technical Assistance for Self-Advocacy project in Kansas, produced an *Advisor's Guidebook for Self-Advocacy*, written by Jeff Woodyard, containing information and advice on the nature of self-advocacy, the development of a group, the role of the adviser, problems that may be encountered, and a list of groups and resources in America.*

People First International has suggested the following 'Pointers to Help the Helper':

- *Patience*: Patience for the self-advocacy process is critical. There is a tendency to rush handicapped people to move faster than they are ready to do, and to put together a movement that is not really theirs. Patience allows the helper to see the smallest changes. Patience says that the movement will take years and years; that we are at a given point in time, and that we have a long way to go.

- *Generating Excitement*: Generating excitement is a 'gut level' characteristic and you can tell an excited helper by looking. An excited helper shows involvement, facial expression, and 'pizzaz'. A helper must be able to laugh and cry, to be compassionate, and to be angry. An excited helper spreads the spirit of the movement to the group. It is not useful to the movement if helpers are neutral.

- *Having a Vision*: Helpers must realise that self-advocacy is a lengthy process and that growth and development happen slowly. Helpers with vision will persevere and overcome any obstacles, especially traditional professional barriers. Some people just will not believe that handicapped people can and do achieve what is actually

*The *Guidebook* is available from the Kansas University Affiliated Facility, address in Appendix Six.

happening with People First. Without helpers having belief and vision in the process, the movement would be a sham. There would be no movement continuing without the vision and support of the helpers.

- *Finding Other Helpers*: Helpers need other helpers. It is lonely without peers to share and reflect ideas with. It is the exceptional person who will actually show the energy and vision to be involved in a movement such as People First.

- *Financial Concerns*: Most self-advocacy groups have no ongoing funding for the organisation and for carrying on the day-to-day work that happens. Support for self-advocacy is critical but it doesn't have to be financial support. In Oregon the support for the movement to date has been through in-kind services such as donated time of the helpers, donated use of agency phones, duplicating machines, and transport. Due to the limited income of handicapped people, People First members pay only $1 yearly membership fee, which is used to defray mailing costs. Helpers should explore potential financial resources for the movement, which could be through donations and grants. Special attention should be paid to any requirements that are tied to receiving money. Obviously a strong financial base is nice to have, but it is imperative that the self-advocacy motive behind People First does not get lost in the lust for money. Helpers must continually evaluate whether or not the movement would dissolve without financial support; if so, then the core group needs to re-align the emphasis of the movement to avoid such heavy dependence on funds.

- *Defining Roles*: Helpers should avoid spending time and energy defining roles. It is easy to get caught up in word games, role games, definition games and power games. The games of defining roles take the energy away from what the helpers should be concentrating on. The distinction between the handicapped people and the helpers is for discussion only. In practice the helpers and the handicapped members must put aside roles and work together. In this movement the power belongs to the members. The professional who is involved with the movement must learn to be comfortable in accepting a secondary role.

If there is glory to the movement, it belongs to the People.

The Rewards of Being an Adviser

Advising a self-advocacy group is one of the most rewarding activities an individual can undertake. It is a privilege to be able to be with people who are learning to value themselves, who are finding the courage within themselves to speak out and to try to change their worlds. As an adviser to a self-advocacy group, you will greatly increase your circle of friends, because many members of the group will probably become your personal friends. You must learn new skills in order to impart those skills to leaders and group members, and you must also be fearless enough to face your own attitude deficiencies, as revealed in your behaviour towards mentally handicapped people.

Finally, we who are not mentally handicapped can learn a great deal from the members of a self-advocacy group. Many of us are relatively unassertive in our own lives. We may have difficulty standing up for our own rights or expressing our thoughts and feelings to others. The mentally handicapped people who learn assertiveness and begin to practise it may become models whose example nudges you yourself towards greater self-assertion.

To enable helpers or potential advisers to review their own values and to understand the way in which society's values have been damaging to handicapped people historically, and still are today, we would very strongly recommend two books:

Normalisation, by Wolf Wolfensberger, published by the National Institute on Mental Retardation, Toronto, Canada, 1972.

The Principle of Normalisation: A Foundation for Effective Services, by John O'Brien, published by the Georgia Advocacy Office, Atlanta, Georgia, USA, 1980.

Both books are available in Britain from the Campaign for Mentally Handicapped People (address in Appendix Six, as are the addresses of NIMR in Toronto and the Georgia Advocacy Office). Alan Tyne of CMH has prepared a version of John O'Brien's book specially adapted for British readers.

5 LEARNING SELF-ADVOCACY

We hold these truths to be self-evident, that all men are created equal, that they are endowed by their Creator with certain unalienable Rights, that among these are Life, Liberty and the pursuit of Happiness.

Declaration of Independence of the
United States, 4 July 1776.

Designing a Curriculum

There have been a number of attempts in America to design courses to teach self-advocacy and related skills to mentally handicapped people. Of course, the whole process of involvement in a self-advocacy group is likely to be a major learning experience for individuals, but in this chapter we discuss some specific areas where direct teaching may be very useful. This teaching can take place on an ad hoc basis, or can be incorporated into courses in colleges or training centres. Mentally handicapped people who have already developed skills, knowledge or experience can be involved in the teaching alongside non-handicapped people.

Some materials that have been developed to assist in this teaching are reproduced in the Appendices, especially the manual on self-advocacy from the Nebraska Advocacy Office (Appendix Two). This manual was based on an earlier draft by Patty Henderson of the Protection and Advocacy Agency in Honolulu, Hawaii, entitled *You Have the Right to Speak for Yourself or to Have an Advocate Speak with You.* Some other examples of American and Canadian teaching materials are mentioned in Chapter Two.

The most comprehensive attempt to design a whole course on self-advocacy, which has been adapted and used in many parts of America, is *Life, Liberty and the Pursuit of Happiness: A Self-Advocacy Curriculum* by Betty Hallgren, Annette Norsman and Daniel Bier, produced by the Wisconsin Association for Retarded Citizens (address in Appendix Six) in 1977. This course is designed to take place over a twelve-week period, with one two-hour session per week. It is recommended that class size should not exceed fifteen and that there be two instructors.

The following is the rationale behind the Wisconsin curriculum:

The right to life, liberty and the pursuit of happiness may be self-evident, but it has never been self-enforcing. For people with developmental disabilities the struggle to establish basic human rights has been long and frustrating. Historically, individuals with a developmental disability have been devalued by and segregated from societal mainstreams by reason of their supposed inability to make a contribution to society. When they were perceived as a menace, they were treated as criminals. When they were perceived as sick, they were treated as patients. The consequence of these perceptions, the societal Catch 22, is that it is very difficult – if not impossible – to contribute to a society from which one has been excluded.

We know that an individual's capacity to protect and exercise his basic human rights is directly dependent upon the economic, legal and human resources which are available to him. A substantial consensus of opinion now acknowledges the need to provide these resources to people with developmental disabilities in order to establish their first-class citizenship. Advocacy is a movement which endeavours to establish and implement systems which will represent and safeguard the rights and interests of individuals who are impaired or disadvantaged to the degree that they have difficulty effectively representing their own interests in society. Self-Advocacy is that component of the advocacy movement which is directed towards increasing the knowledge and understanding of basic human and civil rights and responsibilities, and is a pre-condition to meaningful citizenship.

Many people with developmental disabilities have been denied opportunities to learn their rights and responsibilities as American citizens and members of the human family. Even more unfortunate is the fact that many people with developmental disabilities have been 'programmed', by families and professionals alike, to believe that they are second-class citizens not deserving of the same dignity and respect afforded their non-disabled peers.

We contend that ignorance of human and civil rights and responsibilities combined with a perception of oneself as a second-class citizen and inferior human being, have created (and will continue to create) substantial barriers to the success of programmes and services designed to facilitate the physical and social integration of disabled individuals into societal mainstreams.

Just as Citizen Advocacy will change negative attitudes and break down additional barriers to integration among the general public, Self-Advocacy training will raise the consciousness of developmentally disabled people and help them to develop the knowledge and self-respect they need in order to demand the rights and dignity to which they are legally and morally entitled.

Using short talks illustrated with films or slides, exercises, and small or large group discussions and sharing of experience, the twelve sessions of the Wisconsin curriculum cover the following topics:

Session One: Each person is an individual with a unique self that should be positively valued.

Session Two: We are all members of the human family; differentness should be respected; all people have certain capabilities and certain limitations.

Session Three: All citizens have certain rights and certain responsibilities.

Session Four: All citizens have a right to live in and participate in their community; community services should exist to help citizens to do this.

Session Five: The purpose of laws, and how citizens can participate in the law-making process.

Session Six: The circumstances in which rights can be limited; entitlement to legal process and appeal; guardianship.

Session Seven: Rights and responsibilities in how and where we live; the right to live in the community, and to make choices about living arrangements.

Session Eight: An administrator or planner responsible for providing comprehensive community residential services is invited to talk to the group and answer questions.

Session Nine: Rights and responsibilities in learning and work; the right to adequate education to equip people for work; overcoming barriers to handicapped people working.

Session Ten: Two administrators or planners from the areas of vocational rehabilitation and adult education are invited to talk to the group and answer questions.

Session Eleven: Self-advocacy; decision-taking and choosing between alternatives; pursuing strategies of problem-solving; assuming responsibility for protecting one's own rights and interests.

Session Twelve: Review of what has been learned.

A very similar curriculum has been prepared by the Texas Association for Retarded Citizens, condensed to take place as a one-day workshop, with the following intensive nine-hour timetable:

8.00	Registration.
8.30	Introductions.
9.00	Individuality.
9.30	Film.
10.00	Discussion on valuing one's uniqueness and respecting differentness.
10.30	Coffee.
10.45	Rights and responsibilities, with slides and discussion.
12.00	Lunch.
1.00	Responsibilities of citizenship; 'belonging' to a community.
2.00	Laws and the law-making process, with exercises.
3.00	Tea.
3.15	How rights are sometimes limited; legal process and appeal.
3.45	Self-advocacy, with slides.
5.00	Finish.

At the University of Kansas, where the Technical Assistance for Self-Advocacy (TASA) project was based, there was in the late 1970s an 'Assertiveness Training Task Force', producing material designed to help people (for example women as part of the women's rights movement) to be more assertive in the responsible protection of their rights. TASA worked with this group to develop some courses of assertiveness training for developmentally disabled people, as part of the process of developing self-advocacy skills. Assertiveness is defined as standing up for one's rights, and honestly expressing one's feelings, beliefs and opinions, without violating the rights of others. It is contrasted with passivity, or not standing up for one's rights, and aggression, which is pursuing one's own rights in a way that dominates or humiliates others and hence infringes their rights.

Using ideas from all these American sources, we try in this chapter to outline some suggestions for training or curriculum content that can help individual mentally handicapped people in the process of personal, individual self-advocacy or in the process of working with others in a self-advocacy group. There is a great need for development work to take place on training for mentally handicapped people in all these areas in the future.

Values

Just as it is important for helpers or advisers to have a personal set of values that is conducive to helping individual and group development, it is of course important for handicapped people themselves to have these values. There is the added dimension that these values include the way the person perceives himself and his place in the world. Unfortunately, many handicapped people have simply learned the set of values that is common in ordinary society, and they may view themselves and other handicapped people as of low worth and status, capable of few achievements – dependent people who should show continual gratitude to others for their existence, and who are not able to participate in decision-taking or in community life. On the other hand, it is greatly to the credit of some mentally handicapped people that, despite a lifetime of experiences that would tend to reinforce these perceptions, they are resilient enough to retain a belief in their own value as individuals, and in the value of other handicapped people too.

There is a need for strong teaching of mentally handicapped people in order to reinforce the positive values that they have, and to counteract the negative perceptions that their experiences may have caused. The aim of this teaching is to give each person a set of beliefs about himself and other handicapped people that will engender self-confidence, motivation and direction in the person's everyday life, and a respect for other handicapped people and a willingness to work with them to pursue common interests. Such beliefs will be along these lines:

- I am a unique individual who has a value and worth that is as great as that of anyone else.
- Being different does not mean being less valuable.
- Everyone has capabilities and limitations.

- People should not be judged on their capabilities or limitations, but rather on the extent to which they have tried to use their capabilities and overcome their limitations.
- The courage and example of people who have overcome severe limitations is as great as that of people who have shown great natural capabilities.
- Every person, given the opportunity, can use his capabilities and overcome his limitations, and hence be a valuable citizen.

It is important that these values be taught to handicapped people, not because of any notion that they should identify with other handicapped people because they themselves are handicapped, but because it is only by the adoption of these values by *all* of us that the place of handicapped people in society can be improved. For this reason it may be ideal if handicapped people can learn these values in the company of other students who are also learning the same lesson, be they helpers of self-advocacy groups or other non-handicapped students.

The teaching can be done through discussion and exchange of experiences, and through accounts of achievements by handicapped people. The *People First* film could be used. In Britain there are several other films available for hire from Concord Films (address in Appendix Six) that might be useful:

- *The Special World of Nigel Hunt*, about a man with Down's syndrome who wrote a book about his experiences;
- *We're Outsiders Now*, showing a group of mentally handicapped people moving out of an institution into a home of their own;
- *Joey*, the story of Joseph Deacon, the mentally handicapped man who wrote his autobiography with the help of three similarly handicapped friends;
- *Stepping Out*, an Australian film showing impressive drama and mime by mentally handicapped people;
- *Like Other People*, about a severely physically handicapped couple who wish to get married.

Other useful material might include the story of Helen Keller, who was both blind and deaf but overcame these severe limitations. And a handicapped person who has made impressive achievements could be invited to speak to the group. For members of People First of Nebraska, a source of renewed appreciation of the worth of handicapped people was a talk at their convention by a very severely physically handicapped man who communicated through a machine operated by his foot.

Rights
The issue of rights is central to self-advocacy. There are two kinds of rights – human rights that apply to everyone by common agreement, and legal or civil rights that apply to people in a certain country by virtue of laws or regulations passed by law-makers in that country. Some of the main areas for possible teaching are:
* What are rights?
* What are some important human rights?
* What are some important legal or civil rights of handicapped people?
* How are laws made, and how can citizens be involved?
* How can rights sometimes be limited?
* What safeguards apply in cases of limitations of rights?

What Are Rights?
The *Self-Advocacy Workbook* written by Nancy Gardner for the TASA project (see Chapter Two) has many succinct statements and definitions. 'Rights' are simply defined as the rules that help make people equal. 'It is important to know what your rights are so when someone tries to take one away you can stop them.'

An approach to teaching the concept of rights might be to get the group to suggest some rules that would help to make handicapped people more equal to non-handicapped people. This can be an introduction to other lists of human rights that have been suggested or agreed by other people, and to some legal rights (or rules) that have been laid down in formal legislation. The need for agreement among lots of people in order for a right to be established can be discussed, and experiences can be recounted by individuals of attempts to take away their rights.

It can be pointed out that rights apply to everyone, by virtue of their being a human being and a citizen of their country, and they can only be taken away in very special and rare circumstances. Simply being handicapped or different is not a good enough reason on its own for a right to be denied to a person.

Important Human Rights.

A group can draw up its own list of rules that it would like to see adopted, to help ensure equality between handicapped and non-handicapped people. The list can then be reviewed to see what problems there might be in gaining general agreement to those 'rights'. In the end a 'Charter of Rights' might be drawn up, that the group is willing to work to get general agreement on and to see enforced.

To assist the group in deciding on important human rights, there are many sources of lists of rights drawn up by others; some are declarations of the rights of everyone, some apply specifically to disabled or mentally handicapped people, and some apply to people in special circumstances like living in a hospital or residential establishment.

The *Self-Advocacy Workbook* (TASA) gives this basic list:

- The right to life
- The right of choice
- The right to freedom
- The right to try to be happy
- The right to make up your own mind
- The right to choose the people you want to be with
- The right to be listened to
- The right to eat what you want
- The right to go to bed when you want

An obvious source of ideas for incorporation into a Charter of Rights is the United Nations Declaration on the Rights of Mentally Retarded Persons. Two other UN Declarations of Rights are the Universal Declaration of Human Rights and the Declaration on the Rights of Disabled Persons. All three of these are reproduced in Appendix One. It should perhaps be noted that, although the Declaration on the Rights of Retarded Persons represented an impressive breakthrough when it was achieved through international action by parents of mentally handicapped people in the 1960s, it is in some ways very weak. Phrases like 'as far as possible' and 'aware that certain countries can devote only limited efforts to this end' occur as get-out clauses in the Preamble. The words 'to the maximum degree of feasibility' in Article 1 are a dangerous inclusion: what rights might be denied by invoking this clause? Similarly, the wording of Article 7 is disastrous: to imply that in some circumstances the rights in Articles 2, 3, 4, 5 and 6 can be denied is almost to render the whole Declaration meaningless. These inclusions are in marked contrast to the phraseology of the Universal Declaration of Human Rights, which is un-equivocal in its demands. The Universal Declaration may therefore be a more useful source of genuine rights for mentally handicapped people than the Declaration on the Rights of Retarded People.

Another source of ideas for a Charter of Rights is to be found in attempts to delineate standards for service provision. A good example in Britain is the STAMINA papers produced by the National Society for Mentally Handicapped Children and Adults. STAMINA stands for 'Standards that are Minim-ally Acceptable', and the papers define these standards for a range of services for children or adults and suggest action by local parents' groups to achieve them. We reproduce in Appendix One the standards from the STAMINA paper concerned with residential services for mentally handicapped adults. Such a list could be adopted as a Charter of Rights for mentally handicapped people receiving residential services.

One of the objectives of those concerned with the establish-ment and protection of rights is to turn agreed human rights into formalised legal rights. One example is the right to receive services in the 'least restrictive environment'. This is widely accepted as a human right of handicapped people. For example the Jay Report on Mental Handicap Nursing and Care, published in Britain in 1979, states: 'An individual has the right to live, learn and work in the least restrictive environment appropriate to that particular person.' In America, however, this has now become a legal right, enforceable by the courts, and this right has been a major factor in the extensive deinstitutionalisation of mentally handicapped people in America in the last decade. Another example is the right to an individualised written plan for how services will help to meet your needs: this too is now a legal right in America.

It should be stressed in teaching about human rights that they apply to all people, regardless of degree of handicap. We should always remain aware of the need to pursue and protect these rights even for the most severely handicapped people.

Legal and Civil Rights

These rights will vary in different countries. In America a number of basic rights are legally guaranteed under specific laws or under the US Constitution. TASA's *Self-Advocacy Workbook* lists the following:

- The right to worship the way you choose.
- The right to 'due process' and the right to appeal. This includes the right to know what is happening and why your rights are being restricted (like if you have to go to a special education class instead of a regular class). It also includes the right to ask for a change in the decision if you do not agree with it, plus the right to know exactly how long your right will be restricted.
- The right to petition for change. This includes the right to ask for a rule to be changed if you think it is not a good one.
- The right to equal protection, which includes the right to have the same laws that everyone else has apply to you, too. No one can take away your rights just because you have a disability.
- The right to vote.
- The right to least restrictive environment. This includes the right to live and work as independently as you are able. It also includes the right to the same services everyone gets.
- The right of informed consent. This includes the right to know all of your choices or options before you make up your mind.
- The right to Individual Programme Plans, including the right to be in a programme where people work out a plan, with your help, just for you and what you need. This also includes the right to ask questions about the programme when you do not understand something.

Specific laws can be identified that it might be useful for individuals or self-advocacy groups to know about. In Britain and America there are laws concerning the right of mentally handicapped children to education. In the United States there are laws concerning discrimination, access to buildings, and transport (see the manual on self-advocacy reproduced in Appendix Two). In Britain the Chronically Sick and Disabled Persons Act gives some important entitlements to handicapped people.

One of the most necessary things to teach mentally handicapped people about legal rights is that simply having been labelled 'mentally handicapped' for schooling, medical or social work purposes, is not a reason in itself for a person's legal status being different from that of anyone else (see Chapter Six).

A person may wish *herself* to be formally recognised as having a certain category or degree of disability in order to become eligible for particular benefits or entitlements, and teaching can be given on what these benefits are and how to get them. Pamphlets giving this information are usually readily available.

Or other people may wish the person to be legally recognised as 'incompetent' to protect her from exploitation or harm, or to prevent her from becoming involved in situations that she is assumed not to be able to understand. In America this will usually take the form of the person being placed under the legal guardianship of someone else, who must give permission for the handicapped person to do certain things, and can take certain decisions on behalf of the person and have certain controls over her. In Britain, legal guardianship is used only very rarely, but there are circumstances in which the competence of a mentally handicapped person can be challenged. This question is discussed further in Chapter Six.

An understanding of guardianship, and the procedures whereby the competence of a person can be challenged, are possible areas for teaching. Perhaps the most useful information that can be given concerns where the handicapped person can go for advice on his legal position, in any specific instance.

Even if a handicapped person is under guardianship or subject to other forms of restriction, she is still entitled to equal protection under the laws of his country. This is a very important principle to teach. For example, mentally handicapped people, whatever their circumstances or legal status in other respects, have equal rights with everyone else to protection from assault or theft. Some mentally handicapped people live in conditions where they are subject to constant risk of assault or theft of their property. (See for example *Looking at Life*, an account of the experiences of handicapped people in a number of residential establishments in Britain, written by Alan Tyne and published by the Campaign for Mentally Handicapped People, 1978; other examples were shown in a television film, 'Silent Minority', broadcast in Britain in June 1981, in which mentally handicapped people in two institutions were pictured tied to a post or herded into an outdoor 'cage' during the day.) These are serious infringements of the civil and legal rights of these people, which are condoned or actually perpetrated by professional people. Mentally handicapped people are as entitled to legal protection and redress in these circumstances as anyone else would be.

Other important areas of knowledge are: rights on being questioned by the police; rights relating to treatment by neighbours; rights in relation to discrimination in jobs, housing or education; consumer rights; rights in relation to medical or other treatment (quality, consent, access to records, etc.); rights to further education for adults; and rights to public housing.

The Law-Making Process

People can be taught how laws are passed, and the role that all citizens can play in electing the politicians that make the laws. They can also be given an understanding of the role of pressure groups and special interest groups in influencing civil servants and politicians. There can be teaching about political manifestos, and how to choose which of several candidates to support. Teaching can include information about both local and national government. Voting procedures can be practised.

Handicapped people can be taught that playing a role in choosing the people who make decisions that affect our lives, and pass the laws that protect or restrict us, is one of the most important abilities that we have in democratic countries.

Limitations of Rights

There are two kinds of limitations to rights: legal limitations and personal limitations. The rights of some people in society (e.g. property owners) can be protected only by limiting the rights of others (e.g. burglars). There are, therefore, legal procedures for limiting people's rights in certain circumstances. Again, the important point for handicapped people to understand is that simply being handicapped is very rarely, if ever, a sufficient reason in itself for a person's rights to be limited. There must be other circumstances that apply. Also, there are regulations that govern the legal limitation of people's rights, and formal procedures laid down that have to be gone through. A handicapped person, regardless of degree of handicap, is entitled to have these regulations and procedures properly followed if his rights are legally limited. How to obtain easy access to good legal help and advice is important information to have.

Personal limitations can prevent a person from exercising all of her rights effectively. In this case, the individual should learn where to get, and how to press for, every assistance to enable him to develop new skills or to exercise rights – she may need the help of other people, or special aids and equipment. A person who cannot get to a polling station on her own to vote in an election, for instance, must have a way of getting help to do so. (The concept of working with a personal advocate can be introduced here.)

Safeguards

Mentally handicapped people should know to whom they can go if they are in trouble, if they think they are being wrongly treated or if their rights are being infringed. A major safeguard for them will be membership of a self-advocacy group, whose leaders and advisers will be good people to approach initially for help or advice. People might also usefully find out the names and addresses of helpful professionals, and of their political representatives, and how to contact them in case of need. There also has to be some teaching on what sorts of issues are appropriate to raise with particular people. The usefulness of membership of other groups, such as trade unions, students' organisations, or tenants' associations can be explored.

Personal strategies for tackling infringements of rights can be taught. The TASA *Workbook* suggests.

- Ask questions about why your rights are being limited. Keep asking questions until you understand what is happening.
- Write down the answers you are given, or get the answers on tape. Get as much information as you can. Make sure it is correct.

- Get a friend to help you if you want to. Some towns have services that can help you get a friend who knows about advocacy.
- Find out what all the choices are. Pick out the ones that are best for you.
- Decide what you think about what is happening. Decide what steps you need to take to reach your goal.
- Know who to talk to and who is in charge. Go to the person who makes the decisions.
- Know and use your rights. The main ones to remember when your rights are being limited are: the right to know all the information; the right to appeal and ask for a change in the decision before you agree; the right to know what is happening all the time and why it is happening.

Responsibilities

Side by side with rights go responsibilities. The TASA *Workbook* uses the analogy that, just as we have to pay money for some things we want, we have to 'do our duties' to get our rights. Another approach to teaching this concept might be to point out that if we wish to have our own rights respected, we must respect the rights of other people, and this involves behaving towards them in a responsible way. We must also not waste our rights by using them carelessly or without adequate preparation or information.

Examples in the *Workbook* include the responsibility to register as a voter ahead of time and to know who the candidates are, before exercising the right to vote; the responsibility to come to work every day, to be on time and to do the job as well as you can, when exercising the right to work and make money; and the responsibility to learn to wait at the right bus stop, have the money for the fare, and know how to get where you need to go, before exercising the right to use the public bus.

A teaching group can discuss and generate its own list of other responsibilities in relation to other rights it wishes to pursue.

Responsibilities can also include more general aspects of behaviour such as courtesy and consideration for others, and following rules of meetings. These can be the subject of additional teaching for individuals if required.

Problem-Solving and Decision-Taking

Any change that a person or group wishes to achieve can be thought of as a 'problem'. As discussed in Chapter Four, mentally handicapped people need help and teaching in being able to recognise and delineate alternative approaches or solutions to problems, to consider the advantages and disadvantages of each alternative, and finally to decide on the best one. A teaching exercise can be carried out in which a problem is put forward and the group suggests alternative solutions or actions to help. These are all listed and the group discusses the points for or against each one. Finally a vote is taken on which alternative is best.

A special example of a 'problem' is the election of group officers or representatives. Simulation exercises can be held in which alternative candidates are put forward, their relative merits discussed, and a final choice made through voting. For those who require it, additional teaching on how to vote can be arranged. Use aids to voting, such as the shoe-boxes used by Project Two (see Chapter Four).

Making a Plan of Action

Once decisions have been made, they need to be carried through, and mentally handicapped people are likely to need help and teaching in how to do this. Teaching might include:

- specifying the goal clearly;
- splitting down the goal into steps or tasks or actions that are required on the way;
- listing the strengths available for meeting each step, i.e. skills or special interests that people have, good relationships already existing, help available;
- deciding, on the basis of the strengths, who will be responsible for achieving each step, and how they might go about it;
- setting target dates by which each step will be achieved;
- keeping any necessary records, and ensuring good communication between the people involved.

Simulation exercises can be carried out using tasks like planning a picnic, planning an election, planning a convention, planning a meeting with a politician to discuss a grievance, planning an appeal against a decision, or planning an award to someone who has given good service.

Teaching might include suggestions for how to use meetings

with other people effectively to achieve things, using such materials as the booklet *How to Work with the System – and Win* (see Chapter Two and Appendix Four).

Communication

The greater the general communication skills of mentally handicapped people, the better will they be able to practice self-advocacy and join successfully with others in a group. An important aspect of teaching skills of self-advocacy is therefore to work on improving communication skills. People can be helped to express themselves better; to speak more clearly; to use gesture, eye contact, body posture and facial expression more successfully to convey interest and enthusiasm while conversing; to pay attention; and to listen better.

The *Advisor's Guidebook for Self-Advocacy*, written by Jeff Woodyard for TASA and available from the Kansas University Affiliated Facility, suggests some exercises to develop communication skills:

- People 'act out' emotions non-verbally, while others identify which emotions are being demonstrated: shyness, sorrow, joy, suspicion, anger, happiness, fear, indifference, frustration, hope.
- One person describes himself to another, who then gives feedback on the way facial expressions, gestures, eye contact and posture were used; they then switch roles.
- People practise using brief verbalised expressions of interest and understanding: 'I see', 'Yes', 'Really', 'That's interesting', 'Great'.
- People practise phrases that indicate willingness to continue or expand a conversation: 'I'd like to hear more about that', 'What happened next?', 'What will you do about that?', 'Let's discuss that now'.
- People practise paraphrasing what someone has just said, to indicate that the communication has been understood: 'So you're getting a new job?', 'If you move into an apartment, you think you'll be happier', 'So John keeps annoying you, does he?'
- People practise reflecting the mood of another person: 'You seem sad about that', 'You look angry', 'You seem tired', 'You sound very pleased with the way things have turned out'.

A further area of very useful teaching is of course in reading and writing. Another is use of the telephone.

Assertiveness

As mentioned at the beginning of this chapter, a major contribution of TASA was to point out the importance of training for handicapped people in assertiveness, and to work with others at Kansas University to produce relevant training materials. The *Advisor's Guidebook* suggests the following exercises:

- People practise giving answers that are assertive, passive or aggressive in response to someone asking if they may smoke.
- People practise expressing the following statements in an assertive way, a passive way and an aggressive way: 'It's time for me to leave', 'No, I don't want to join your club', 'It certainly is warm in here.'
- People practise responding with a refusal to orders such as 'Go to the store!' or 'Take these out to the car!' Feedback is then given on whether the person appeared comfortable in refusing; whether he made eye contact; whether he hesitated; whether posture, gestures, tone, expression and volume were assertive, or too passive or aggressive.
- People practise positive assertiveness, with feedback. People make positive statements such as: 'I like you', 'You look very nice', 'You're a nice person', 'I appreciate your patience', 'You work hard'. And they give positive replies such as: 'Thank you for saying so', 'I'm glad you think so', 'I'm happy that you appreciate me', 'Working hard is important to me'.
- People practise responding to a salesman trying to sell them an encyclopaedia they don't want, with feedback on their performance. Then people practise being the salesman, also with feedback.

What Is Advocacy?

There can be teaching on the nature of advocacy, and the components of advocacy, as outlined in Chapter Three. The distinction between expressive and instrumental tasks can be discussed, and examples given of good practice in each area. The concept of citizen advocacy can be explained, and discussion and teaching can take place on how to seek an advocate and how to work with one. The ways in which members of self-advocacy groups can be advocates for each other can be explored.

What Is Self-Advocacy?
Self-advocacy is defined in the TASA *Workbook* as follows: 'Self-Advocacy is speaking or acting for yourself. It means deciding what's best for you and taking charge of getting it. It means standing up for your rights as a person.' Thus defined, self-advocacy is of course something that can be carried on by just one person, for himself. And it is clearly something of universal application, not just for handicapped people. The concept of self-advocacy can be explained on two levels – that of a universal phenomenon of individual people speaking or acting in their own interests, and that of the very special phenomenon of handicapped people joining together to speak and act on each other's behalf.

Personal self-advocacy involves developing the skills and knowledge outlined in this chapter, to the best of one's ability, and using them to achieve for oneself as many choices and opportunities as one can. Personal self-advocacy counteracts the deadening effect of other people always making decisions for you. It gives motivation and direction to one's own life. Teaching personal self-advocacy can include helping people to outline choices, take decisions and prepare plans in relation to things they would like to achieve or change in their own lives.

The concept of group self-advocacy can be taught through information about the self-advocacy movement, by inviting members of existing groups to give talks and show slides of their work, and by showing and discussing the film *People First*. A practical exercise in setting up and running a group might be attempted, if students are not already involved in an existing group. If they are, the meaning of self-advocacy can be discussed in relation to what the group does at present and how it might function in the future.

Community Involvement
Both the Wisconsin curriculum and the Texas curriculum mentioned earlier in this chapter include a session on rights and responsibilities relating to living in the community. One

concept that can be taught is that of 'belonging' to a community – using its facilities, taking part in its institutions and contributing to the life of the community. Lists can be made of community resources that people could learn to use, such as libraries, adult education facilities, sport and leisure facilities, museums and galleries, churches, shops, pubs and eating places. Organisations that people might join can also be listed, for example clubs concerned with hobbies, sport, voluntary work, music, drama, conservation, civic affairs, politics, religion.

Alongside discussion of the rights people have to live in the community, to have choice of where and how and with whom they live, to have privacy and possessions, and to have the chance to develop skills for greater independence, the responsibilities of community living can be explored. These might include respect for public property, obedience to national and local laws, becoming as informed as possible about community affairs, taking part in an informed way in local elections, and being proud of one's community.

Leadership and Running a Group
Some mentally handicapped people will have a leadership role in a self-advocacy group, and may benefit from the teaching of leadership skills. These might include extra experience and guidance in evaluating alternatives; persuading others; making plans; and reviewing strengths so as to allocate responsibility for particular steps in a plan. Other skills that might be taught are those of helping people to evaluate the success of their actions; encouraging and supporting people (especially when they undertake new tasks); controlling meetings without aggression; drafting agendas, letters or press releases; planning future activities of a group to strike a balance between formal meetings, recreation and other events; canvassing for election; organising elections, conventions or other events; and fundraising.

Allied to the development of leadership skills, there may be a need to teach greater understanding of the processes involved in running a group: for example the importance of voting procedures; the functions of a committee and of individual officers; ways of involving all the members; how to achieve necessary compromises in cases of strong disagreement or difficulty; how to achieve agreement on rules for the group, such as rules of membership or of behaviour at meetings; and ways of recruiting new members.

As part of a teaching process, leaders can be helped to gather information about other self-advocacy groups and ways can be explored of communicating with them or cooperating with them in events or in pursuing issues. The same can be done with other local self-help or special interest groups. A greater understanding of local government and politics, and the operation of service agencies, can also be imparted.

Public Speaking

Training can be given in public speaking, including how to prepare in advance what one wishes to say; how to organise a talk, using examples, stories or visual aids to add interest; how to project oneself to an audience; and how to answer questions. Simulation exercises can take place, and practice, supervision and feedback can be given on real occasions when talks are given. Invitations to give such talks can be actively solicited from different groups, to give a range of opportunities to speak to audiences of different size and composition in a range of different settings. Making tape or video recordings to provide examples and feedback in teaching is extremely useful. Tape or video recorders can also be used by individuals to practise speaking.

A large part of the skill of public speaking is developing self-confidence. Given this, there is no reason why people with relatively poor communication skills should not, with help, take part in public speaking, as is illustrated in the *People First* film.

Helping and Supporting Others

In a self-advocacy curriculum there may be some teaching designed to enhance skills of understanding the problems and needs of others and of helping and supporting others in overcoming their problems. Simulation exercises and role-play can be used, and people can share their own experiences. Some input may be given on how certain experiences might make people depressed, poorly motivated, angry, aggressive, lethargic, disinterested, or physically or mentally unwell. Ways of approaching and forming relationships with people with these

162   *We Can Speak for Ourselves*

problems might be discussed. In this, as in most teaching of mentally handicapped people, it is best to keep discussion and teaching to specific concrete examples. One useful fact to remember, one that can be a rich source of examples for discussion, is that many of the more able handicapped people are likely to have had considerable experience of helping to care for more severely handicapped people. Often mentally handicapped people have considerable helping skills.

A Vision of the Future
Finally, a useful teaching exercise, which can help to motivate and give further direction to individuals, is to discuss with them the hopes and aspirations they have for themselves or their self-advocacy group in the future. What will they or the group be doing in one year, five years, ten years, twenty years? Views can be exchanged on the problems likely to be encountered in achieving these dreams of the future, while healthy idealism can be encouraged and supported. Mentally handicapped people can look forward to achieving, through their own efforts, a better life, greater liberty, and more opportunities for the pursuit of happiness.

6 SELF-ADVOCACY IN BRITAIN

Dear Sir,
   There are people in the Centre who have been through soul
destroying experience being treated as second-class citizens.
   Would you give us more information on *People First* and
self-advocacy as we think this can help us.
   Yours faithfully . . .

>   *Letter from a mentally handicapped person*
>   *attending an Adult Training Centre in*
>   *England.*

The CMH Conferences
From Friday evening, 14 July 1972, to Sunday afternoon, 16
July 1972, the first national conference of mentally handicapped people in Britain was held at Castle Priory College in
Wallingford, Oxfordshire. It was organised by the Campaign
for Mentally Handicapped People (CMH) and was called 'Our
Life'.
   A number of hospitals, local authorities and voluntary
organisations in different parts of England had been invited to
send mentally handicapped delegates, by themselves or accompanied by staff. Twenty-two mentally handicapped people
attended: eight lived in hospitals, five in local authority hostels,
one in a hostel run by a voluntary organisation, two in a
privately run village community, and six lived at home with
their parents or relatives. In her report of the conference (*Our
Life*, available from CMH, address in Appendix Six), Ann
Shearer describes the degree of handicap of these delegates as
follows:
   'The group fell well within the middle to top range of people
we call mentally handicapped. Two of the participants found it
particularly hard to follow the thread of a discussion and
express themselves clearly even when asked a direct question;
one needed help with washing and dressing; one was incon-
tinent at night. Several had epilepsy; one delegate was nearly
blind, one deaf and two others had additional physical
handicap. None, however, found it impossible to contribute to

the discussions about the way they lived and worked and saw people around them.'

Fifteen non-handicapped people were present; six were staff who had accompanied delegates; six were members of CMH; one person represented the Centre on Environment for the Handicapped; and three people had been invited as independent chairpersons for the group discussions.

The programme was organised around three main 90-minute discussion sessions, with the themes: 'How would we like to live?', 'How would we like to work?' and 'What would we like to do with our leisure time?' There was an hour at the end of the conference for groups to report back to a plenary session. Interspersed between these main sessions were shared meals, an introductory session on the first evening, painting, films, a football match, a boat trip on the river Thames, a supper party with invited guests, and an evening chamber concert. The conference programme, and some notes on organisation from the *Our Life* report, are reproduced in Appendix Five, and some of the comments made by delegates in the discussions are quoted at the end of this chapter.

CMH organised a second conference in 1973. It was held at an Adult Training Centre in London, with delegates from outside London being accommodated in the homes of participants who lived closer, and its title was 'Listen'. Since that time CMH has organised about a dozen events deriving from the idea of these conferences, and still does so. Reports on some of the early conferences were published, and are still available from CMH:

- *Our Life*, report of the first conference, held in July 1972;
- *Listen*, report of the second conference, held in May 1973;
- *A Workshop on Participation*, report of a conference held in June 1973;
- *Participation with Mentally Handicapped People*, report of a conference held in July 1974, with a wider discussion of the principles and ideas behind such events;
- *Working Out*, report of a conference held in June 1975, which had as its theme the experiences of people in work or in trying to find jobs.

The titles of the third and fourth of these reports reflect an important change in the thinking of the organisers of the CMH conferences about their purpose, following the first 'Our Life' event. At the first conference about 40 per cent of the people present were non-handicapped. After the conference there were many indications of its value to the mentally handicapped people who attended, but it had also clearly made a deep impression on the non-handicapped participants. Many had found it an exciting and important personal revelation of the potential of mentally handicapped people, the value of what they have to say, and the possibilities of forming a new and much more equal kind of relationship with them.

During the next few years, CMH came to look on the conferences and events that they organised not so much as conferences for mentally handicapped people in which they could express a voice of their own – though this was always an important element – but as events during which mentally handicapped and non-handicapped people could join together on an equal basis to explore a new relationship of sharing. This was done through trying to arrange that about half the delegates would be mentally handicapped and half non-handicapped; insisting that non-handicapped and handicapped people shared bedrooms, washing facilities, meals and free time (usually being paired with people they did not previously know); expecting that in discussions people would ask and answer questions on a completely equal basis, so that a discussion about 'where we live' would be a sharing of information about where everyone in the group lives, not just about where mentally handicapped people live; and arranging activities in which everyone could share equally without the non-handicapped people having obviously more competence than others – for example painting, making and playing simple percussion instruments, learning country dancing, dancing to pop music, learning yoga, going to church or to the pub or for a walk or for a visit to a local historic house.

The occasions came to be called 'participation events' rather than 'conferences'. Paul Williams has described the philosophy behind them in a paper called *Our Mutual Handicap*, available from CMH. Handicapped people have problems in relating to us, and we have problems in relating to them. The events have the aim of giving people an opportunity to work on reducing this 'mutual handicap': mentally handicapped people have a welcome chance to express themselves and to share activities with non-handicapped people, while non-handicapped participants have the unusual chance, sometimes approached with trepidation, to share their lives for a short time on an equal basis with mentally handicapped people. Learning and growth can take place amongst all participants – if anything, especially among the non-handicapped people present.

This idea has been very fruitfully pursued by CMH in recent years, and there is no doubt about the value of these participation events. However, one effect of this change in orientation has been that the events are no longer seen as clear examples of self-advocacy for mentally handicapped people. Now, not so much importance is placed on what the handicapped people say, but more on the relationship that is set up between handicapped and non-handicapped people. Conversations somehow become more 'ordinary' and less worthy of note, and it is more difficult to write them up or to produce a conference report.

The reports on the 'Our Life' and 'Listen' conferences remain, however, powerful British examples of how mentally handicapped people can be given a voice of their own, and of how valuable and interesting the things are that they have to say. There is scope for the idea of straightforward conferences for mentally handicapped people to be revived in Britain, to take place in addition to CMH's participation events. The ideal would be for such conferences to be initiated, and largely organised, by mentally handicapped people themselves.

Other Examples of Mentally Handicapped People Speaking for Themselves

There are many other examples in Britain of mentally handicapped people speaking with a voice of their own. These include other conferences and participation events, books written by mentally handicapped people, appearances by mentally handicapped people on television, and surveys of the views of mentally handicapped people.

Other Conferences and Participation Events

One group of mentally handicapped people from Harrow, near London, did go back from one of the early CMH conferences and organise one of their own. A small committee of mentally handicapped people, with the help of just one or two non-handicapped people, decided on a programme and on themes for discussion, and held a small non-residential conference of their own. A report was prepared afterwards listing the concerns of delegates and some demands for change. One particularly strong issue was the low remuneration given to mentally handicapped people for the work they do in training centres.

In January 1980, CMH, in cooperation with the King's Fund Centre, ran a one-day course in London on participation events, and in May 1981 CMH ran a similar one in Edinburgh in cooperation with the Area Five Action Group in that city. Following both these, a number of participants went away and organised small similar events for mentally handicapped people they knew or worked with. It is probable that several other small conferences of mentally handicapped people have been held under the auspices of other organisations or individuals over the last few years.

Books by Mentally Handicapped People

At least two books written by mentally handicapped people have been published: *The World of Nigel Hunt* by Nigel Hunt, a man with Down's syndrome, published as long ago as 1967 by Darwen Finlayson; and *Tongue Tied* by Joseph Deacon, published in 1974 by the National Society for Mentally Handicapped Children and Adults. Mr Deacon's book was followed by a television programme in which he spoke about his life. Mr Deacon died in December 1981.

Mr Deacon was a mentally handicapped man who had additional severe physical handicaps that made communication extremely difficult. He had been resident in an English mental handicap hospital from 1928. Another handicapped resident in the hospital befriended Mr Deacon, learned to understand his attempts at communication and translated them for the staff. Painstakingly over many years, Mr Deacon told the story of his life, his friend translated it to a third friend who could write, and a fourth friend slowly typed it. Following publication of the final book, Mr Deacon and his three friends gave many public appearances, including a very success- ful tour of Holland, after which the Dutch people raised a substantial sum of money to enable the four men to move into their own self-contained house in the hospital grounds.

The story of Mr Deacon and his friends is a small but amazing example of self-advocacy by mentally handicapped people. Two brief extracts from the book are given at the end of this chapter.

Appearances on Television

On several occasions mentally handicapped people have been interviewed on British television in the ATV programme 'Link', primarily aimed at disabled viewers and their families. In 1979 two of the organisers of the Harrow conference, mentioned earlier – Gillian Oliver and John Lumbus – were featured in a ten-minute interview which is thought to be the first extended interview of its kind with mentally handicapped people on British television. In 1980 David Ward of the Avro ATC Students' Council (see later in this chapter) was interviewed on 'Link', in part about his attendance at a CMH participation event. In June 1981 'Link' devoted a whole programme (30 minutes) to self-advocacy by mentally handicapped people, which included excerpts from the film *People First* and a discussion with four representatives of the Avro Students' Council – David Ward, Terry Green, Barry Woodwood and Hugh Townsend. [ATV is now Central TV]

A film called *We're Outsiders Now*, also shown on 'Link' (and available for hire from Concord Films, address in Appendix Six), has a commentary by one of the mentally handicapped people shown moving from hospital into a group home.

Surveys of the Views of Mentally Handicapped People

A number of surveys of the views of mentally handicapped people have been undertaken in Britain. One took place in the London Borough of Wandsworth in 1974, and the results were published in a report called *Project 74* by the Research and Planning Section of Wandsworth Social Services Department. All the mentally handicapped people living in the Borough's hostels or attending their Adult Training Centres were interviewed. Here are some of the results:

Of those attending ATCs, 62 per cent preferred creative activities to industrial contract work; 38 per cent really disliked the contract work they did. Despite the fact that very few people ever get placed in jobs from ATCs, 76 per cent of people said they would like jobs. Clearly there was a gap here between the expectations people were given, and reality. One in four of those brought to the centres in mini-buses said they would prefer to come by public transport.

Asked about their home lives, 68 per cent said they had not chosen the colour of their bedroom walls, but of these four out of five would like to. Forty-four per cent did not have their own door key, but two thirds of these would like to. Thirty-one per cent did not have their own bedroom, but nearly all would like to. Twenty-five per cent did not choose their own bedtime, but three out of four of them would like to. Generally, those who were interviewed who lived in hostels were more restricted than those who lived at home.

Fifty-seven per cent said they had serious girlfriends or boyfriends, and of those who did not over half would like to have one. Eighty-one per cent of those with serious girlfriends or boyfriends said they would like to get married.

The Wandsworth survey was interesting because not only did the research worker interview the mentally handicapped people about their views, he also asked their parents and the staff who worked with them what they thought their answers would be.

There was very considerable underestimation by parents and staff of the extent to which the handicapped people saw eventual placement in a job as the aim of their being at an ATC, and of the extent to which they had serious friendships with the opposite sex.

At the end of the Wandsworth interview, people were asked to make three wishes. Some wished for pets or sweets, to go swimming, for more money, that their favourite football team would win on Saturday, or to live to be ninety years old. Some were perhaps a bit unrealistic, wishing to go to university or to join the Army. But very many made perceptive, sensitive wishes: for a happy life; for peace of mind; to be always good to each other; to learn to read better; that we never die in a war; for all the fighting to stop in Ireland; that roads be safer; to get my girlfriend to meet my parents; to see my brother in Australia. The views expressed were clearly not only interesting, but often well thought out and responsible. The report states:

It might be thought that the responses of mentally handi-

capped people will often be random and confused and if taken
literally will mislead rather than help those responsible for
providing services. Basically we think that the responses of
the mentally handicapped should be taken seriously because, in the main, they were able to make appropriate,
unprompted responses to open-ended questions such as
where would they like to live or what job would they like to
do. The level of non-response was low – between ten and
twenty per cent. The replies show a serious concern for all
those matters which concern everyone: personal relationships, state of mind, acquiring material things, getting away,
work, health. Wherever it has been possible to check the
consistency of the replies to related questions this has been
done. In all cases apparent inconsistencies could on reflection be construed as reasonable responses. Overall, such
checks as have been made do indicate that the responses
should be taken seriously. Moreover, experience does
suggest that taking account of the views of the mentally
handicapped can make an important contribution to improving services.

Several other surveys of services have included the views of
mentally handicapped people. For example a recent survey of
group homes in the Exeter district by Nick Booth, psychologist at the Royal Western Counties Hospital in Devon, asked
the opinions of residents themselves. Broadly speaking they
were well satisfied with life in the group homes, but they
thought the training arrangements to equip people with skills
before moving into the group homes were unsatisfactory. The
report concludes:

Residents do have opinions and it is recommended that
these should be listened to and, wherever possible, incorporated into the process of decision making. If hospital
policy is to be geared towards the benefits of its clients, then
those clients' opinions about the benefits are crucial.

Committees in Adult Training Centres

At present, the most promising development in Britain from
which the establishment of a self-advocacy movement along
the American lines seems possible, is the emergence over recent
years of many trainee committees or student councils in Adult
Training Centres. (Some of these centres in Britain have

changed their name to 'Social Education Centres', reflecting a general change in emphasis away from industrial contract work towards full-time teaching of social skills; we retain the term ATCs here.)

Bronach Crawley of the Hester Adrian Research Centre, University of Manchester, is carrying out a three-year study on the feasibility of committees in ATCs as a means of developing self-advocacy. She is writing up her work as a Ph.D. thesis. During 1980, she carried out a postal survey of ATCs and obtained replies from 391 centres, 83 per cent of all centres in England and Wales. She discovered that 87 of these centres (22 per cent) had some form of committee, and a further 36 centres (9 per cent) had previously had a committee that was no longer functioning.

A typical committee has about seven members elected (for one year) by the other trainees in the centre, meets every week or fortnight, has a member of staff attending each meeting, has officers of the committee, and has a written agenda and minutes. A few committees have been in existence for up to eight years, but there has been an upsurge in numbers in the last two or three years.

The committees vary tremendously in the way they function. In quite a high proportion, the staff member plays a dominant role, acting as leader or chairperson at meetings. In some cases, however, the groups have begun to function effectively with very little staff help. Many of the committees are at present solely concerned with matters directly relevant to the centre – planning or organising social events, making suggestions and expressing views about activities and in some cases having a disciplinary function if rules are broken by individuals in the centre. Some groups produce a news-sheet or magazine.

The following is an account of one group which is probably fairly typical of a committee that is just beginning to function well, with great potential for exploring the possibilities of self-advocacy further. The group is the trainees' committee at the Ditton Walk ATC in Cambridge, and the account is by Ivan Molyneux, Senior Teacher at the Centre:

The idea of a trainees' committee was first discussed with the staff and myself many months before we started. Questions and doubts about the committee were numerous. Would the more able trainees take over the discussions? Would the committee break down if there were no staff to coordinate the meeting? What would be discussed? How would they report back? Would a member of staff have to be present all the time? Would it be possible to involve non-verbal trainees? Would staff feel threatened? How would the questions be related back to the staff as well as the trainees?

All these questions and more were discussed in considering the merits of setting up the trainees' committee, but the manager and I were anxious that the trainees should have some say in the running of their everyday affairs. It was with all the doubts in mind that we decided to go ahead by selecting two trainees from each unit of the centre. It was decided that the staff would select the first trainees, so as to have a good cross-section of people who were communicative and those who would need encouragement from their own peers to help them speak.

The committee started with ten trainees. They were each asked if they would like to take part in the group, and only one showed any reluctance to join (he has now started to come along). After the initial group was chosen by the staff the committee was able to choose its own members. Since this has happened the group has swollen to twelve. The committee meets once every week on a Wednesday afternoon, when they are able to use the staff room without restriction.

The committee selects a different chairperson each week; the person can refuse to chair the meeting if he or she wishes. Minutes are taken by using a tape recorder. Afterwards I and the chairperson play back the recording and pick out the relevant parts between us. The minutes are duplicated by one of the committee so that each member has a copy for the next meeting. If I am sitting in on the group I will take the minutes, but we will still sort them out together. Every fortnight at our own staff meetings I report on what has happened at the trainees' meeting.

The format of the meetings is more or less on the same lines as ordinary meetings, but without all the red tape. I normally attend the meeting every two weeks to report back to the committee what the staff have decided at their last meeting. The chairperson asks for comments regarding the minutes, then he or she asks if there are any problems that the members have brought to the meeting from the trainees in the centre.

The committee then discusses the problems and any other questions that are raised by the members themselves. The discussions are quite informal and sometimes become very noisy, with everyone trying to speak at once. At these times I remind the chairperson to bring the meeting to order.

The committee members discuss any questions that are brought to them from staff or trainees. The questions are usually concerned with the general running of the centre. Examples have been: broken locks in the toilets; the danger to less able trainees of people running in the corridors; the possibility of having orange and lemonade at lunchtime instead of water; whether staff should be allowed to smoke in the different units when trainees were not allowed to; and whether staff and trainees should use first names or surnames in addressing each other.

One problem that has arisen in the committee is the tendency for the more communicative of the trainees to take over the meeting and for the others to get little say in what is being discussed. As the group is still only in its infancy, these problems should soon disappear.

The Senior Training Centre at Mitcham in the London Borough of Merton has annual elections for the officers of its trainees' committee. Canvassing takes place during the two weeks before an election, with candidates making speeches to groups of trainees. Voting is by ballot, with photographs of the candidates on the ballot papers. During 1981 the committee agreed to a suggestion by the centre manager that there should be an independent President of the committee, chosen from outside the centre. A local businessman who has a mentally handicapped brother and himself has a physical disability was invited to be the President. He attends most of the committee's meetings, helping to formalise procedure and acting as an independent adviser to the group.

As we have made clear in previous chapters, it takes a long time to develop the self-advocacy skills of mentally handicapped people, and many centres have found that there has to be strong initial direction from staff. At the Lisson Grove Social and Education Centre in the City of Westminster in London, for example, an initial attempt to form an elected committee with freedom to meet without substantial staff intervention was not successful. It was decided to re-form the committee under much stronger direction, and each staff member selected a student from his or her own tutor group to join the committee. Initially, questions for discussion were proposed by staff. Each committee member has a notebook in which to write the question; the book is taken to the tutor group for each student to record a 'yes' or 'no' answer to the question; results are pooled at the next committee meeting and appropriate action decided following the decision. Two staff members sit on the committee and gradually assist members to propose questions for consideration and to run meetings effectively themselves. The work of this group is an excellent example of careful help to enable all students in the centre to be involved in decisions, and potential student leaders to develop the required understanding and skills for self-advocacy.

Another example of strong initial staff involvement is at the Perryfields ATC in Worcester. The suggestion that a committee be formed came from staff, staff selected the first members, and staff sit in on meetings and often adopt the role of chairperson. However, now the committee itself selects new members when a member drops out or needs to be replaced; the group is becoming more cohesive and it is hoped that the staff can begin to reduce the extent of their interventions in meetings.

In some cases a committee develops functions that are best served by staff remaining on the committee in partnership with trainees, even when members have developed skills of running meetings themselves. One example is at the Crown Hill Workshops in Sheffield, where the committee is considered as a joint council between representatives of the trainees and the management, and this committee is given formal responsibilities for health and safety in the centre. One particularly interesting feature at Crown Hill is the use of tape recorders and videotape to improve the verbal and behavioural skills of committee members.

At Conisbrough ATC in Yorkshire, the whole centre is run as a partnership between staff and trainees. Much self-advocacy and equality between trainees and staff is fostered on a day-to-day basis. In addition, there is a committee elected annually by the trainees. The method used is very similar to that adopted by Project Two in Omaha: those nominated stand behind their own ballot box; each trainee can distribute five voting slips according to her choice. The committee meets without any staff attendance, unless this is requested by the committee.

There are committees in centres in Scotland as well as in England and Wales. An example is at the Dalgairn ATC at Cupar in Fife. Four trainee representatives are elected to serve on a committee with two staff members, in order to give the trainees more say in the running of the centre.

One of the strongest ATC committees in Britain is at the Avro Centre at Southend in Essex. This group has moved beyond the stage of being primarily concerned with the day-to-day life of their own particular centre, and has started to pursue some much wider, and more political, issues. For example, recent activities have included exchange visits with other centres; showing the film *People First* to a large invited meeting of parents, staff and friends, followed by open discussion; soliciting invitations from local colleges running courses for professional staff, for the group to talk to the students on those courses; negotiating within the social services department that the people attending the centre should be referred to as 'students' rather than 'trainees'; inviting a representative of the National Union of Students to visit the centre, which has led to all the students being enabled to become NUS members; and soliciting an invitation from Brian Rix, Secretary-General of the National Society for Mentally Handicapped Children and Adults, to travel to London to meet him in his office.

In June 1981 four members of the Avro Students' Council were invited to the studios of ATV to record an interview for the 'Link' television programme, broadcast nationally on Sunday mornings. They were interviewed about their views and about the work of the Council by Alan Tyne of the Campaign for Mentally Handicapped People, and in the final programme the interview was shown between excerpts from the film *People First* and an interview with Brian Rix in which he acknowledged his society's role in encouraging and supporting self-advocacy by mentally handicapped people in Britain.

One of the factors in the emergence of activities and interests in the Avro Students' Council that approach the concerns and actions that characterise true self-advocacy as described in earlier chapters, has been the extremely sensitive and careful support given to the group by the centre manager and by the staff who have advised the group. This approach is illustrated by the following account of the Council, and of her role in its activities, by Carol Scott, instructor at the centre and current adviser to the group:

I have worked with the Avro Students' Council since moving to the Centre in 1980. The Council had been running for two years before I was invited to join them as an adviser. The Councillors are democratically voted for each year by the people attending the Centre. Since it was first formed it has always had an adviser. Until recently we have been meeting once a week for an hour and a quarter. We have now had to extend that time to at least two hours a week, sometimes longer, in order to cope with the issues the Councillors have involved themselves in.

I find my title 'adviser' to the Council rather deceptive and far too grandiose. I do advise when and where needed, but this usually means just a short explanation of a particular procedure that could be followed if they require more information about a subject under discussion. An example of this was how to contact the National Union of Students concerning membership, and to suggest that an invitation to one of their officers might be more beneficial than requesting a leaflet.

The word 'adviser' is particularly deceptive because the advice and insight I myself have gained during the last six months have been the most rewarding of my four years working with people who attend Training Centres. The advising is a two-way process in which we learn from each other. Indeed I am left with no doubt at all that it is we who work within ATCs that are the people most in need of advice and better understanding.

I feel very strongly that, given the opportunity in the right atmosphere, people can express themselves and are very aware of what their needs are and how these can best be met. It is vitally important to establish the fact that what they say will be taken note of and acted upon. In some instances the language used may be termed 'restricted', but what they need or would like still comes across very plainly if we listen with an open mind.

In some instances the Councillors I work with have had criticism levelled at them, and no doubt will continue to have this. They have made mistakes, but my answer to this is: what council or group of representatives in our wider society have not? Some Councillors have said what others have classed as 'silly or irrelevant things'. My answer to that is: all those who have never committed this deadly sin, please stand up! For those who deceive themselves and do stand up, then an invitation to any local authority council meeting should soon put their minds at rest! I do not doubt that the Council will continue to make mistakes or say what others may think irrelevant. These are not only excellent learning situations but emphasise the biggest point, that is that we are all human and entitled to that privilege. If we afford this to ourselves it is not unreasonable to ask or demand that the same privilege be shown to those people who attend ATCs.

As the Council is branching out more and more, meeting other student councils and becoming involved in the local Society for Mentally Handicapped People, my role will be to fade further into the background. With so many difficulties affecting ATCs, I feel the time will soon be here when it will be those people who attend the Centres who will bring about the changes needed in society's attitude towards them, and will demand a better service than they are receiving at the present. And I do not doubt for one moment that they will do a far better job of it than we have ever done.

Bases for Further Self-Advocacy Development

The Future Development of ATC Committees
Over and above the need to develop the understanding and skills required for self-advocacy among the mentally handicapped people attending ATCs, there are three major problems that most of the present committees seem to be facing: inward-looking agendas, conflict of interest in the staff who help or belong to committees, and poor contact between committees and the trainees they represent.

As discussed in Chapter Four, inward-looking agendas are to be expected in the early stages of a group's development, and may be necessary while the group learns the skills of holding meetings, and slowly increases its appreciation that there are wider issues of relevance to mentally handicapped people as a whole that could be discussed and acted on. While an adviser to a group should tolerate very inward-looking agendas until the group has begun to develop these skills and appreciation, there will come a time when the group's further progress will require a wider vision. This might be achieved by the adoption of a statement of purpose or a constitution that outlines some important general issues that the group wishes to pursue (as in the Avro Students' Council constitution reproduced in Appendix Five). It is important that a group should be allowed to move from any original notion of its purpose that may have been conceived by staff, to a new formulation of purpose devised by the group itself. Often the current purposes of ATC committees, as stated by staff, are related closely to the educational aims of the centre, and are concerned with such things as maintaining discipline, assisting in the management of the centre, fund-raising for the centre, or organising social events at the centre. It is probable that, when the group itself is able to draw up a statement of purpose, these functions will not figure so prominently in them.

Possible conflict of interest for an adviser to a committee is clearly a risk in this change. An adviser who is a member of staff has a vested interest in the purposes of the group as seen by the centre management, and may thus be unable to assist the group impartially to devise and pursue its own purposes. Even before that time arises, conflict may occur between an adviser's role in the group and his responsibilities in and loyalty to the centre. For example, the group might be severely critical of centre management and might wish to take strong action that would place an instructor in a difficult position if he or she went along with it. In many cases, adequate safeguards against this conflict of interest damaging the group's development will be provided by good awareness of this possibility by the adviser and the centre management. An even better safeguard might be to bring in independent people to advise the group, as has happened at the Mitcham Centre.

In many centres there seems to be little involvement of the trainees who are not on the committee, other than in voting in occasional elections to the committee. Among other disadvantages, this means that trainees are likely to have very little idea what they are electing people for. Some centres, like Lisson Grove in London, have good arrangements for committee members to represent small groups of trainees effectively, by regularly consulting them and reporting back to them. The suggestion we would like to make, that we have not seen tried in any centre yet, is that all trainees in a centre should be considered members of a self-advocacy group that is *represented* by the committee, and meets regularly as a whole body under the leadership of the committee. For a long time proceedings are likely to be chaotic, but given tolerance, perseverance and skill the notion that all trainees can play an active role in a group can be explored and pursued.

Because of these three problems of present purpose, possible conflict of interest on the part of advisers, and lack of involvement of the people represented by committees, it is probably best to consider most of the ATC committees as akin to the 'support groups' in the People First International model of development of self-advocacy, rather than as full self-advocacy groups. When committees that have begun to find solutions in these three problem areas come together to form independent groups with wider membership and wider purpose, then the potential for a strong British self-advocacy movement will begin to be more fully realised.

There is no doubt, however, that the establishment and continuing growth of ATC committees, the excellent work of many of their advisers, and the good support of many centre managers have laid a firm foundation for this exciting and challenging future development.

Other Potential Support Groups

In many local authority hostels, in homes run by voluntary organisations, and in some hospitals, regular meetings of residents take place and an attempt is made to involve residents in decisions. Some recent attempts to do this have taken place with an awareness of what self-advocacy is, and with the intention of working towards the establishment of a self-advocacy group. For example, following a one-day course on participation held by CMH in Edinburgh in 1981, an attempt is being made to set up a group for some of the residents at Gogarburn Hospital, Edinburgh. Such groups all have the potential to become 'support groups', as in the People First model of development of self-advocacy, and to join together with each other and with ATC committees to form full self-advocacy groups. Groups of mentally handicapped students attending Colleges of Further Education also have this potential.

An Independent Self-Advocacy Group

At least one initiative has already been taken in Britain to develop a self-advocacy group that is independent of service provision. Early in 1980 the Society for the Mentally Handicapped (a local parents' group) in the London Borough of Camden raised with the mental health sub-committee of the social services department the need to consult with mentally handicapped people themselves about services and facilities. It was suggested that a self-advocacy group be set up, with secretarial help from the Borough Council. The Society for the Mentally Handicapped got together a group of mentally handicapped people who they felt might be interested in the idea. It was agreed to call an open meeting for mentally handicapped people from local group homes, hostels and ATCs. Ten people turned up and it was decided to form a group. One person was elected Group Convenor by secret ballot, and the group discussed the recent closure of a disco that had been enjoyed, and a strongly held view that ATCs should offer more creative work rather than routine jobs. The group is still slowly getting started. It currently meets at a community centre every few months. There have been some problems in gaining the promised secretarial help, but it has been agreed that the group's minutes and reports will be seen by the mental health sub-committee and, if desired, by the social services committee itself.

Clubs for Mentally Handicapped People

Another potential part of the foundation for the future development of self-advocacy in Britain is the existence in most parts of the country of leisure clubs for mentally handicapped people. Some of these clubs operate independently and go by a wide variety of names (for example the 'Seven O'Clock Club' in Oxford), but many call themselves 'Gateway Clubs' and are affiliated to the National Federation of Gateway Clubs (address in Appendix Six). Most of these clubs were initiated by local parents' groups and many of them continue to be operated by committees that are dominated by parents or by other non-handicapped members of the local group. Many of the clubs make extensive use of young non-handicapped volunteers, who may play a large part in running the group. Generally, the purpose of the club is seen fairly narrowly as providing organised leisure opportunities for mentally handicapped people, with an emphasis on games, sports, dancing, entertainment, social events, outdoor pursuits such as camping, holidays sometimes, and occasionally creative activities such as painting, craftwork, music appreciation or drama. Some of the clubs are well integrated with youth clubs for non-handicapped young people, sharing premises and activities with them. In a few cases, some of the mentally handicapped members themselves are on the organising committee and have a strong say in the planning and general control of the group's activities.

Within these clubs there are many opportunities offered for individual self-advocacy, and there is enormous potential for development of a self-advocacy role by the groups; but there is a general lack of awareness of what self-advocacy is or of its potential. Some of the perceptions of mentally handicapped people by the organising committees and by non-handicapped volunteers in the clubs would need to be modified if true self-advocacy were to be pursued. They would need to regard themselves more in the role of self-advocacy advisers, with the considerations that go with this role that we have outlined in Chapter Four. Much greater involvement of mentally handicapped people themselves in the organisation and management of the clubs is required as a first step in the direction of self-advocacy.

Nevertheless, it is quite possible that, given interest in and support for self-advocacy within these clubs, they will form the basis for the British self-advocacy movement of the future. As we have said in an earlier chapter, self-advocacy can be allied with enjoyment and fun, although it does not itself consist of enjoyment and fun. As long as leisure opportunities and social enjoyment are not seen as the *sole* aims of a group, they can play a very important part in creating group cohesion and identity and as a vehicle for pursuing other purposes of the group; the expertise of many clubs in this area would no doubt be extremely valuable within the context of a broader-based self-advocacy movement. Of course, it is also possible that there is a place for organised leisure clubs for mentally handicapped people, that do not attempt to be part of a self-advocacy movement at all.

Resources for Teaching Self-Advocacy

With the increasing emphasis on social education in ATCs, and increasing provision by Colleges of Further Education of courses for mentally handicapped people, many opportunities are being opened up for devising curricula to teach self-advocacy skills. There is also an awareness in special schools for mentally handicapped children (for example the Beaufort School in Birmingham) that specific skills can be taught in school to equip pupils for later self-advocacy, with particular emphasis on skills of self-determination, making choices, solving problems and taking decisions.

There is a need for the development in Britain of materials such as those produced by the Technical Assistance for Self-Advocacy Project in Kansas. It is likely to be very unsatisfactory to try to use American materials in a British context. Such material can give ideas and point directions, but it cannot supply the required detailed content. This needs to be the subject of hard work and effort in other countries. There is no alternative.

Particularly useful would be British manuals or packages or sets of teaching aids, designed for direct use by mentally handicapped people or by their teachers, on:

- Rights
- What is self-advocacy
- Assertiveness training
- Procedures for meetings, committees, elections and voting
- The principles of normalisation

These could be incorporated in the curricula of schools, colleges or social education centres to help many more individuals to develop skills of personal self-advocacy and active participation in the self-advocacy movement.

Possible future sources of these materials are difficult to predict, but the most likely agencies to produce them one day are probably: the Hester Adrian Research Centre, Manchester

University, where work is in progress under the direction of Dr Edward Whelan to produce teaching packages on a wide range of topics for use in centres and colleges; or the National Society for Mentally Handicapped Children and Adults; or the Campaign for Mentally Handicapped People; or indeed the self-advocacy movement itself if it can gain financial support to commission these aids.

There is also a need for written materials and training courses to be developed to aid advisers to self-advocacy groups. Again, American material is available, but can only be of use in giving ideas, not detailed information, in other countries. British materials may come from the sources mentioned above, especially from the Hester Adrian Research Centre as a follow-on from Bronach Crawley's study of ATC committees. Courses for advisers might be established by agencies such as Castle Priory College (the Spastics' Society's staff training centre at Wallingford in Oxfordshire) or the British Institute of Mental Handicap (address in Appendix Six). Castle Priory College already runs occasional courses on self-advocacy by mentally handicapped people at which the *People First* film is shown and the potential for developing self-advocacy in Britain is discussed. The courses are open to handicapped people themselves as well as to staff, potential advisers and other interested non-handicapped people.

The Campaign for Mentally Handicapped People and its sister body the CMH Educational and Research Association (addresses in Appendix Six) have been active in running courses which, while not specifically designed to foster self-advocacy, have helped to lay good foundations for its development. CMH continues to organise occasional 'participation events'. CMHERA has a programme of workshops that it can put on in any part of the country, on values, the principles of normalisation, individual programme planning based on nor-malisation principles, advocacy and participation. In conjunction with Castle Priory College, CMHERA has organised several four-day in-depth courses on normalisation which include substantial consideration of values. These courses would provide a useful basic orientation for potential advisers of self-advocacy groups. CMHERA is also looking for effective ways of recruiting and involving mentally handicapped people themselves in these courses.

The Rights of Mentally Handicapped People in Britain
One of the parts of American materials that would require substantial rewording for use in Britain is the information on the rights of mentally handicapped people. Many of the general principles outlined in Chapter Five will apply, but reference needs to be made to British laws and other sources of rights in Britain.

Human Rights

Britain is a full signatory of the United Nations Declarations of Rights reproduced in Appendix One. It is also a signatory to the European Convention of Human Rights, adopted by fifteen European nations, in 1950.

There is indeed increasing awareness of the human rights of mentally handicapped people in Britain. For example, here is an extract from a paper on 'The Rights of the Mentally Handicapped' by A. Nicholls, N. Beasley, S. Gittens and A. Grimley, published in *Resources, Responsibilities and Rights*, the report of the 1977 annual congress of the Association of Professions for the Mentally Handicapped (available from APMH, address in Appendix Six):

Any discussion of the human rights of the mentally handicapped must start from the premise that mentally handicapped persons are part of the human race and not another species of animal. Their rights therefore are exactly the same as [those of] any other human being. What has to be stated is that exercise of those rights should be assisted where the handicap makes for difficulty, and not arbitrarily removed, reduced or ignored by those whose parental or professional responsibility is to nurture and develop the capabilities of the mentally handicapped.

It is often stated that the aim and object of the care of the mentally handicapped is to develop as far as possible the independence of function in society. Part of that independence must include the expression of preference and exercise of choice and judgment, which in their turn demand consultation *with* and not just *about* the client. Like all other members of society it must be accepted that there exists the right to a choice of associates, place and mode of living and of livelihood and of leisure activity and the right to refuse that which is considered unacceptable.

They [mentally handicapped people] have the right to be protected from exploitation not only from those who would take advantage of them as consumers of goods or services but from those who would subjugate their individuality to the interests of the regime or organisational convenience of hospitals, hostels, training establishments, schools; or the personal convenience, interests or prejudices of social workers or parents (whether natural or surrogate).

They have the right to like, to dislike, love or loathe other human beings, handicapped or non-handicapped, and the right to form strong emotional and physical relationships. They have a right to be *believed* and not to have any complaint or plea they may express dismissed as being unworthy of attention, particularly as regards complaints concerning their treatment by police officers, hospital and hostel staff, foster parents and their natural parents.

They have the right to freedom from exploitation by the local authorities themselves in the matter of work performed in ATCs. For example, many authorities operate laundries in ATCs to do work for other sections of social service departments. Training for this work could extend for a period after which it becomes no less contract work than that done for outside industry. If the mentally handicapped are occupied long-term in laundry work they should be paid at the appropriate rate for the job and become members of the appropriate union.

To sum up – the mentally handicapped begin with the same rights as every other human being. What has to be guarded against is the appropriation and arrogation of those rights away from the mentally handicapped, particularly by those whose duty is plainly to protect those rights. No amount of rationalisation can excuse abuse of the trust reposed in professional workers in this respect, for there is no reason why these rights should not be regarded as sacred and inviolable.

There have been several recent attempts to define human rights of mentally handicapped people in Britain, perhaps the most important being the *Report of the Committee of Enquiry into Mental Handicap Nursing and Care* (the Jay Report), published by HMSO in March 1979. Other examples include the King's Fund Paper *An Ordinary Life*, published in March

1980 by the King's Fund Centre (address in Appendix Six), the National Development Group's Checklist of Standards, entitled *Improving the Quality of Services for Mentally Handicapped People*, published by the Department of Health and Social Security in 1980, and the NSMHC & A's STAMINA papers, an extract from which is reproduced in Appendix One.

The Jay Report includes the following specifications of rights of mentally handicapped people:

- Mentally handicapped people have a right to enjoy normal patterns of life within the community;
- Any mentally handicapped adult who wishes to leave his or her parental home should have the opportunity to do so;
- An individual has the right to live, learn and work in the least restrictive environment appropriate to that particular person;
- An individual has the right to make or be involved in decisions that affect himself or herself.

Legal Rights

The legal rights accorded to particular citizens of a particular country are a complex matter on which expert sources of advice and knowledge should be consulted. We do not attempt, therefore, to describe in detail the legal rights of mentally handicapped people in Britain. We give some sources of information and advice on legal and civil rights in the next section of this chapter. The remarks here are intended to give a broad general indication of the sorts of issues that self-advocacy groups in Britain might try to become more informed about, through seeking facts and advice from properly qualified and knowledgeable sources.

As a broad generalisation, mentally handicapped people in Britain have the same civil and legal rights as anyone else. It is important to recognise that simply having been to a special school, or receiving special services intended for 'mentally handicapped people', do not make a person's legal status different in any way at all from that of other people. Differences between the rights of mentally handicapped people and anyone else arise only if the person herself, or someone else, wishes to emphasise the person's disability for a particular purpose.

There are four particular circumstances in which this may

happen, and it is as well for self-advocacy groups to be aware of them:

First, it may be of benefit to a mentally handicapped person or her family for her to be classified as having a particular type or degree of disability, in order to receive the various benefits to which she may be entitled by virtue of that disability. It is important for a self-advocacy group to be clear about what benefits are entitlements due to a mentally handicapped person's family by virtue of their having a dependent member, and what benefits are entitlements due directly to a mentally handicapped person herself. For example, if a mentally handicapped person has additional expenses that may qualify her for an increase in benefits, she has a right to be assessed for this increase on the basis of *her* needs, and not those of her parents. This has been an important factor, for example, in recent moves to require mentally handicapped people to pay for their attendance at ATCs: this is a payment that mentally handicapped people themselves are required to pay, not their parents, and they thus have a right to be assessed for an increase in benefit on the basis of the hardship that *they* will be caused, not their parents.

Second, the liberty of mentally handicapped people can be severely restricted by society, in certain rare circumstances through the provisions of the 1959 Mental Health Act: for example if the mentally handicapped person commits a criminal offence of a violent or destructive nature. There are two issues here of which a self-advocacy group should be aware. First, the definitions of 'mental disorder' in the Mental Health Act are extremely vague. (As Lord Chief Justice Goddard once said: 'As far as I can see, I am psychopath myself, and so is everyone else!') There is thus plenty of scope for argument, if necessary, about whether an individual person has been appropriately classified. It can also sometimes be the case that a person loses her freedom for much longer if she is detained under the Mental Health Act, than she would if she received a prison sentence for the same offence.

Most mentally handicapped people do not have to worry about these provisions of the Mental Health Act, as they apply only to a very few mentally handicapped people.

Third, if a person has special needs for care, or is considered to have needs appropriate to residence in social services or hospital accommodation, that person's housing rights may be affected. It is wise for self-advocacy groups, on behalf of their members, to seek information about housing options, rights to be on local authority housing lists, and any restrictions or additions to these rights by virtue of members' disabilities. A long-term task for self-advocacy groups might be to work towards establishing the same rights to housing options for all mentally handicapped people as there are for ordinary people in society.

Finally, there are some circumstances in which the competence of a mentally handicapped person can be challenged. If this occurs it may restrict the person's ability to enter into contracts, to vote, to marry, to make a will, to have control over her financial affairs, etc. Correspondingly it is possible for mentally handicapped people themselves to claim that they were incompetent at the time of signing a contract, for example, in order to be released from that contract.

In these circumstances, there has to be some concrete evidence that the person is or is not incompetent in the particular context of the challenge of her competence. As we have already pointed out, simply having a label of 'mental handicap' in one's medical or social work case-notes is not sufficient reason for restriction of a person's rights or responsibilities. Many mentally handicapped people can therefore expect to be able to enter into contracts, to vote, to marry, to make a will, to have post office and bank accounts, to take out insurance, etc., just as any other citizen can, without any query as to competence. The more severely handicapped a person is, however, the more likely it is that someone will query her ability to understand what is involved in some or all of these areas.

The best safeguard for a mentally handicapped person is probably to have a network of friends, preferably including such people as doctors, social workers, clergymen, magistrates, lawyers, whom she can call on to vouch for her competence in particular circumstances. This is an area where self-advocacy groups can do some pioneer work in providing support, information and good advice in enabling many mentally handicapped people to extend their present rights.

If a person who is likely to be called 'mentally handicapped' wishes to enter into an important agreement or sign an important document, for example making a will, marrying, or opening a bank account, it is always advisable to seek advice on the legal position in each specific instance in order to avoid possible problems at a later date.

As we have discussed in Chapter Five, it is vitally important that people should not be allowed in their dealings with mentally handicapped people, to get away with infringements of the ordinary civil and legal rights that apply to everyone, such as the rights to protection and redress in case of assault or theft. As a further example, young mentally handicapped people in Britain have exactly the same rights to further education under the various Education Acts as any other young person. Denial of educational rights to a mentally handicapped person is as serious an infringement of rights as denial of education to a potential university entrant, and mentally handicapped people are entitled to have just as much fuss made if this happens.

Resources and Support for Self-Advocacy
The addresses of the organisations listed in this section are given in Appendix Six.

Concord Films is a non-profit-making organisation that has an extensive catalogue of films available for hire, on a wide range of topics concerned with handicap. Some of the films that may be useful in teaching self-advocacy to mentally handicapped people have been mentioned in Chapter Five.

CMH – the Campaign for Mentally Handicapped People – still runs 'participation events' and is a source of information and advice on rights, particularly housing and voting rights, on which it has some publications.

CMH Educational and Research Association runs training workshops relevant to potential members or advisers of self-advocacy groups.

Network for the Handicapped is a legal advice centre for handicapped people, which will answer correspondence at any time. It holds an open meeting weekly where people may discuss legal problems or queries with qualified lawyers and legal experts. Network is particularly interested in the rights of mentally handicapped people, and is a good source of advice on rights to welfare benefits.

MIND – the National Association for Mental Health – has a

legal advice department, directed at the time of writing by Larry Gostin who is Britain's foremost expert on the legal and civil rights of people who are mentally handicapped or mentally ill. MIND has pamphlets and other written guidance available on these rights.

The National Council for Civil Liberties can be consulted about general civil rights and also has pamphlets available on these. The NCCL is a good source of advice in any cases of severe infringement of liberty.

The National Society for Mentally Handicapped Children and Adults is a good source of advice on welfare rights and on the particular rights of mentally handicapped people. The Society has a Welfare Rights department which produces a package of information called *Communications* which is sent regularly to subscribers, and includes up-to-date information on rights and allowances. There is also a general information department from which booklets or fact-sheets on rights are available.

Castle Priory College runs occasional courses on self-advocacy by mentally handicapped people.

The Child Poverty Action Group produces a *National Welfare Benefits Handbook*, and is a further source of information on welfare rights.

The Consumers' Association is a source of information on consumer rights.

The Association of Professions for the Mentally Handicapped has information on rights and can suggest further sources of advice.

RADAR – the *Royal Association for Disability and Rehabilitation* – publishes a guide to *Housing Grants and Allowances for Disabled People* and is a good source of information on the general rights of disabled people.

The Disability Alliance publishes an annual *Disability Rights Handbook*, and will answer individual queries.

The National Corporation for the Care of Old People and *Age Concern* have information available on the rights of elderly people, much of which is applicable to younger handicapped people. In particular, the NCCOP published in 1980 a book called *Rights and Risk* by Alison J. Norman which is an excellent discussion of human, civil and legal rights of relevance to all handicapped or disadvantaged people.

In particular local areas, useful sources of information and advice are:

- Local Authority Housing Departments;
- local offices of the Department of Health and Social Security;
- Citizens' Advice Bureaux;
- local Consumer Associations;
- local Welfare Benefits Advice Centres (for example Claimants' Union);
- local Community Action Groups;
- local Legal Advice Centres (the Legal Action Group produces a *Directory of Legal Advice and Law Centres*).

Citizen Advocacy in Britain

We have discussed in earlier chapters how the existence of independent supports and structures to assist the process of 'citizen advocacy' – the linking up of non-handicapped advocates with handicapped protégés so that the advocate can represent the interests of her protégé as if they were her own – can be invaluable in assisting the development of self-advocacy too.

In Britain, the first tentative steps are being taken towards initiating some citizen advocacy. A consortium of voluntary organisations – One-to-One, the NSMHC & A, the Spastics Society, MIND and the Leonard Cheshire Foundation – have formed an Advocacy Alliance (address in Appendix Six) which is to mount a pilot project to provide and support independent advocates for residents in a number of mental handicap hospitals in England. Proposals have been drawn up for training potential advocates. Further information is available from the Coordinator of the Advocacy Alliance, Robert Sang, at the address given in Appendix Six.

Keeping in Contact

As a self-advocacy movement develops in Britain it will be useful if groups can keep as much contact with each other as possible. It is suggested that, until an accepted central focus of coordination is established, groups or individuals who are interested in or are beginning to practise self-advocacy keep in contact with the following people and groups (the addresses of the organisations in italics are in Appendix Six):

- Bronach Crawley and Edward Whelan at the *Hester Adrian Research Centre* in Manchester;
- Paul Williams at *Castle Priory College*;
- *CMH – The Campaign for Mentally Handicapped People*;
- *The National Society for Mentally Handicapped Children and Adults*;
- *The Advocacy Alliance*;
- *The Avro Adult Training Centre Students' Council.*

Links with America

British groups might also like, as suggested for any group in Chapter Four, to correspond with People First International and United Together (addresses in Appendix Six).

CMH set up a travel fund in 1979 to assist mentally handicapped people to visit services or groups in other countries. This fund is very small and is not able to support many people, but so far it has assisted a British man who is mentally handicapped – Alan Salomon from Kent – to travel to America to visit services and to meet with two self-advocacy groups, the Boston Mohawks and Squaws and Project Two in Omaha; and an American man – Tom Houlihan from Project ˙ Two – to visit Britain (see Chapter Four). Tom spent some time with the members of the Avro ATC Students' Council, as well as visiting services, organisations and individuals all over England.

'I left my heart in England,' says Tom in his contribution at the end of Chapter One. It would be a fitting tribute to the courage and self-determination of the people like Tom who have built up the self-advocacy movement in America, if the movement could be fostered in Britain in partnership with such American friends.

And maybe one day self-advocacy by mentally handicapped people will spread the world over.

The New Voice in Britain

The following quotations from mentally handicapped people in Britain begin with some verbatim comments by delegates at the CMH 'Our Life' and 'Listen' conferences, held in 1972 and 1973, taken from the conference reports, which in turn were based on tape recordings of the proceedings. There follow two extracts from Joseph Deacon's book *Tongue Tied*, and some personal accounts kindly supplied to us by members of several ATC committees.

Our Life

'It's nice to be able to talk to someone, a thing we haven't been able to do for years and years until a short time ago. Until the beginning of this year we haven't been able to do such things. Well, we could say things, but not without being told to shut up.'

'If you protest, sometimes they will take it, other times they won't take any notice. Whatever I think, I'll say. I say a bit much sometimes, I don't know if it's always wise.'

'When I was little I watched my mother. I had a little cooker of my own. I'd like to watch other people bake, but that was a long time ago.'

'People call me – "Are you a mongol?" I am not. "Are you a handicap?" I am not. But I'm just on the border, on the edge of it I am.'

'Some people get the wrong idea. They can't see that "mentally" doesn't always mean you're wrong in the head.'

'They asked me if I enjoyed being called a resident, and I told them I'd always been a resident as far as I'm concerned – whatever you say won't make any difference. We'll still be patients here, won't we? It doesn't make any difference, does it? It would be nice to be called a resident if I went somewhere else.'

'You mustn't give the staff cheek. I call them "sir" for a joke sometimes, and salute, but you have to be careful. It's like the Army, you see – the staff are in charge, that's why they wear uniform.'

'They don't tell you about changes until the last minute, or they don't really tell you at all, things you'd like to know. If you go for a medical examination, you'd like to know how much you weighed, how you were, how you were getting on. You don't know whether you're going to die next week or whether you'll live to be a hundred. I feel I'd like to know.'

'We used to go out three on the pass. You weren't allowed to leave your partners. Oh no, you weren't allowed to leave your partners. You had to be back at six o'clock. If you weren't back at six o'clock, if you left it a bit too late, you lost your half day for good – sometimes for good altogether. You weren't allowed to leave the town, weren't allowed to go out of the district, only when you were with your parents.'

'Some people, you go to the house and they say, "Oh, she'll be one of the family," and as soon as the social worker's back's turned you're a maid or something like that. I went to a house once, about five years ago, and they said I was going to have all this and that, and as soon as the social worker went, there I was scrubbing floors and polishing. I mean, I didn't go to do that work.'

'If I went in a factory they'd all pick on me, so I wouldn't be very happy in a factory. I'm happy now where I am, so I'm going to stick there. I've got nothing to grumble at. I'll finish my training first.'

'I ought to be working somewhere different, but I've got to wait until they send word for me. I'd like to go on making crackers until they get a job outside for me. I'd like to make Christmas and birthday cards in an ordinary factory when I go out. I'd like about £7 a week. That will be enough for me till I get used to it, and I can get a bit more later on.'

Listen

'You don't like to be domineered too often; we're not kids, we're over twenty-one. We're not stupid, we don't like to be domineered. Staff say don't be so cheeky, they don't like you to speak your mind up. If I didn't speak for myself I wouldn't be where I am today. I used to be shy and people just trod on my toes. I don't like to be domineered too much. It's not right. People have to have a life of their own.'

'When they have conference meetings like this we're having now, it's just the nursing staff and doctors – only what they say. I think that's wrong, because I think myself they should let the patients stand up on their own two feet – you know what I mean?'

'When you're in hospital and you talk to the doctor or someone like that you get a bit nervous, you know, of really saying what you do want. It's all right now because the nurse is here; he can say that I'm not frightened to speak up for what I do want. They don't give you a chance, there's nothing in the papers or anywhere about jobs or things like that. The lady I work for says there are some changes – if I want a job I've got to stand up for my own rights.'

'Your mother's your best friend; when you've lost her, you've lost a good friend. There's nothing like being at home; my mother was good to me and I was good to her. My mother was used to arguing with me, but I never took any notice. I used to go into the other room and have a lie down. Since I've lost my mother, my sisters don't come to see me. Sisters these days don't want to know you. They could come to see me; one's got a car, but they don't. When they get married they've got no time for you. My mother was nice to me and I was nice to her, but now I've lost all contact. I can't help it. Your mother's your mother. When you haven't got your mother you're done for.'

'I was told I've got no brains where I live – how do you think I felt? Very sarcastic, some of them. There's a limit to teasing anyone, but some of them go too far – beyond the deep end, as they say. I wouldn't mind it occasionally, but they do it too often – crack a joke. If you retaliate they don't like it. That's not fair, is it?'

'The doctor, he's got eyes like steel, they look right through you. I can talk to you lot because your eyes aren't like his eyes.'

'If you're in hospital you get hospitalised. If you're in the ward for very long, with staff and everything, you're not allowed to think for yourself. No independence, privacy or self-respect. You're told to do this and that, go to wash the floor and scrub the kitchen. We're not allowed any more freedom than that. It's very strict, you feel like running away from places like that. If you had freedom, you'd stay there. I think probably many would stay there. They wouldn't want to run away from places if they were like home.'

'My business is to get away, right away altogether so I can forget all about my lifetime in the past. You can't help thinking about it because you're still in the same county as the hospital where you were. You must get right away, so you can forget. I'm looking forward to the future. That's what my ambition is – to get things organised if I can.'

'These sorts of things should have been done years ago – to take the patients, able-bodied people, away from the hospitals into the hostels, and let them work and keep themselves. Get more out and take less back into the hospitals; cut them down as much as possible. It's no good bringing patients from the hospitals into the hostels if you're going to send some back; you might just as well leave the patients where they are. If I had my way, I'd pick all the able-bodied patients and make them go into the hostels. The poor invalids and cases like the very bad epileptics, you don't mind them keeping them. But able-bodied people like yourself and myself, good pair of hands, good limbs, pair of legs, who can keep themselves, should be made to go out.'

'The nurses haven't let me down; they've given me great pressure to go on my own way, live as I want to, to keep myself. If people like to put themselves forward, no one knows what can be done till they speak their mind. Nurses help people who want to be helped.'

'You can go into a hostel and be hospitalised even though you're in the hostel. No freedom – like a little animal or dog. If they say you've got to go to bed you've got to go, you can't go on your own. You can't choose. You've got no life of your own, you're not independent or anything. You come in and they take it all away.'

'A hostel would be good, to mix with younger people. If you stay on your own you get fed up. But if you're in a hostel you can enjoy yourself, go out with other people – ice skating and things like that. I'd go horse riding once a week.'

'I can't read and write, that's what's done me. I used to walk about the streets for hours and hours, staying out on street corners. I've got no contacts to write to now. It's too late I think, now I'm getting on in years.'

'I would like to go back to evening classes if I can, and learn to read and write, try to write a bit – my address. But when I pick up a pen my hands go funny.'

Two Extracts from 'Tongue Tied'
by Joseph Deacon

I

When I was fit to go back to work, I was told that I couldn't go as the lift had broken down; anyway, by the time Ernie had got to know, and climbed the stairs, I had thought of an idea. I said to him, 'You see that bread basket over there? You could ask Tom to put me in it, and him and Michael could carry me down the stairs.' They all agreed, so I was carried down the stairs in the bread basket; the staff kept an eye on us until I was safely at the bottom and put in my chair, then I was off to work. . . .

II

My friend Ernie said to me, 'How would you like town parole?' I said to Ernie, 'It is up to the authorities of the hospital', and I said to Ernie, 'It is taking a big risk'. And I turned round to Ernie and said, 'There is no harm in trying'. I said to Ernie, 'This is a free country'. Ernie asked the two charge-nurses about it. First of all they were not on Ernie's side. They were thinking of the traffic, which they were right to do. Mr Atkins and Mr Eaton saw Mr Bowden. We did not hear any more for three months. Mr Ryves down at the Training Centre took us out to Littlehampton for the day one Friday, and he let Tom, Ernie and me and Michael go down the town by ourselves. We would not cross until the traffic was clear. Mr Ryves was watching from the other side of the road, and when we got back to the coach that Friday, I got a good report when we got back to the hospital. On Wednesday Mr Ryves went to the office; the following week we got our town parole.

Terry Green
Member of the Avro ATC Students' Council, Southend

I went to school in Colchester. It was a boarding school for backward children. I liked it sometimes, but I did not like it all the time. There, some boys were good and some were bad. I was happy at school with the staff and teachers; they looked after me when I was ill. I liked the things I did at school – sums, writing, reading, dancing, going out on Saturdays with the boys to parks and the pictures, and shopping and long walks with the staff. I missed all this when I went to hospital.

When I went into hospital my mum and dad took me to the place called a clinic where I stayed for two weeks. The staff took all my own things away and I put on pyjamas and dressing gown and slippers. I had a blood test and the staff saw how high it was and how much it registered. The reason I went into hospital was that there was no centre for me to go to. I did not know about going into hospital to live.

When I went in I felt very sad and I was very upset. I was with a lot of bad patients. It was all too much for me on the ward. In the day I went to a workshop where I did a lot of woodwork for a long time. After I did woodwork they put me in a place where I did a lot of printing and a bit of book making and a bit of setting up the print and putting it on the machine. At weekends I went out with some of the boys on Saturday afternoon to the pictures and shopping. We all got back by seven o'clock. On Sunday I went to the wards to see what the staff and patients wanted from the shop. When I came back from going to the shop I went back to the wards with the things and I gave them to the staff. I went to church with the boys, and in the afternoon I went over to the hall to wait for my mum and dad to see me from two o'clock until four o'clock.

I did not have a visit every week, only when my mum and dad could come up to see me in the hospital. But when my mum didn't come to see me she sent me money in a letter to spend in the hospital shop, or go out to spend it. I went over to the hall when it was time for my mum to come up in dad's car. Then I went out into the car park. My mum and I went over to the canteen for a cup of tea and cake to eat. Then we went in the hall until it was time for mum and dad to go home. I said goodbye and I went back to the ward.

In the evenings I watched TV with the boys and I played games sometimes. And I went out to play indoor games with other hospitals. On Tuesday evenings I went over to the hall to see a show, and on Wednesdays I went to a club over at the hall. On Friday I went to the hall for dancing with the girls. I did country dancing with some people outside once a month on Monday evening.

I slept in a room with some of the other patients. The rooms were big and we all had our own lockers to put our things in, but no key. The hospital had a lot of wards and a church, a sweet shop, a workshop, a club room and a hall, a clinic and a farm, a lot of bungalows and a big kitchen, a club house for staff and a big nurses' home, a store, a needle-room and a big playing-field, a canteen and a big laundry room, and a lot of gardens. The staff and patients at the hospital, and doctors and nurses – some were all right and some not all good. Some of the patients were very bad on the wards. They had fights and went too far with their words. The doctors were very good with all the patients. They made us better. The staff looked after us the same too.

I was a patient in the hospital for ten years. I was very happy there. I made a lot of friends on the ward where I was. There was no centre or work at home for me until 1971. Then a social worker came to see me in hospital. She told me about leaving and coming home for good to go to a centre in Southend. It was a bit sad for me to go out of hospital. I went home for my holiday, and after that I was sent to Maybrook Centre.

I made a lot of friends in the centre. I played football, tennis, and I did a lot of woodwork and I went on holidays with the staff, and outings. I did some cooking and reading and writing. I went shopping for the staff and other people. On Friday we did what we liked in the afternoon. In 1979 I came to a new centre called Avro, where we all do some work.

I would not like to go back to the hospital again. I spent ten years in there and that is a long time to be there. It was too long. When I was there, lots of patients had fights and staff hit the patients on the wards and beat them up too. I have been out of hospital for a long time now and I am living at home. I go to work in the centre in the day-time and go home at night-time. I have got lots of friends at the centre. I've got my own little job in a bar at Southend Airport. I work with an ex-West Ham player; his name is Brian Dear.

I still see my friends in other centres when I go to play football and darts. They all come up and see me and talk to me. I sit down with them when I have my dinner. I would like to work outside. I don't care what job it is as long as it's work for me to do. I want to stay living at home with my mum because I would not like to go in a group home or hostel or be back in hospital again.

Barry Woodwood
Member of the Avro ATC Students' Council, Southend

I became a student councillor last September. I take my role very seriously. My job is to find out the feelings and problems of the group I represent and bring it into the council and talk about it. Some problems we can sort out ourselves; other problems have to be taken to the staff meeting by Carol, our friend and adviser.

We have decided not to do just those things that affect us in the centre, but to also do things about what affects us outside the centre. We contact other councils and talk to them about the 25 pence charge that we don't agree with. We talk about the word 'student' instead of 'trainee' because we feel we should be called students as we are adult men and women.

We are also doing a project on group homes, that we will be asking the local Society for Mentally Handicapped Children and Adults to take up. I think this is very important because we should be allowed to lead our own lives and be independent.

I have been speaking out in the centre lately because of the staff cuts that have meant we have lost a lot of our groups we used to go in. I have been saying that unless something is going to be done about this we will refuse to be shut in the workshop all day.

Hugh Townsend
Secretary of the Avro ATC Students' Council, Southend

The council began when the trainees from Ashleigh and Maybrook came to settle at Avro and they became candidates. The Chairman was David Bawn. We thought 'trainee' was degrading and had no meaning to it at all, so we had the word 'trainee' changed into 'student', which we are supposed to be. We have had a long battle over this with Essex County Council and we won't give up until we win. We are full-grown adults and we want to be treated like any other person. We have the same feelings as any other adult. We will fight the 25 pence attendance charge that was put down on us. The social services are cutting down the staff and so there will be less groups at the centre. I don't agree with the cutbacks on staff and groups; it means you get fed up in the workshop all day with nothing much to do. But the National Union of Students are backing us up. It means we have the right to more education outside the centre, and to become real students and to be more independent, and social services cannot put a stop to it.

Pauline Regan
Member of the Students' Committee at the Lisson Grove Social and Education Centre, City of Westminster, London
On Friday morning we have a meeting. We have two staff sitting in, and nine students. They were picked by their tutors, one from each tutor group. If we have got any ideas we tell the two staff, and if they have got any ideas they tell us. We've all got separate books. We write the questions down in them to remind us what we've got to ask our tutor group. In the book there are names and little boxes to put their answers. In the meeting we count up the votes.

We've talked about what collage people wanted on the wall for Christmas, whether people like loud music at discos, and who wanted to take part in the hockey match. John wanted to start a bike club, so we asked our tutor groups who had ridden a bike without falling off. Yvonne asked the students if they thought it would be a good idea to start a collection for some more records.

John Sims
Chairman of the Trainees' Committee at the Mitcham Senior Training Centre
I have been Chairman before, in the past – I don't know how many years ago. I do the same type of work as before. I read out the agenda point by point, throw it out openly to the

committee, and we make decisions on it. There is the Treasurer's report, Secretary's report, report back on the Friends of the Centre committee meeting, report back on the last trainees' meeting, minutes and matters arising from them, and any other business. Things discussed usually are ideas to go forward to the Friends of the Centre meetings, like outings and boat trips, and ideas from the suggestion box. We talk about broken equipment, and about changes round in the different sections, and management meetings. I can co-opt trainees to the committee; if they go to the management meetings then they can report back to the committee.

We meet every fortnight in the staff room. Our President comes every time. If we get through the meeting quickly it takes half an hour; it can take longer – one or one and a half hours. It varies. If we have urgent business or important points, we invite the Manager or Senior Instructor. Sometimes it's difficult because members go out for work experience and they are not always here. It is also possible they may leave to get a permanent job and I've lost a committee member. All the members could go and then I would have no committee – it's possible.

We have our President. We had an Inauguration in the dining hall so all the trainees could see. Representatives from the committee and from the Merton Society for Mentally Handicapped Children and Adults, and the Director of Social Services, sat on the stage. At the same time we had a presentation for the Assistant Director who retired.

Since the Inauguration our meetings have changed from informal to formal. When we got our President we knew we no longer had it informal. We take one person at a time to speak. The President helps us with the minutes. We have elections every year. We canvas and lobby our friends to vote for officers and committee members: Chairman, Vice-Chairman, Secretary, Treasurer, Public Relations Officer, and two representatives for the Friends of the Centre meetings.

Patrick Dockerill
Member of the Trainees' Committee at the Ditton Walk
ATC, Cambridge

When the group first started I did not think it would work, but in fact I was wrong, as people brought many ideas. Chairing the group can be difficult, depending on what happens during the week. Sometimes too much time is spent talking about individuals rather than more general things. I myself have learned how to deal with people more fairly and to be more democratic and less selfish since I have been chairing some of the meetings. The group gives the trainees more independence and more responsibility. We have to depend on the staff less. I have got to know the staff better as I have had to talk over problems with them. One thing I would like to see is the meetings to be open to more people so that they can have their say and see what is going on, because sometimes when we report back from meetings people do not listen or may not be there.

APPENDICES

1 MATERIALS ON RIGHTS

1 The United Nations Universal Declaration of Human Rights

Whereas Member States have pledged themselves to achieve, in cooperation with the United Nations, the promotion of universal respect for and observance of human rights and fundamental freedoms,

Whereas a common understanding of these rights and freedoms is of the greatest importance for the full realisation of this pledge,

Now, therefore, the General Assembly proclaim this Universal Declaration of Human Rights as a common standard of achievement for all peoples and all nations, to the end that every individual and every organ of society, keeping this Declaration constantly in mind, shall strive by teaching and education to promote respect for these rights and freedoms and by progressive measures, national and international, to secure their universal and effective recognition and observance, both among the peoples of Member States themselves and among the peoples of territories under their jurisdiction.

1 All human beings are born free and equal in dignity and rights. They are endowed with reason and conscience and should act towards one another in a spirit of brotherhood.

2 i) Everyone is entitled to all the rights and freedoms set forth in this Declaration, without distinction of any kind, such as race, colour, sex, language, religion, political or other opinion, national or social origin, property, birth or other status.

  ii) Furthermore, no distinction shall be made on the basis of the political, jurisdictional or international status of the country or territory to which a person belongs, whether it be independent, trust, non-self-governing or under any other limitation of sovereignty.

3 Everyone has the right to life, liberty and security of person.

4 No one shall be held in slavery or servitude; slavery and the slave trade shall be prohibited in all their forms.

5 No one shall be subjected to torture or to cruel, inhuman or degrading treatment or punishment.

6 Everyone has the right to recognition everywhere as a person before the law.

7 All are equal before the law and are entitled without any

discrimination to equal protection of the law. All are entitled to equal protection against any discrimination in violation of this Declaration and against any incitement to such discrimination.

8 Everyone has the right to an effective remedy by the competent national tribunals for acts violating the fundamental rights granted him by the constitution or by law.

9 No one shall be subjected to arbitrary arrest, detention or exile.

10 Everyone is entitled in full equality to a fair and public hearing by an independent and impartial tribunal, in the determination of his rights and obligations and of any criminal charge against him.

11 i) Everyone charged with a penal offence has the right to be presumed innocent until proved guilty according to law in a public trial at which he has had all the guarantees necessary for his defence.

   ii) No one shall be held guilty of any penal offence on account of any act or omission which did not constitute a penal offence, under national or international law, at the time when it was committed. Nor shall a heavier penalty be imposed than the one that was applicable at the time the penal offence was committed.

12 No one shall be subjected to arbitrary interference with his privacy, family, home or correspondence, nor to attacks upon his honour and reputation. Everyone has the right to the protection of the law against such interference or attacks.

13 i) Everyone has the right to freedom of movement and residence within the borders of each State.

   ii) Everyone has the right to leave any country, including his own, and to return to his country.

14 i) Everyone has the right to seek and to enjoy in other countries asylum from persecution.

   ii) This right may not be invoked in the case of prosecutions genuinely arising from non-political crimes or from acts contrary to the purposes and principles of the United Nations.

15 i) Everyone has the right to a nationality.

   ii) No one shall be arbitrarily deprived of his nationality nor denied the right to change his nationality.

16 i) Men and women of full age, without any limitation due to race, nationality or religion, have the right to marry and to found a family. They are entitled to equal rights as to marriage, during marriage and at its dissolution.

   ii) Marriage shall be entered into only with the free and full consent of the intending spouses.

   iii) The family is the natural and fundamental group unit of society and is entitled to protection by society and the State.

17 i) Everyone has the right to own property alone as well as in association with others.

  ii) No one shall be arbitrarily deprived of his property.

18 Everyone has the right to freedom of thought, conscience and religion; this right includes freedom to change his religion or belief, and freedom, either alone or in community with others and in public or private, to manifest his religion or belief in teaching, practice, worship and observance.

19 Everyone has the right to freedom of opinion and expression; this right includes freedom to hold opinions without interference and to seek, receive and impart information and ideas through any media and regardless of frontiers.

20 i) Everyone has the right to freedom of peaceful assembly and association.

  ii) No one may be compelled to belong to an association.

21 i) Everyone has the right to take part in the government of his country, directly or through freely chosen representatives.

  ii) Everyone has the right of equal access to public service in his country.

  iii) The will of the people shall be the basis of the authority of government; this will shall be expressed in periodic and genuine elections which shall be by universal and equal suffrage and shall be held by secret vote or by equivalent free voting procedures.

22 Everyone, as a member of society, has the right to social security and is entitled to realisation, through national effort and international co-operation and in accordance with the organisation and resources of each State, of the economic, social and cultural rights indispensable for his dignity and the free development of his personality.

23 i) Everyone has the right to work, to free choice of employment, to just and favourable conditions of work and to protection against unemployment.

  ii) Everyone, without any discrimination, has the right to equal pay for equal work.

  iii) Everyone who works has the right to just and favourable remuneration ensuring for himself and his family an existence worthy of human dignity, and supplemented, if necessary, by other means of social protection.

  iv) Everyone has the right to form and to join trade unions for the protection of his interests.

24 Everyone has the right to rest and leisure, including reasonable limitation of working hours and periodic holidays with pay.

25 i) Everyone has the right to a standard of living adequate for the

health and well-being of himself and of his family, including food, clothing, housing and medical care and necessary social services, and the right to security in the event of unemployment, sickness, disability, widowhood, old age or other lack of livelihood in circumstances beyond his control.

ii) Motherhood and childhood are entitled to special care and assistance. All children, whether born in or out of wedlock, shall enjoy the same social protection.

26 i) Everyone has the right to education. Education shall be free, at least in the elementary and fundamental stages. Elementary education shall be compulsory. Technical and professional education shall be made generally available and higher education shall be equally accessible to all on the basis of merit.

ii) Education shall be directed to the full development of the human personality and to the strengthening of respect for human rights and fundamental freedoms. It shall promote understanding, tolerance and friendship among all nations, racial or religious groups, and shall further the activities of the United Nations for the maintenance of peace.

iii) Parents have a prior right to choose the kind of education that shall be given to their children.

27 i) Everyone has the right freely to participate in the cultural life of the community, to enjoy the arts and to share in scientific advancement and its benefits.

ii) Everyone has the right to the protection of the moral and material interests resulting from any scientific, literary or artistic production of which he is the author.

28 Everyone is entitled to a social and international order in which the rights and freedoms set forth in this Declaration can be fully realised.

29 i) Everyone has duties to the community in which alone the free and full development of his personality is possible.

ii) In the exercise of his rights and freedoms, everyone shall be subject only to such limitations as are determined by law solely for the purpose of securing due recognition and respect for the rights and freedoms of others and of meeting the just requirements of morality, public order and the general welfare in a democratic society.

iii) These rights and freedoms may in no case be exercised contrary to the purposes and principles of the United Nations.

30 Nothing in this Declaration may be interpreted as implying for any State, group or person any right to engage in any activity or to perform any act aimed at the destruction of any of the rights and freedoms set forth herein.

2 The United Nations Declaration on the Rights of Mentally Retarded Persons

The General Assembly,

Mindful of the pledge of the Member States of the United Nations under the Charter to take joint and separate action in cooperation with the Organisation to promote higher standards of living, full employment and conditions of economic and social progress and development,

Reaffirming faith in human rights and fundamental freedoms and in the principles of peace, of the dignity and worth of the human person and of social justice proclaimed in the Charter,

Recalling the principles of the Universal Declaration of Human Rights, the International Covenants on Human Rights, the Declaration of the Rights of the Child and the standards already set for social progress in the constitutions, conventions, recommendations and resolutions of the International Labour Organisation, the United Nations Educational, Scientific and Cultural Organisation, the World Health Organisation, the United Nations Children's Fund and of other organisations concerned,

Emphasising that the Declaration on Social Progress and Development has proclaimed the necessity of protecting the rights and assuring the welfare and rehabilitation of the physically and mentally disadvantaged,

Bearing in mind the necessity of assisting mentally retarded persons to develop their abilities in various fields of activities and of promoting their integration as far as possible in normal life,

Aware that certain countries, at their present stage of development, can devote only limited efforts to this end,

Proclaims this Declaration on the Rights of Mentally Retarded Persons and calls for national and international action to ensure that it will be used as a common basis and frame of reference for the protection of these rights.

1 The mentally retarded person has, to the maximum degree of feasibility, the same rights as other human beings.

2 The mentally retarded person has a right to proper medical care and physical therapy and to such education, training, rehabilitation and guidance as will enable him to develop his ability and maximum potential.

3 The mentally retarded person has a right to economic security and to a decent standard of living. He has a right to perform productive work or to engage in any other meaningful occupation to the fullest possible extent of his capabilities.

4 Whenever possible, the mentally retarded person should live with his own family or with foster parents and participate in different

forms of community life. The family with which he lives should receive assistance. If care in an institution becomes necessary, it should be provided in surroundings and other circumstances as close as possible to those of normal life.

5 The mentally retarded person has a right to a qualified guardian when this is required to protect his personal well-being and interests.

6 The mentally retarded person has a right to protection from exploitation, abuse and degrading treatment. If prosecuted for any offence he shall have a right to due process of law with full recognition being given to his degree of mental responsibility.

7 Whenever mentally retarded persons are unable, because of the severity of their handicap, to exercise all their rights in a meaningful way or it should become necessary to restrict or deny some or all of these rights, the procedure used for that restriction or denial of rights must contain proper legal safeguards against every form of abuse. This procedure must be based on an evaluation of the social capability of the mentally retarded person by qualified experts and must be subject to periodic review and to the right of appeal to higher authorities.

3 The United Nations Declaration on the Rights of Disabled Persons

(The Preamble of this Declaration is very similar to that of the Declaration on the Rights of Mentally Retarded Persons.)

1 The term 'disabled person' means any person unable to ensure by himself or herself wholly or partly the necessities of a normal individual and/or social life, as a result of a deficiency, either congenital or not, in his or her physical or mental capabilities.

2 Disabled persons shall enjoy all the rights set forth in this Declaration. These rights shall be granted to all disabled persons without any exception whatsoever and without distinction or discrimination on the basis of race, colour, sex, language, religion, political or other opinions, national or social origin, state of wealth, birth or any other situations applying either to the disabled person himself or herself or to his or her family.

3 Disabled persons have the inherent right to respect for their human dignity. Disabled persons, whatever the origin, nature and seriousness of their handicaps and disabilities, have the same fundamental rights as their fellow-citizens of the same age, which implies first and foremost the right to enjoy a decent life, as normal and full as possible.

4 Disabled persons have the same civil and political rights as other human beings; article 7 of the Declaration on the Rights of

Mentally Retarded Persons applies to any possible limitation or suppression of those rights for mentally disabled persons.

5 Disabled persons are entitled to the measures designed to enable them to become as self-reliant as possible.

6 Disabled persons have the right to medical, psychological and functional treatment, including prosthetic and orthotic appliances, to medical and social rehabilitation, education, vocational education, training and rehabilitation, aid, counselling, placement services and other services which will enable them to develop their capabilities and skills to the maximum and will hasten the process of their social integration or reintegration.

7 Disabled persons have the right to economic and social security and to a decent level of living. They have the right, according to their capabilities, to secure and retain employment or to engage in a useful, productive and remunerative occupation and to join trade unions.

8 Disabled persons are entitled to have their special needs taken into consideration at all stages of economic and social planning.

9 Disabled persons have the right to live with their families or with foster parents and to participate in all social, creative, or recreational activities. No disabled persons shall be subjected, as far as his or her residence is concerned, to differential treatment other than that required by his or her condition or by the improvement which he or she may derive therefrom. If the stay of a disabled person in a specialised establishment is indispensable, the environment and living conditions therein shall be as close as possible to those of the normal life of a person of his or her age.

10 Disabled persons shall be protected against all exploitation, all regulations and all treatment of a discriminatory, abusive or degrading nature.

11 Disabled persons shall be able to avail themselves of qualified legal aid when such aid proves indispensable for the protection of their persons and property. If judicial proceedings are instituted against them, the legal procedure applied shall take their physical and mental condition fully into account.

12 Organisations of disabled persons may be usefully consulted in all matters regarding the rights of disabled persons.

13 Disabled persons, their families and communities shall be fully informed, by all appropriate means, of the rights contained in this Declaration.

4 Extract from the National Society for Mentally Handicapped Children and Adults' 'STAMINA' Papers

For mentally handicapped people in residential care, the following are essential:

1 That full assessment of educational and social potential and of physical and emotional needs of each entrant for residential placement, is made or is available prior to or immediately after placement.

2 That parents and mentally handicapped adults are provided with full details of local authority options for residential care inside or outside their area.

3 That the selection of options and policy on placement is jointly decided. That the individual adult, parents or nearest relatives, together with the supervisory staff who will have responsibility for the resident, are always included in such joint decisions.

4 That in each local authority area there is a sufficient number of places in residential homes to meet the needs of all the mentally handicapped requiring residential care including those at present in subnormality hospitals who could live in the community.

5 That mentally handicapped adults with severe behaviour difficulties are not excluded from residential care in the community.

6 That homes are in ordinary houses, local to the adult mentally handicapped person's home area where possible.

7 That hostel accommodation offers a variety of rooms – to be alone or to share.

8 That hostels should contain no more than fifteen residents.

9 That hostels are mixed-sex.

10 That there is space for recreational and leisure activities.

11 That there is a warm domestic atmosphere.

12 That furniture is of a varied and not 'institutional' nature.

13 That the kitchen and laundry is 'household' in character and can be used by the residents.

14 That a resident's privacy is respected.

15 That toilets and bathrooms have adequate privacy.

16 That residents take part in decision making.

17 That 'learning through doing' results in residents being involved in the running of their own home.

18 That some leisure activities involve relationships outside the hostel.

19 That there is provision made for holidays (the Chronically Sick and Disabled Persons Act 1970, provides for this).

20 That there is on-going contact with the family, if any, of every resident in a home or hostel.

21 That parents, other relatives and friends are encouraged to visit.

22 That senior staff in homes or hostels have relevant experience and training.

23 That there is support for the staff from professional specialist workers.

24 That specialist services are available as required (speech therapist,

psychologist, etc.).

25 That there is regular evaluation, at least annually, by local authorities of the standards provided in local authority homes.

26 That the resident, parents or relatives are included in discussions on progress.

27 That the Local Society for Mentally Handicapped Children and Adults keeps in close touch with the staff and residents and that staff are encouraged in this by the local authority.

28 That homes run by private individuals or voluntary organisations are given the same degree of support and evaluation by local authorities or health authorities as is provided for statutory services.

29 That there is regular contact between the residential home and the Adult Training Centre to ensure co-ordination of assessments.

30 That each individual in residential care (of whatever category, from special care to minimal support) participates in a regular review of his circumstances.

31 That all assessments are in writing – (adequate records are essential for new staff) – and that all involved in joint consultation and decision-making receive copies.

32 That while no residential placement should become a 'dead-end', there should be regular reviews of the suitability of each placement in consultation with the resident. Regard must be given to the need for security and continuity of residence, in accordance with the wishes of the individual.

33 That consideration is given to the possibility of the individual living independently, and that provision is made on local authority housing lists for this purpose.

34 That social work support is available for those living independently.

2 A MANUAL ON SELF-ADVOCACY

We reproduce verbatim here the contents of *We Are People First: A Book on Self-Advocacy*, prepared by John McGill of Nebraska Advocacy Services, Lincoln, Nebraska. It is based on a similar manual entitled *You Have the Right to Speak for Yourself or to Have an Advocate Speak with You*, by Patty Henderson of the Protection and Advocacy Agency in Honolulu, Hawaii, and on the course curriculum *Life, Liberty and the Pursuit of Happiness* by Hallgren, Norsman and Bier, discussed in Chapter Five.

We Are People First

Each of us is different; we all have certain strengths and weaknesses. We all have the right to be the way we are and to become the way we want to be. Sometimes we think it is wrong to be different and we try to be like another person or group of persons. Being different is good; it is easier to be ourselves than to try to be someone else.

We all have some handicaps. A handicap is only a part of our differentness, and it is not the most important part of us. Sometimes people don't understand this; they may put labels on us and treat us poorly. This is not because they are mean people; it is because they don't understand. We can help teach them; then the world will be a better place for all of us to live in.

We All Belong to the Human Family

We are all members of the human family. We all have things that we can do well and those we can not. Sometimes we treat people based on the way they look or act, but we should not make decisions about people without really getting to know them. We must accept others if we expect them to accept us.

Sometimes we are not treated fairly. People are sent to institutions; people are not paid enough for the work they do. These are just two examples of unfair treatment. You do not have to be treated that way; you can ask for better treatment if you don't think it is good. You can stand up for yourself. You should let people know if you are not happy. This is called Self-Advocacy.

214 We Can Speak for Ourselves

What is Self-Advocacy?

Self-Advocacy means to stand up for your own rights. Self-Advocacy means to speak for yourself and to look for help when you need it. It is the best kind of advocacy because it means you are taking charge of what you want to do.

To be a good self-advocate, you need to know more about your rights and responsibilities. If you know more about your rights, you will be a better self-advocate. If you know about your responsibilities you will be a better self-advocate too.

This book will tell you about the kinds of rights that you have. It will also tell you about your responsibilities. If you study this book, you will be a better self-advocate.

What Are Rights?

Rights are things which belong to you. All people have the same rights.

The United States constitution says that all people are created equal, and all have certain rights which cannot be taken away. It doesn't mean that all people must be treated exactly alike, but it does mean we all have the same basic rights.

There are two kind of rights, these are *human* and *legal* rights. Both kinds of rights are important. Our rights are the main thing we have in common with our fellow citizens. If you have a handicap it does not matter; you still have the same rights.

Sometimes we take our rights for granted. Most of us don't think that having a name and a home, buying a new TV, or choosing our friends, are all rights that we have. We are entitled to do these things because we have rights.

In the past, people with handicaps have had their rights denied. People have been sent to institutions or special schools for example. This book is to help you better understand your human and legal rights and how to use them in a responsible way.

Rights are things we are entitled to because we are human beings, and because of laws that we have made to protect us.

Human Rights are yours at birth. Because you are a person, you have human rights. These rights have been written down in the Declaration of Independence.

Legal Rights are the 'Laws of the Land'. If you have a handicap, there are laws to protect you from unfair treatment. There are penalties for violating these rights. These rights are written down in law books of the city, state, and county.

Human Rights

Human Rights are basic and very simple. They are yours at birth.

These rights are important in being alive and living your life. Basic human rights include:

The right to choice – to choose how you wish to live your life.

The right to life – to be alive.

The right to freedom – to move around as you wish and to be free from other people restricting your movement.

The right to pursue happiness – to learn about the world and to live in the world.

All Human Beings Have These Basic Rights:

- The right to choose where you wish to live;
- The right to choose the people you wish to be with;
- The right to make up your own mind about what you want to do;
- The right to say 'No' when you don't want to do something;
- The right to change things that you don't like.

What Are Rights of Living?

Stop here for a minute and think about the following things:

- Celebrating a special personal holiday, such as a birthday.
- Going shopping with your own pocket money.
- Selecting your own clothes to buy and wear.
- Having friends away from home.
- Dating people of the opposite sex.
- Having a job and being paid a fair wage for a fair day's work.
- Being spoken to when you are present.
- Selecting the food you eat.
- Going to church, or not going to church, as you wish.
- Choosing your bed time.
- Marrying and having children.
- Going to school with other students your age.
- Being able to leave your home to go into the community.
- Not being ignored when you speak.
- Going to the beach because you want to.
- Doing nothing because you want to.
- The right to choose what kind of life you want.

Self-Advocacy Is:

- Knowing your basic human rights;
- Standing up for your rights;
- Taking responsibility for your life;
- Asking for help because you want it or need it.

Self-Advocacy is the best way in which you can protect your own human rights.

Legal Rights

Laws giving you legal rights have been written to give clear instructions as to how your rights must be protected. Laws are very powerful.

As human beings, we agreed on the rights which belong to all of us. We also made some rules and said exactly what we needed to do to protect the basic rights of all people living together in this country.

Legal rights are those which have been given to you because of specific laws. These laws are clear instructions as to how your rights must be protected. There are penalties for not following the law.

There are many important legal rights; we will discuss several of the most basic.

Your Right to Equal Protection

All laws made for all people apply to you; you have the same or equal protection under the law just like any other person. You cannot be denied services that are available to other citizens, just because you have a handicap. Equal protection means that you can demand the right to services which are being provided to all other citizens.

If you are put into an institution, *just because you are mentally retarded*, then your rights under the law are being violated.

If you are denied a job, for which you are qualified, *just because you have epilepsy*, then your rights under the law are being violated.

If you can't go to the school in your area, *just because you have cerebral palsy*, then your rights are being violated.

Your Right to the Least Restrictive Environment

You have a right to live, learn, work, and move around in the place which restricts your freedom in the least possible way that is needed to help you.

If you receive services, they must be provided in the 'least restrictive' way necessary to help you. It means that no one should be cut off from the kind of life that others enjoy, just because of a handicap. Anyone who thinks that a person's special needs require services apart from the rest of us, must prove that it is the best for that person.

In Learning: You have the right to go to school in the least restrictive school necessary to properly teach you.

In Living: You have the right to live as independently as you can, in the community you choose.

In Working: You have the right to work in a place that helps you be as productive as you can be.

In Moving About: You have the right to move around in a society which is free from physical barriers, like steps if you are in a wheelchair.

Your Right to Informed Consent

Consent means to allow someone to do something. We give consent to be operated on by doctors, to be taught by teachers, or to allow our children to go on field trips. Informed consent simply means that you must be given all the information necessary so that you can give your consent.

Informed consent means that you or someone you trust, must be given all the information, including all of your options, before you agree to something. You can refuse if you want to.

Informed consent means that you do not have to agree to something unless:

1 It has been completely explained to you, or
2 To someone you trust and have chosen to help you decide, and
3 You have been given all the information about what other choices you have.

If you do not understand the programme plan which has been developed for you, and you agree to it anyway, then you have not given *informed consent*.

If you agree to be sterilized even if you don't understand what the operation does, you have not given *informed consent*.

If you agree to go to a charity workshop because you are told it is the only place you can work, you have not given *informed consent*.

Your Right to Due Process

Sometimes, a person's rights are restricted, either for their own benefit or to keep them from hurting others. In order to restrict a person's rights legally, due process must take place.

Due process means telling you what is happening before and while it happens. Here are the steps:

1 There must be strong evidence to prove that restricting the person is necessary to keep him or her from hurting themselves or others.
2 Evidence must be presented at an open hearing or meeting.
3 The person must be allowed to attend and take part in the meeting.
4 If the person disagrees, they can appeal.
5 The restriction can only be for a certain amount of time; it must be reviewed to see if it is still necessary.

If you or your child is evaluated for special education and you are not told before the evaluation started, then you have not had *due process*.

If you are terminated from a programme or service without knowing why, then *due process* has not been followed.

If you are moved from one place to another without having had a say, then you have not had *due process*.

Your Right to Appeal

Appeals are ways of solving disagreements. You have a right to appeal something that you think is unfair.

Sometimes you might disagree with what your caseworker wants you to do. When this happens, it is best to talk with him or her directly to find out their reasons. If you still don't agree, you have a right to appeal and to ask to have the decision changed.

You may also appeal if you feel:

1 Information was withheld;
2 You did not have a choice;
3 Services were too slow;
4 Your caseworker has been unfair;
5 You don't have enough help.

If you are moved into a boarding home and you don't want to be there, but no one in authority will listen to you, then you have not had your right to *appeal*.

If you are fired from your job and you feel it was unfair, but no one will listen to your concern, then you have not had the right to *appeal*.

If your child is placed in a special education class and you do not like the programme, but the principal won't talk to you, then you have not had the right to *appeal*.

Self-Advocacy Is:

* Knowing your basic legal rights;
* Standing up for your rights;
* Taking responsibility for your life;
* Asking for help because you want it or need it.

Self-Advocacy is the way in which you may protect your legal rights.

Some Laws You Should Know

In the past few years, there have been several laws passed which further protect your rights. They are very powerful. You can use them to fight discrimination. Discrimination is when you are treated differently or unfairly because of your handicap. Someone once said, 'No people are free until all people are free.' What does that quote mean to you?

[Here follow brief summaries of the provisions of key US civil rights and 'access' laws.]

Self-Advocacy Is:

● Knowing the basic laws which protect your rights;
● Knowing these laws also provide for your special needs;
● Standing up for your rights;
● Taking responsibility for your life;
● Asking for help because you want or need it.

Self-Advocacy is using the law to protect your basic legal rights.

Can My Rights Be Taken Away?

No, the rights of any person living in the United States of America may not be taken away. But they may be restricted. This may be done to protect you, or to provide you with special help.

Any time any of your rights are restricted, due process must be followed. The three major ways in which your rights may be restricted are:

Restrictive Programmes: If you are placed in a programme which is specifically for developmentally disabled people, due process and informed consent must be followed. Restriction from normal activities of everyday life is a restriction of your basic rights.

Guardianship: This is a method by which the responsibility for your actions is given to someone else. The guardian is allowed to make decisions for you. Often, it is felt that this is in your best interest. Guardianship limits your ability to make decisions for yourself; guardianship restricts your rights in being your own person.

If You Break a Law: If you break a law or violate the rights of other people, you may find your rights restricted through a court of law. Your rights may be restricted through confinement in a jail or other institution. If you violate the rights of other people, your rights may be restricted.

When Rights of Human Beings Are Restricted:

- Due process must be followed;
- Informed consent must occur;
- You have the right to appeal the decision to restrict your rights;
- You can petition for change.

Anytime you think your rights are being taken away or restricted without due process, ask for help.

Self-Advocacy is standing up for your own rights.

What Are Responsibilities?

Responsibilities are things which others expect us to do. Being responsible means being trusted. Responsible people know what their own rights are and respect the rights of others. If you are responsible, it means that you care about other people's rights, it means that you try to do everything possible to make our community a good place for *all* of us to live.

Responsible People ask questions anytime they do not understand:

- What is happening;
- What is being said to you;
- What choices have been given to you;
- What you have been asked to agree to or sign.

We Can Speak for Ourselves

What Should You Do?

If you feel that your rights are being taken away or are not being thought of . . .

If you feel that you are not getting the correct information about the choices of services for you . . .

If you feel that you are being pressured into something, or are just not certain what to do . . .

Then You Should:

- Get more information;
- Ask for help from a helping agency or from a friend;
- Think about what questions you need answered.

Steps In Self-Advocacy

These steps are the same if you do it by yourself or if you have an advocate to help you. You and your advocate work together. The first thing you need to do is to be able to explain what the problem is. Then you should set a goal to solve that problem.

Planning for Self-Advocacy

- Get your information together. Make sure it is true. Include whom you talked to, what they said, and when you talked to them.
- If you have an advocate, make sure he or she knows the full story.
- Look at your facts, look at your rights, and decide what you can do.
- If you need more information, find it out. Don't take people's word for things – you and your advocate need to get the information yourself from people you know.
- Figure out what the choices are and pick the best choice for you.
- Decide the steps you are going to take to reach your goal.

Remember

- Anytime you begin to ask questions about the 'status quo', or about why things are being done a certain way, you are likely to feel some resistance.
- Advocacy involves being willing to continue your plans, even though there is resistance.
- Try not to use pressure unless you need to – but make sure you have your information together so you can when you want.
- Write everything down – time, date, what happened, whom it happened with. That is documentation.

In Addition, You Can . . .

- Use the 'chain of command' and go to the person who is the main boss.
- Find a friend of the person you are trying to convince and ask that person for help.
- Have a back-up plan if the first one fails.
- Call a meeting with all the people involved – make sure that someone is taking notes.
- Agree on dates by which certain things are supposed to happen. Make certain those things happen by those dates, or find out why not.
- Know your rights as a person and your legal rights as a person with a handicap.

Self Advocacy Means . . .

- Getting all of the information;
- Deciding what you want to do;
- Finding out what and who will support you in doing what you want to do;
- Knowing your rights and responsibilities;
- Beginning to change the way things are.

Self-Advocacy is speaking out on behalf of yourself and taking charge of what you want to do.

Self-Advocacy is the best kind of advocacy.

Review Questions

This review will give you an idea of how well you understood this book.

The answers are at the end.

Answer Yes (you agree) or No (you don't agree).

1 We should try hard to be like someone else because being different is not good. _____

2 We should not make decisions about people without really knowing them. _____

3 All human beings have the same basic human rights. _____

4 Self-Advocacy means letting other people make decisions for you. _____

5 Legal rights are only given to people who vote in elections. _____

6 Due process means telling you what is happening before and while it happens. _____

7 Informed consent means that you have agreed to a decision even if you do not really understand what is happening. _____

8 If you have a guardian, your right to make decisions on behalf of yourself is restricted. _____

9 If you consent to being sterilized even if you don't understand the operation, you do not have a right to change your mind. _____

10 If you live in an institution, you do not have a right to say what you want because your counsellor always knows what is best. _____

11 If you apply for a job and you can do the work but are not hired because of your handicap, there is nothing you can do. _____

12 If you go to a public building and cannot get up the steps to the door and there is no ramp, your rights are being violated. _____

13 If you are not receiving a public school education, it is because the school can do nothing for you, and you have no rights under the law. _____

14 Responsible people know what their own rights are and respect the rights of others. _____

15 The first thing to do if you have a problem in getting services, is to threaten to sue the agency. _____

16 There will probably be some resistance when you try and change things that have been done a certain way for a long time. _____

17 The best type of advocacy is Self-Advocacy. _____

18 Which of the following is Self-Advocacy:
_____ Knowing your rights?
_____ Taking responsibility for your life?
_____ Asking for help if you want or need it?
_____ Standing up for your rights?
_____ Knowing the laws that protect your rights?

ANSWERS

1 No	10 No
2 Yes	11 No
3 Yes	12 Yes
4 No	13 No
5 No	14 Yes
6 Yes	15 No
7 No	16 Yes
8 Yes	17 Yes
9 No	18 All

3 MATERIALS FROM PROJECT TWO

1 Information Sheet Produced by Project Two
(originally prepared for a convention workshop)

Starting a Local Group – Why and How

Project Two:

- Has officers:
  The Chairman is the boss and calls and runs the meetings;
  The Vice-Chairman takes over for the chairman when needed;
  The Treasurer keeps the bank account;
  The Secretary takes minutes and does other organisational things under the direction of the chairman.
- Is sponsored by the Association for Retarded Citizens.
- Has speakers and an agenda at each meeting.
- Does social things together, too.
- Votes on:
  definite goals for the group;
  speakers desired;
  committee members.
- Sets up committees to accomplish goals.
- Has regular meeting times (third Friday of every month).
- Sends meeting minutes and notices to all members.
- Has good members who come to most meetings, pay attention during meetings, and help each other. Some are good at numbers but can't read; some can read but can't write; some can write but can't speak well. The skills of each person are used to help the group, and that way everyone can participate in his own way.

2 Resolutions, Goals, and Statements Adopted by People First of Nebraska, August 1978

I   Philosophical Statements:

   1 We believe that we are people first, and our handicaps are second. We wish people would recognize this and not give us a tag like 'handicapped' or 'retarded'.

   2 We believe that we have to fight for our own rights, and that

unless we do we won't get them.

3 We believe that people shouldn't just stay at home and feel sorry for themselves and ask for pity; there's a beautiful world out there, and we want to be part of it.

4 We believe that we should work to destroy the physical and mental restrictions on *everybody*, not just on ourselves.

5 We believe that it is important to get people out on their own.

6 We believe that it is wrong for the public to run us down and treat us badly.

7 We believe we can win this fight, if we work together.

II Realization of Our Rights:

1 We have the right to stand up for what we believe in.

2 We have the right to live where we choose.

3 We have the right to equal pay for equal work.

4 We have the right to date, marry, raise a family, or get a divorce.

5 We have the right not to be threatened with being sent to an institution.

6 We have the right to have enough money to live on; this can be through money we've earned, or through food stamps, welfare, and SSI. We shouldn't be denied these if we need them.

7 We have the right to better pay in training.

8 We have the right to organize groups for helping ourselves.

9 We have the right to go to high school or college.

10 We have the right to take trips and vacations and to have access to transportation.

11 We have the right to have a drink.

12 We have the right to be treated like human beings, to be treated with respect and not to be called 'epileptic', 'stupid', or 'retarded'.

13 We have the right not to be pushed and bossed around.

III Statements Relating to Services:

1 There should be better contracts in the workshops.

2 The workshops need to be improved.

3 More money is needed for the programmes so that we can have new, better ones instead of the old ones. The world is changing and the programmes must change right along with it.

4 The workshops are too crowded; something must be done about this.

5 The staff (houseparents, foster parents, nursing home staff) shouldn't be so bossy. They have no right to tell us we can't go anywhere without them, or to tell us what to do.

6 People should not be placed in crowded places and foster homes; they should be placed in places that are right for them.

7 When we get frustrated, our staff should leave us alone instead of pushing and pushing.

8 We should treat each other with respect instead of being bossy toward each other, in the hostels and at work.

9 There should be separate workshops for physically disabled persons. (It's not appropriate for physically disabled persons to be served with retarded persons, nor are their needs the same.)

10 Physically disabled persons should not always have to wait to get the help they need.

11 Beatrice State Developmental Center should be closed; people have the right to get out of there.

12 We all know of situations where people were abused in the institution. This is wrong, and we must speak against it.

IV Action Goals

1 That a group like Project Two be started in every city and town.

2 That we form a committee which would represent all of us, that would get the communities behind us and get a statute that would guarantee all our rights.

3 That we have another convention next year.

4 That we show the federal, state and local governments that we can destroy any barriers that are put up in front of us; that we show them how we feel about being shut out.

5 That we work to pass a law prohibiting any business, church, or other organization from discriminating against us.

3 People First of Nebraska Convention Agenda, 1979

Saturday, 6 October

1.00 p.m.	Welcome. Ollie Rector and Nancy Loomis, Leaders.
1.15 p.m.	Speaker. Randy Kitch.
1.45 p.m.	Film: *People First.*
2.30 p.m.	Coffee and doughnuts.
2.45 p.m.	Workshops:
	Rights and Responsibilities;
	How to Stick Up for Yourself;
	Starting Your Own Group;
	How to Make Rules for Your Group.
3.45 p.m.	Back in large group. Workshop reports.
4.30 p.m.	Room 246: Videotape on Ray Loomis.
	Room 346: Hospitality Room.

6.00 p.m.   Steak Dinner.
8.00 p.m.   Disco Dance and Contest.
Sunday, 7 October
  7.30 a.m.   Breakfast.
  8.30 a.m.   Convene in large group. Pat Miller and Christ Corso,
               Leaders.
  9.30 a.m.   Workshops:
               Self-Advocacy;
               How to Stick Up for Yourself;
               Keeping a Group Going and Growing;
               Changing Public Attitudes;
               How to Advise a Group (for helpers).
10.30 a.m.   Elections.
12.00 noon   Adjournment and lunch.

4 Press Release from Project Two
7 November 1979.   For Immediate Release.

Project Two, a group of adults with mental handicaps, will hold a
press conference on Monday, 12 November, at 9.30 a.m. to kick off a
campaign to protest at the alleged abuse of a child at the Beatrice
State Developmental Center.

The press conference will be held at the offices of the Greater
Omaha Association for Retarded Citizens, 3212 Dodge.

Project Two, which feels that abuse is all too common in
institutions, hopes to exert pressure to speed the movement of
residents out of the state institutions and back to their home
communities. Their decision to undertake this effort arose after
Jonathan Allen, a 10-year-old Bellevue boy, was allegedly abused at
Beatrice on 23 October. Many Project Two members were residents
of Beatrice at one time and their experiences there have intensified
their concern about this particular incident.

The group's campaign has three goals. These are:
1 to tell the public, state legislators, and state and local officials, of
  the need to bring Beatrice residents back to their own communities
  and to prevent community residents from being placed in Beatrice;
2 to insist that all people should be treated humanely and with
  dignity, regardless of their handicaps, age, or other problems; and
3 to support the family of Jonathan Allen.

After the press conference, the group intends to appear on various
local talk shows and to meet with state legislators about their
concerns. Members have met to inform themselves in regard to this
specific incident of alleged abuse and on the ability of community
based programs to serve even the most handicapped persons in small,
more normal settings.

5 Statement by Project Two at Their Press Conference, November 1979

We believe people should be treated like human beings – with kindness and fairness and love. We are upset that a child may have been abused at Beatrice. Jonathan Allen could not defend himself. We believe that it is the responsibility of the State of Nebraska to provide more care and to watch over its residents more carefully.

We also believe that all the people should be moved out of Beatrice into their own communities. We believe that all people, no matter how handicapped they are, can live in their own communities. We think that the money that is being spent right now to keep people in Beatrice should be spent to bring them back here.

We are Project Two, a group who believes that we are people first and our handicaps come second. Some of us have lived in Beatrice, and that's why we are so upset about what may have happened to Jonathan. Our experiences have taught us how important it is for people to be treated well.

Some of us have lived in ENCOR residences. Some of us have visited these residences in the last week. We know that people can be served humanely in their own communities. We urge the people of Nebraska to support these program. We intend to keep fighting for our goals. In the next few months, we will be speaking to community organizations and on talk shows. We will also be talking to our state senators about our experiences and our concerns.

Are there any questions?

4 OTHER AMERICAN MATERIALS ON SELF-ADVOCACY

The materials reproduced in this Appendix were all produced or made available by the Technical Assistance for Self-Advocacy Project at the Kansas University Affiliated Facility, Lawrence, Kansas, between 1978 and 1981.

1 How to Form a Self-Advocacy Group
1 Meet with disabled people and explain what self-advocacy is on a personal level and a group level.
2 Show the *People First* film.
3 Have a question and answer period with the group or a discussion.
4 Ask the people if they want to form their own self-advocacy group.
5 Explain the jobs of the officers (group leaders).
6 Elect officers – president, vice-president, secretary, treasurer.
7 Hold regular meetings
   ● weekly or monthly
   ● time
   ● place
8 Pick an advisor to the group to help the group organise.
9 Talk about the *purpose* of the group.
10 Talk about what the group wants to do (goals).

2 Recruitment Procedure
Membership recruitment is essential for any organization for growth, strength, and support. The more individuals who are involved in the organization, the more successful the organization will become. The purpose of the recruitment process is to stimulate interest and support from outsiders, and thus obtain more members.

There are several ways to recruit members, which are:
1 Word of mouth. The starters of the organizations can stimulate an abundance of interest just by talking to friends, relatives, and anyone with whom they associate.
2 Using the media (TV, radio, newspapers, newsletters) to get the name and purpose to the general public. A newspaper article is a good method for reaching people in a fast, accurate manner. Make

sure to give the name, address, and phone number of the contact person of your organization for access for people who want to join. Every organization needs a good public relations program to establish good communication with the public at large, and the media is the best source for accomplishing this needed program.

3 Giving presentations in schools, rehabilitation centers, other advocacy groups and to civic groups as another method of stimulating interest and recruiting people.

The important element in recruiting members is to have your organization's purpose, mission, and goals really concrete and in black and white so you will have a solid foundation in which people can believe and trust. Then present the concept in a positive and clear manner. Any organization needs active members and recruiting can obtain this type of member. Another important element to remember is that you cannot force people to join. Just present the facts and tell them their involvement is wanted and needed, but never pressure people to join.

3 Officers' Responsibilities

President

- To be in charge of all meetings;
- To call each meeting to order;
- To get opinions from every member at every meeting;
- To maintain order at meetings by allowing only one person to speak at a time;
- To plan meetings: write the agenda, follow the agenda, and set time limits or pace the meeting;
- To use standard Rules of Order;
- To work with the advisor on an ongoing basis.

Vice-President

- To be present and active at all meetings;
- To take charge of a meeting when the president is unable to attend;
- To make sure all other officers fulfil their responsibilities.

Secretary

- To take notes of each meeting;
- To make formal meeting minutes from the notes;
- To include the treasurer's and committee reports in the minutes;
- To make copies of the minutes and make sure every member has a copy;
- To file the minutes;

- To find out the agenda for the next meeting from the president;
- To make sure the next meeting's agenda is mailed to every member;
- To mail out information.

Treasurer

- To receive and record dues from each member;
- To keep records of money coming into the group from donations or fund-raising activities;
- To keep records of money spent – when, by whom, and for what reason;
- To keep and file all receipts and treasurer's reports;
- To report what money was received, what money was spent, and what the balance is, at each meeting;
- To make sure the treasurer's report is included in the minutes.

Member

- To attend all meetings;
- To get to meetings on time;
- To read and understand the agenda;
- To know and follow standard Rules of Order;
- To know when and how to propose a motion;
- To voice ideas and opinions on the topics listed in the agenda;
- To have respect for the officers and for each other – everyone has a right to be heard and to vote;
- To make sure the officers do their jobs;
- To nominate and vote for responsible officers;
- To volunteer for committees of choice.

4 Typical Self-Advocacy Meeting Agenda

1 Call to order by the president.
2 Role call (checking and recording who is at the meeting).
3 Reading of minutes by the secretary.
4 Approve minutes.
5 Reading of letters written to other groups, agencies, or people, and reading of mail received.
6 Treasurer's report.
7 President's report.
8 Committee reports.
9 Old business.
10 New business.
11 Special program.
12 Adjournment (group agrees to leave).

Suggestions:

A   A person or persons in the group should be responsible for bringing refreshments if desired.

B   Meetings should occasionally have guest speakers, films, slide and tape presentations, etc.

C   A date, place, and time should be arranged for the next meeting.

D   The officers should stimulate the interest and encourage discussion of all group members.

E   The officers should emphasize being punctual to meetings as well as regular attendance.

F   Don't let the meetings go beyond 2 hours in length.

G   A ten or fifteen minute break should occur about half-way through the meeting.

H   Plan a short period for socializing right after the meeting.

I   Standard Rules of Order should be followed.

5 Steps in Decision-Making

1 Identify the problem or situation.
2 Define the problem (state what's wrong).
3 Collect information about the problem and its cause(s) (what would help you solve the problem).
4 Consider solutions (what things can you do to solve the problem).
5 Choose the best solution.
6 Follow through (implement) the solution of choice.
7 If the chosen solution does not bring the desired results, try another way.

6 Twelve Principles of Advocacy

1 Know your case well and *document* your facts.
2 Know the opposing case and the possible arguments and strategies. (Role play this.)
3 Operate from a sound base of support.
4 Know your resources and your allies.
5 Intervene at a high enough level to get the job done.
6 Take a positive approach; reinforce. Assume the agency really wants to help the clients.
7 Demonstrate to the system how it is interfering with its own goals.
8 If there has to be a battle (overt), only do so after completion of steps 1 to 7.
9 If you have to battle, don't pussyfoot. Know how far you have to go and take it to the limit.
10 Strengthen the client group. Self-advocacy is the most powerful kind of advocacy.
11 Be aware of client vulnerability. Let the clients know the risks.

Beware of exploitation.
12 Before you begin, know the risks and weigh them against possible gains.

7 Fund-Raising Procedure

Any organization must do fund-raising at some point to establish a financial foundation for the organization to operate. Organizations cannot be productive without some type of financial support. There are several ways to obtain financial support. They are: grants, donations, and fund-raising activities.

Fund-raising activities can range from sponsoring a dance to a 'ping-pong-a-thon'. The essential element that an organization must have is membership involvement. Members must be actively involved and dedicated for a fund-raising project to be a success because a project takes organization, hours of work by every member, and a good public relations program to stimulate the community about the fund-raising project.

The basic steps of organizing any fund-raising project are:
1 Appoint a fund-raising steering committee.
2 Decide on a fund-raising project – dances, bake sales, any event that will draw the interest of the public.
3 Decide on a place, date, time, and the costs. Note any regulations about printed raffle tickets, or any tax liability.
4 Send news releases to the media – TV, radio, newspapers, etc.
5 Develop promotional materials – leaflets, brochures, posters.
6 Display posters in store windows, on school bulletin boards, etc.
7 Try to speak to civic groups about the philosophy of your organization and the purpose of the fund-raising project.

The success of the project depends on community support and involvement to the fullest degree. The members of the organization must be stimulated and full of energy all through the fund-raising campaign.

8 Your Constitutional Rights

Freedom of Religion
No one can keep you from worshipping or not worshipping however you want to.

Freedom of Speech
No one can keep you from saying anything you want as long as it is the truth.

Freedom of the Press
No one can keep you from writing and publishing anything you want

so long as it is the truth.

Freedom of Assembly and Petition
No one can keep you from meeting together with your friends or other people or keep you from telling the government when something bothers you.

Right Against Unreasonable Search and Seizure
No one can come to your house and legally take something you own without permission from a judge.

Right to Jury Trial
If you are arrested, you have the right to a hearing from a Grand Jury before you are sent to trial – if you must go to trial, it must be held quickly, it must be held near where you live, witnesses must be brought against you, and you can have a lawyer to help you.

Right to Due Process
You cannot be put in prison for a long time or have your property taken away from you without having a chance to defend yourself in court.

Right against Excessive Bail
If you are arrested, you have the right to be released before trial by posting a reasonable bail.

Right against Cruel and Unusual Punishment
If you are convicted of a crime, the punishment given you must be legal and reasonable.

Right to Equal Protection under the Law
Laws must be written and enforced so that they apply to everyone in an equal and fair way.

Right to Vote
Everyone who is 18 years or older, has the right to vote in elections if they have registered to vote.

9 Planning a State Convention
(From *Self-Advocacy: A Basic Right* by Barbara Welter, John Hanna and Randy Kitch, published by the Kansas University Affiliated Facility, Lawrence, Kansas, in 1978.)
1 Select a group of disabled individuals and advocates to organize the convention or at least assist in the organizational process.
2 Have regular meetings to maintain communication.

3 Decide on a convention location, which should be near the centre of the state so nobody will have a long distance to travel.
4 Select a hotel, checking on meeting rooms, accessibility, food (consider special dietary needs) and amenities.
5 Obtain a list of agencies serving disabled people.
6 Appoint a representative in every county to help promote the convention. Send packets of self-advocacy and convention materials to representatives, advisors and agencies. It is suggested that the representatives have some experience in organizational work or be given guidance by an adviser.
7 Involve the media – TV, radio, newspapers and newsletters – to develop public relations.
8 Plan an outdoor cookout or banquet in the evening to create a friendly and relaxed environment. It will also promote a 'group' attitude.
9 Draw up posters and send to county representatives.
10 Decide on a theme for the convention.
11 Show the film *People First* at the convention.
12 Require pre-registration.
13 Select speakers and chairpersons to conduct the convention.
14 Discourage having 'professionals' on the program. The convention is for the disabled individuals to communicate and the professionals to listen.
15 Make every effort to schedule the convention when it is least likely to conflict with other planned gatherings of audience members, common vacation weeks or holidays, or periods of predictable extreme weather.
16 Solicit the aid of local chamber of commerce officials and hotel operators.
17 Make sure emergency medical services will be readily available.
18 Ensure there is provision on the forms sent to representatives and advisers for entry of any special dietary or medical requirements for prospective participants.

A successful convention depends on involvement. The best way to accomplish this is to meet with people with disabilities, and groups and agencies serving disabled people, to produce interest and excitement.

10 How to Work with the System – and Win
by Barbara Noone Gibbons and Jacqueline Osborne
(This is the written content of an illustrated booklet published by the Kansas University Affiliated Facility, Lawrence, Kansas, in 1981. The booklet is adapted from *Negotiation: A Tool for Change* by Steven Taylor of the Developmental Disabilities Rights Center at the Center on Human Policy, Syracuse, New York.)

Many times people have different ideas on how things should be done. For example, sometimes people disagree over which television show to watch, or sometimes people disagree over the location of a group home. To get people to change their minds – and do what *you* want – you need to know what to do and say. That's why this booklet was written.

In order to change people's minds you need to:
- Know exactly what you want;
- Know exactly what the other person wants;
- Figure out the best way to make that person understand what you want.

What *is* the best way to make people understand what you want? First of all, try simply telling them. Tell people exactly what you want and why. Sometimes they will agree with your ideas. Sometimes they won't. However, listen carefully to what they say. Show that you can listen. If they agree to what you want, let them know you appreciate their help. Tell them 'thank you'.

If, though, you try this and it doesn't work, you should probably try another way. First of all, check to see if anyone else agrees with your idea. Explain what you want to other people (staff, consumer groups, friends, advocates, family). You may be surprised by the people who agree with you.

Next, write a letter to the people whose minds you want to change. Ask them to come to a meeting with you. If necessary, have a friend help you write this letter. Remember, there's no sense wasting your time with people who don't have the power to change what you want changed. Talk to the people who can help you. Be sure the letter includes:
- The purpose of the meeting (for example, to talk about the location of a group home);
- The names of the people you want at the meeting;
- The date, time and location of the meeting.

A few days later, call the people you want at the meeting and make sure they are coming. If they refuse to meet, then you must *get tough!* Ask them what day or time would be better to meet. If they still refuse to meet, go to someone higher up than them. Tell other people in your town what is going on (for example, let your newspaper know that someone is opposing the location of a new group home).

Once people agree to meet, it's time to get your act together. Get a group of people together to go to the meeting with you. Be sure that everyone understands the problem and what you want to change. Remember, if they have four people at the meeting, *you* should have at least four people at the meeting. Don't let them outnumber you. Get together before the meeting. Practise what you want to say. Develop your plan of action: write an agenda (a list of things to talk about); pick someone to do most of the talking for the group; try to figure out what the other people will say about each thing on the agenda, and think of answers for any possible complaints they might have; know all important facts and laws that might affect the decision; know what you *will* and *will not* accept as an answer.

Some things to remember for the real meeting:

- Don't let the other people sit behind a desk or at the head of a table. This gives them control over the meeting. Be sure to have everyone sit at the table, or have no table at all – just chairs.
- If the other people call you by your first name, you should call them by their first names. If someone insists on being called 'Mr' Jones, you should insist on being called 'Mr' Smith. Make everything equal.
- Bring all papers and materials you might need to the meeting. Put them in the order you will use them. If you are going to hand out papers, make sure you have enough for everyone.
- Use a tape recorder or take notes so you can remember what everyone says during the meeting.

As soon as everyone gets to the meeting, *you* should begin the talking. Thank everyone for coming. Say why you are all meeting. Give your side of the story. Answer questions as clearly as possible. Listen to what the other people have to say.

But watch out! They may have their own plan. Stop them if they say things that disagree with their actions (like saying they want you to be independent when they insist on you being in bed by ten each night). Stop them if they say they agree with you but can't do anything about it (they should get hold of someone who *can*). Stop them if they say they don't have the money to do what you want. This is where your homework comes in. Know the agency's budget. There usually *is* enough money, it's just a matter of how it's spent. Tell them this. And know where other funds can be obtained before you go to the meeting. Remember, a lack of money doesn't mean that your rights can be violated.

Stop them if they say that they are the experts and know best. Remember, *you* are the expert because it affects *your* life. Stop them if they say that you should be thankful for what you have, or that things could be worse. Stop them if they say you're too emotional or that you don't understand how things are done.

Whatever happens at the meeting, remember that it's very important to:

- Explain your position clearly;
- Listen to what the other people have to say;
- Know what you want and need.

If you still haven't reached an agreement by the end of the meeting, you should tell the other people that you don't think you're getting anywhere. Suggest another meeting. If necessary, leave the meeting. Remain calm even if you're angry. If you have to leave the meeting, do so in a polite way. Don't give the other people a chance to say you're too emotional and don't deserve what you want.

The final steps to getting what you want are:

- Establish timetables: write everything down to be done and the date it's to be finished; say who is responsible for doing each thing; develop a plan for change.
- Write a letter outlining what went on at the meeting and what was decided. Make sure the leader for the other side gets a copy of this letter. You may want to send the letter by registered mail to make sure it arrives.
- If they say they'll do what you want, hold them to it.

A final note . . . This is not the end. It is just the beginning – the beginning of a lot of work for *you*. Working with the system is not an easy job. It takes a lot of time and energy. Hopefully, however, this book will make that job a little bit easier – and life a whole lot more independent.

5 MATERIALS ON SELF-ADVOCACY FROM BRITAIN

1 The Campaign for Mentally Handicapped People
Guidelines for Organising Conferences of Mentally Handicapped People

(From *Our Life* by Ann Shearer, the report of the first British national conference of mentally handicapped people; the report was published by CMH in 1972.)

1 Conferences should be arranged in the ordinary way which, amongst other things implies that:
- they are well prepared and properly structured;
- they take place in an ordinary conference setting;
- the delegates are treated as ordinary conference delegates;
- reports of the meetings are written and published.

But it must be recognised that this will be the first experience for many and they must be helped to understand it, e.g. use of conference materials must be carefully explained to each individual on arrival. The opening session must be used to explain the purpose of the meeting, the use of results, conference procedure and work in groups.

2 Where possible handicapped people should be involved in the conference arrangements.

3 Participants should be invited in the normal way by writing direct to the individuals or by writing to organisations requesting them to approach individuals to ask if they would care to attend. The organisations concerned should be encouraged to pay conference fees and travel expenses in the usual way. Delegates themselves should cover their own personal expenses at the meeting.

4 The programme used here – its timing, balance of work and leisure and of small group to large group sessions – was successful and we would recommend it as a basis in future.

5 We felt it was helpful for staff from various institutions to accompany delegates, not so much as helpers and supervisors but to support them on return home in communicating results to authorities and in helping to put ideas into practice.

The conference should, of course, offer equal quality accommodation to staff members and other delegates with normal sharing of facilities.

It should be made clear to staff that they are welcome at sessions but only as observers and at most to encourage conversation but without commenting on or affecting ideas; also that they will be expected to help in organisation of recreational activities and in personal support to the people they accompany and others who turn to them. Delegates who are not accompanied by staff should be introduced to one of the organisers as someone who will advise them on any problem.

6 Delegates should be allowed maximum freedom possible in making personal decisions, e.g. about use of their time, attending sessions, when to go to bed, etc.

7 We chose not to have any publicity at the meeting, but if newspaper, radio or TV reports of the conference are made the delegates themselves should make statements.

8 The delegates should receive the conference report and the conference organisers should be prepared to offer continuing support, e.g. in arranging follow-up meetings locally if delegates request this.

2 Programme of the 'Our Life' Conference, 1972

Friday, 14 July

5.30 p.m.	Reception of participants at Castle Priory College. Distribution of conference material.
7.00 p.m.	Supper.
8.00 p.m.	Welcome and Introduction. Division into groups and getting to know each other. Coffee bar open at 9.30 p.m.

Saturday, 15 July

8.45 a.m.	Breakfast.
9.30 a.m.	*How would we like to live?* Group discussion.
11.00 a.m.	Coffee.
11.30 a.m.	Painting on the lawn.
12.45 p.m.	Lunch.
2.00 p.m.	*How would we like to work?* Group discussion.
3.30 p.m.	Films.
4.00 p.m.	Tea.
4.30 p.m.	Football match or free period.
6.00 p.m.	Boat ride on the Thames.
7.30 p.m.	Supper party with guests from Oxford.
8.30 p.m.	An Evening of Music with The Van Walsum Ensemble – Christopher Nicholls : Flute Andrew Cauthery : Oboe

Robert Codd : Bassoon
Howard Davidson : Clarinet
Russell Hayward : Horn
Coffee bar open at 10.00 p.m.

Sunday, 16 July

8.45 a.m.	Breakfast.
9.30 a.m.	*What would we like to do with our leisure time?* Group discussion.
11.00 a.m.	Coffee.
11.30 a.m.	A ride in the country or records in the coffee bar (most people had another working session).
1.00 p.m.	Lunch.
2.00 p.m.	Reports of groups and final discussion.
3.00 p.m.	Tea.
4.15 p.m.	Depart for Didcot station.

3 The Constitution of the Avro Adult Training Centre Students' Council

1 There will be 10 councillors who will attend Council meetings for one year.
2 Every September there will be a voting day when every person attending the Centre can vote for the people they want to be their representative.
3 Only those people attending the Centre can vote for councillors.
4 For people who cannot read the names on the voting form, the list will be read to them by a person who can read, but each person must choose for themselves the people they want to vote for. The person who reads the list must not say who to vote for. Each person can vote for 10 people on the list.
5 Every person's vote will be private and secret. When they have filled in the form it will be put in a sealed ballot box.
6 Each person can only fill in one form. Their name will be ticked off a list when it is given to them. If they make a mistake on the form, they must hand it in before being given another one. The spoiled form will then be torn up.
7 Polling booths that are private must be provided before voting takes place.
8 Every person who attends the Centre has the right to put their name forward to become a councillor.
9 Two weeks before voting day there will be an election campaign when people who want to become councillors can make a poster and give a speech saying why they feel they can represent others, how they can help to improve the Centre and deal with people's

problems and complaints.

10 When the voting has finished the box will be unsealed and the votes counted. The counting can be done by the staff but there must be at least two people who attend the Centre present who can read and count to make sure the counting is correct.

11 The ten people with the most number of votes will be announced as that year's Council.

12 Councillors will be expected to take their place on the council very seriously.

13 The Council will meet once a week and every councillor will be expected to attend if they are in the Centre on that day.

14 Once the Council is formed they will decide among themselves who will be Chairman, Vice-Chairman, Secretary and Treasurer.

15 The Chairman's job will be to bring the meeting to order and make sure that each councillor has a chance to speak. The Chairman will make sure that only one person talks at a time, and the agenda is followed.

16 The Vice-Chairman's job will be to stand in for the Chairman if he or she is absent.

17 The Secretary's job will be to make the telephone calls and write letters dealing with things the Council have discussed. The Secretary must prepare the agenda before the meeting, of matters to be discussed at the meeting.

18 The Treasurer's job will be to make sure that there is money available for stamps, envelopes and paper.

19 Every councillor will keep a file of each week's agendas and minutes.

20 Each councillor will be responsible to one morning group. This means he or she must keep the group informed of what the Council is doing. Most important, he or she must ask the Secretary to put on the agenda any queries or problems the people in that morning group have talked about. The minutes of each meeting will be given to each morning group and discussed.

21 If a councillor decides they no longer want to do the job, the person on that year's voting form who had the most number of votes next on the list can take this place.

22 The aim of the Council is to make sure that we are all treated fairly and as people with our own likes and dislikes.

23 We have the right to be treated like any other human being without being labelled retarded or subnormal.

24 We have the same rights as other people and we will fight to make sure we get them. When we do stand up for what we believe people should have the decency to listen to us.

25 We have the right to go into the community when we please and

do the same things as other people do.

26 We have the right to vote in all elections if we are over 18 years of age.

27 We have the right to become independent and choose where we want to live and who we want to live with.

28 We have the right to love and be with the person we love.

29 We have the right to education and training that will help us to become more independent.

30 We have the right to work.

31 We have the right to say 'no' to something we don't want to do.

32 We have the right to stand up for ourselves, or speak out for others, if we are abused or treated in a degrading way.

33 We have the right to suggest ways of improving the Centre.

34 We have the right to have our point of view listened to, and if we feel we are being treated unfairly, or asked to do something we don't want to do, for this to be discussed with the Manager and Instructor in front of us.

35 The General Assembly of the United Nations have a declaration of rights for disabled people that says:

'Disabled people have the inherent right to respect for their human dignity.

'Disabled people, whatever the origin, nature of seriousness of their handicap, have the same fundamental rights as their fellow citizens, which implies first and foremost the right to enjoy a decent life as normal and full as possible.'

The most important of these is our right to respect for our human dignity. We will fight until everyone knows this and understands this.

We are on the move towards a better understanding and nothing placed in our way will stop us.

4 Key Sources of Information (added for 1991 reprint)

People First London will give advice on the setting up of self-advocacy groups; they also have a regular newsletter.

Values Into Action have produced a series of booklets designed to explain what self-advocacy is and how to set up and run a group. The materials are called *LASA — Learning About Self-Advocacy* and are designed for use by people with learning difficulties themselves, with whatever support they need. VIA also has other publications on self-advocacy.

The National Bureau for Handicapped Students has published a book and a video called *We Can Change the Future*. They are designed to explain to service staff and advisers to groups what self-advocacy is and how to support it.

Skills For People has published a pack of materials designed to help individual people with learning difficulties develop the skills, knowledge and confidence for better personal self-advocacy.

Courses on self-advocacy are put on by Skills For People, the City Literary Institute and Castle Priory College. A course which includes elements of self-advocacy is also available for people with learning difficulties from the Open University (a special version of their course 'Patterns for Living'). Other sources of information include the Norah Fry Research Centre, Bristol, the National Institute of Adult Continuing Education project in Luton, and the Further Education Unit, London.

Addresses of all these organisations are in Appendix 6.

Last-minute Addresses in Britain
Further Education Unit, 2 Orange Street, London WC2H 7WE.
National Institute of Adult Continuing Education, Charles Street Adult Education Centre, Charles Street, Luton LU2 0EB.
People First Wales, c/o SCOVO, 5 Dock Chambers, Bute Street, Cardiff CF1 6AG.

6 ADDRESSES OF ORGANISATIONS

This list has been updated for the 1991 reprint and some organisations referred to in the text may not now appear here — see Postscript below.

America and abroad

Association for Retarded Citizens of the United States, PO Box 6109, ARLINGTON, Texas 76005, USA.

Centre on Human Policy, Syracuse University, 200 Huntington Hall, SYRACUSE, New York 13244-2340, USA.

Centres for Independent Living, World Institute on Disability, 510 16th Street, OAKLAND, California 94612, USA.

G. Allan Roeher Institute (formerly National Institute on Mental Retardation), 4700 Keele Street, Downsview, ONTARIO M3J 1P3, Canada.

Georgia Advocacy Office, 1447 Peachtree Street NE, ATLANTA, Georgia 30309, USA.

International League of Societies for People with Mental Handicap, 13 rue Forestiere, B-1050, BRUSSELS, Belgium.

Kansas University Affiliated Facility, 348 Haworth Hall, LAWRENCE, Kansas 66045, USA.

People First of Canada, G. Allan Roeher Institute, 4700 Keele Street, Downsview, ONTARIO M3J 1P3, Canada.

People First International, PO Box 12642, SALEM, Oregon 97309, USA.

People First of Nebraska, 2501 N Street, LINCOLN, Nebraska 68510, USA.

People First of Washington State, PO Box 381, TACOMA, Washington 98401, USA.

Portland State University, Department of Special Education, PO Box 751, PORTLAND, Oregon 97207, USA.

Project Two, c/o Greater Omaha Association for Retarded Citizens, 3610 Dodge Street, OMAHA Nebraska 68131, USA.

Research and Training Centre on Community Living, Institute on Community Integration, Minnesota University, Pattee Hall, 150 Pillsbury Drive SE, MINNEAPOLIS, Minnesota 55455, USA.

Responsive Systems Associates, 58 Willowick Drive, LITHONIA, Georgia 30038, USA.

Texas Association for Retarded Citizens, 833 Houston Street, AUSTIN, Texas 78756, USA.

Training Institute for Human Service Planning, Leadership and Change Agentry, Syracuse University, 805 South Crouse Avenue, SYRACUSE, New York 13244-2280, USA.

Wisconsin Association for Retarded Citizens, 2700 Laura Lane, MIDDLETON, Wisconsin 53562, USA.

Britain and Northern Ireland

Association of Professions for Mentally Handicapped People, Greytree Lodge, Second Avenue, Greytree, ROSS-ON-WYE, Herefordshire HR9 7HT.

Belfast Self-Advocacy Group, Bryson House, 28 Bedford Street, BELFAST BT2 7FE.

British Council of Organisations of Disabled People, St Mary's Church, Greenlaw Street, LONDON SE18.

British Institute of Mental Handicap, Wolverhampton Road, KIDDERMINSTER, Worcestershire DY10 3PP.

Castle Priory College (The Spastics Society), Thames Street, WALLINGFORD, Oxfordshire OX10 0HE.

City Literary Institute, Stukeley Street, Drury Lane, LONDON WC2.

Community and Mental Handicap Educational and Research Association (CMHERA), 27 Kenilworth Gardens, MELKSHAM, Wiltshire SN12 6AF.

Concord Films Council, 201 Felixstowe Road, IPSWICH, Suffolk IP3 9BJ.

King's Fund Centre, 126 Albert Street, LONDON NW1 7NF.

MENCAP (Royal Society for Mentally Handicapped Children and Adults), 123 Golden Lane, LONDON EC1Y 0RT.

MIND (National Association for Mental Health), 22 Harley Street, LONDON W1N 2ED.

National Bureau for Handicapped Students, 336 Brixton Road, LONDON SW9 7AA.

National Citizen Advocacy, 2 St Paul's Road, LONDON N1 2QR.

Norah Fry Research Centre, Bristol University, 32 Tyndall's Park Road, BRISTOL BS8 1PY.

Open University, Department of Health and Social Welfare, Walton Hall, MILTON KEYNES MK7 6AA.

People First London, Oxford House, Derbyshire Street, LONDON E2 6HG.

Rowntree Memorial Trust, The Homestead, 40 Water End, YORK YO3 6LP.

Skills For People, Haldane House, Tankerville Terrace, JESMOND, Newcastle-upon-Tyne NE2 3AH.

Values Into Action (VIA), Oxford House, Derbyshire Street, LONDON E2 6HG.

POSTSCRIPT, 1991

Introduction
It is ten years since this book was written. We believe that at the time it was the very first substantial book in the world on self-advocacy by people with learning difficulties. A reprint of the book in its original form is worthwhile, since it represents a history of the early development of self-advocacy and contains advice and suggestions that are still valid. This postscript attempts to give an update on more recent developments.

We, the authors, have both changed jobs. Bonnie Shoultz is Associate Director of the Research and Training Centre on Community Integration at the Centre on Human Policy, Syracuse University, New York. Paul Williams is Director of the Community and Mental Handicap Educational and Research Association, in England.

One thing we regret about this book is the terminology we used. The term 'mental handicap' is almost universally rejected by self-advocacy groups themselves. In Britain, the term 'people with learning difficulties' is preferred by most groups, and it is the term we use in this postscript. Unfortunately in this reprint of the original book, the persistent use of 'mental handicap' has had to remain. (It also remains in the title of CMHERA, a fact that it is hoped to change soon.)

If we were writing the book today, the list of acknowledgements would be longer. In particular we need to thank the Centre on Human Policy, Syracuse, and People First London, for support in preparing this postscript.

The original list of useful addresses is now substantially out of date. We have replaced it with a new list of useful contacts for information. As a consequence, some organisations referred to in the text may not now be found in the address list. However, we think that the new address list should enable readers to obtain any information they require.

Update on Project Two and People First of Nebraska
Project Two in Omaha is still in existence, although it now tends to put more emphasis on social activities. It is run under the auspices of the Greater Omaha Association for Retarded Citizens which has appointed a staff member to be Project Two's adviser. It is often better for groups not to be too closely associated, in terms of control and influence, with services or other organisations. Greater freedom may be a useful future

development for Project Two, but we are pleased to report its survival and the continuation of its work. Tom Houlihan is still in regular contact with his friends in England.

Project Two is one of eight local groups or 'chapters' that form People First of Nebraska. One major activity of the group in recent years has been to work directly with the state legislature to remove outdated terminology from legal statutes. In 1987, People First of Nebraska received a grant to employ one of their members, Nancy Ward, as paid Director. She has an advisory board and 'mentors' to help her with record keeping and other office work. Group members form the Board of Directors which sets policy. Shirley Dean, one of the advisers to Project Two ten years ago, is now adviser to People First of Nebraska.

Update on Self-Advocacy in the United States
The Association for Retarded Citizens of the United States recently listed 380 self-advocacy groups, and it is thought this is an underestimate. There are now many statewide organisations, including People First of Washington State, with 45 local chapters, Speaking For Ourselves in Pennsylvania, with six local groups, People First of Tennessee with 12 groups, Speaking For Ourselves of Colorado with 14 local chapters, and many more.

Some examples of their work include the following: People First of Washington runs projects to help individual members with self-advocacy skills. Training materials for members and advisers have been produced and are available at small cost. Through grant funding several people are employed, some with disabilities, directed by a Board of Directors drawn from the members. People First of Tennessee has worked on developing means of monitoring the quality of services that can be used directly by consumers. Speaking For Ourselves of Pennsylvania has concentrated on supporting members on local and state-wide policy-making committees. Speaking For Ourselves of Colorado hosted a national conference of United States self-advocacy groups during 1990. At this conference the decision was taken to form a national self-advocacy organisation for the whole United States.

Self-Advocacy in Other Countries
Self-advocacy has continued to develop in other parts of the world, including Scandinavia, Britain, Ireland, Switzerland, Holland, Australia, New Zealand and Canada. In Canada, the G. Allan Roeher Institute (formerly the National Institute on Mental Retardation) has supported the development of a National People First Project, run by an Advisory Board of members of local self-advocacy groups throughout Canada, and employing a person with learning difficulties and an adviser. The Project publishes a newsletter, *The National Organiser*, which provides information and communication between self-advocacy groups. At present the Project is working on a constitution and developing

its organisational structure, and will soon become People First of Canada.

International Links with Britain

It is interesting that several self-advocacy groups have sought international links from a very early stage in their existence. The state-wide group in Oregon called itself 'People First International', particularly developing links with Canadian groups, and is still in existence under that name. In 1984, People First of Washington organised an international conference in Tacoma to which they gave wide publicity in other countries. Funding was raised in Britain for a group of people with learning difficulties, with some non-disabled supporters, to go to the conference. They came back inspired with the idea of self-advocacy, and founded a group that, unlike most other groups in Britain, was completely independent of services — People First London and Thames Region. Their first newsletter included several letters of support from the international contacts they had made at the conference and had developed since, from as far afield as Australia and the United States.

At the Tacoma conference it was decided that the next international self-advocacy conference would be held in London in 1988, and this duly took place, organised by People First London (as they now are).

One of the British participants at the Tacoma conference was Alison Wertheimer, then Director of CMH — the Campaign for People with Mental Handicaps (now Values Into Action). As a result, CMH made American materials on self-advocacy available in Britain, including those from People First of Washington. CMH also embarked on a project to create some British materials to help people with learning difficulties to understand and develop self-advocacy.

A further link between the United States and Britain came through the work of John O'Brien of Responsive Systems Associates in Georgia. John is a skilled facilitator of self-advocacy meetings and conferences, and has been a regular visitor to Britain since the early 1980s. His facilitation of meetings in both the United States and Britain has served to foster common understandings and links. Two examples are a meeting in North Wales facilitated by John in 1984, which led to a report on participation, and a meeting in conjunction with the annual convention of the American Association on Mental Retardation in 1990, from which a report and audiotape are available (from the Research and Training Centre on Community Living, University of Minnesota).

The international conference held in London in 1988 was a great success and was attended by over 300 people from many countries of the world, including Ireland, Australia, Canada, parts of Europe, and several American states.

Further Developments in Britain

There have been inevitable disappointments in the development of self-advocacy in Britain. For example, the Avro Students' Council was not given the support it needed by the Social Services Department and declined in its activities, morale and pioneering spirit. However, there is much to show that is impressive and exciting.

People First London now has a grant from the Rowntree Trust for an office, staffed by two workers, one of whom is Gary Bourlet, formerly President of People First London. Although particularly concerned to develop and support self-advocacy groups in London, the group is in effect a national body for advice and support to groups throughout the country. Gary and other members of the group are able to give advice by telephone or letter, or in many cases to visit groups to give talks, suggestions and information. A regular newsletter is produced, with information about developments throughout Britain and abroad as well as in London.

People First London organised a national conference of British self-advocacy groups in August 1990 at which the process was set in motion of founding an official national organisation — UK People First. Meanwhile People First Wales was founded in March 1991.

The City Literary Institute in London has for many years run courses on self-advocacy for people with learning difficulties, developed by John Hersov who has been one of the foremost non-disabled supporters of the development of self-advocacy in Britain, making many visits and giving many talks to inspire people with the idea: In 1986 Deborah Cooper and John Hersov produced a book and videotape, *We Can Change the Future*, published by the National Bureau for Handicapped Students, designed to inform and provide a resource for advisers to self-advocacy groups.

A self-advocacy group that has, in alliance with non-disabled people, run many training events to develop knowledge and skills of self-advocacy, is the Newcastle-based group 'Skills For People'. They have an office base with employed staff and funding from a wide range of sources and have published a pack of text, audiotape and videotape called *Speaking For Ourselves*, designed to help individuals develop self-advocacy skills.

CMH (now VIA — Values Into Action) produced their materials to inform and support people with learning difficulties in their development of self-advocacy. They are in the form of five booklets under the title *LASA — Learning About Self-Advocacy*. These cover: an introduction to self-advocacy; starting up a group; running a group; developing the group's work (newsletters, conferences, public speaking); and basic skills that help (communication, listening, decision-taking, problem-solving).

Bronach Crawley carried out a further survey of the extent of self-advocacy in Britain in 1988. This was published by CMH (VIA) under the title *The Growing Voice*, and it shows a substantial increase in the number of groups within day and residential services for people with learning difficulties.

A number of local self-advocacy conferences have been held and several groups have produced reports, newsletters, teaching materials and videos. An example of the latter is a video entitled *The Way We Are*, made and distributed by the Belfast Self-Advocacy Group, Northern Ireland.

The Open University has contributed to the development of self-advocacy by producing a version of their course 'Patterns For Living' for people with learning difficulties and, as part of a follow-up course, 'Changing Perspectives', by publishing an anthology of accounts and expressions of their lives and views by people with learning difficulties: *Know Me As I Am* (edited by Dorothy Atkinson and Fiona Williams and published by Hodder and Stoughton).

Some Themes in the Development of Self-Advocacy

a)   *'Kraft Cheese Advocacy'*
There has been a tremendous tendency to latch onto the word 'self-advocacy' to describe a vast range of activities of people with learning difficulties. Thus, we have heard a group set up to maintain discipline amongst users of a day service described as a self-advocacy group; we have seen pictures of people engaged in childlike finger-painting, and another of people simply having lunch, described as illustrations of self-advocacy; and we have heard at a conference the choosing of what socks to wear in the morning described as self-advocacy. There has even been a tendency to use the term 'self-advocate' as a generic term for anyone with learning difficulties!

b)   *Links with Other Organisations*
To get started and to maintain their activities, self-advocacy groups need a lot of support. Often services, parents' groups and other bodies will very helpfully assist, but there is a risk that the association and consequent control and influence will become too great. In the United States, groups that have been strongly associated with the local Association for Retarded Citizens seem generally to have been less pioneering and effective than genuinely independent groups. In Britain the establishment of independent groups has been very disappointing; there seems almost to have been an assumption that groups will always be associated with a day or residential service.

On the positive side, interest is growing in an alliance between self-advocacy groups of people with learning difficulties and groups of people with other difficulties or disabilities. In the United States, and occasionally in Britain, some groups have opened membership to people with any disability. In Britain, People First London is exploring links with groups of people with physical disabilities, of people with mental health problems, and of people from ethnic minorities. Correspondingly, there is

growing interest in self-advocacy groups of people with learning difficulties within such organisations as the British Council of Organisations
of Disabled People. Also, a number of professional organisations,
parents' groups, universities and other bodies have found ways to support
the self-advocacy movement without dominating it. In America, the
Association for Retarded Citizens of the United States, the American
Association on Mental Retardation, the Centre on Human Policy at
Syracuse University, the Research and Training Centre on Community
Living at the University of Minnesota, and many other similar bodies,
have been helpful. In Britain such supportive organisations would include
Values Into Action, MENCAP, the King's Fund Centre, the Norah Fry
Research Centre at Bristol University, the Open University, the
Association of Professions for Mentally Handicapped People, and the
British Institute of Mental Handicap.

c) *International Links*
It is very encouraging that the self-advocacy movement has developed
an international identity from a very early stage. The international
conferences now take place every four years; the 1992 conference will
be in Canada, and there is a suggestion that the next one may be in Ireland.
It is to be hoped that funding will be made available to enable this
international contact and solidarity to be maintained.

d) *Independent Funding*
A number of self-advocacy groups in the United States, and People First
London and some other groups in Britain, have managed to attract grant
funding to enable them to have an office base and to employ staff, often
members with learning difficulties. As with all grants, this funding tends
to be temporary, and the long-term funding of self-advocacy remains a
problem.

e) *Self-Advocacy and Community Participation*
Self-advocacy has generally developed in the context of philosophies and
changing service practices that are concerned to increase the status and
participation of people with disabilities in society. Self-advocacy groups
therefore often have a primary interest in supporting increased community
participation by members. There has also been a natural affinity between
support for self-advocacy and other developments such as the teaching and
implementation of normalisation and the establishment of citizen advocacy
schemes. The future may see some exciting partnerships between self-
advocacy groups, service planners and community groups to increase the
status and contribution of people with learning difficulties in their
communities.

f) *Self-Advocacy is Difficult*
A theme that has come out of many self-advocacy meetings and

conferences is that speaking up for oneself has costs. People are vulnerable and can be hurt, and often they need a lot of consistent, long-term support. In her surveys, Bronach Crawley has found that up to a third of groups that have started have eventually folded up, mainly because of lack of support, or premature withdrawal of support, from non-disabled people. An atmosphere of trust amongst members, trust by non-disabled supporters in the capacities of the group, and trust by the group in their advisers, is essential.

g)   *The Danger of Isolation*

Some other groups of oppressed people have felt that they need to organise themselves in self-contained independent associations in which they can foster solidarity and devise policies and actions that are their own, without outside control or influence. This has been a successful strategy for many groups, but it is possible that adoption of this course by people with learning difficulties will simply be one more way in which they become isolated from other people. The self-advocacy movement has often seemed to welcome the support of sensitive non-disabled people, and to welcome non-dominating alliances with other groups. It has sometimes been over-zealous 'helpers' who have pushed groups into trying to manage on their own, in pursuit of some concept of 'independence'. The role of adviser to self-advocacy groups remains crucial. Alongside the risk of a premature or unnecessary push to 'independence' are the risks of encouraging unhelpful militancy where that is against the inclinations of the group, and of treating the operation of the group as an educational exercise rather than one of rights.

h)   *A Genuine Voice*

Many individuals and representatives of self-advocacy groups have been genuinely involved as contributors in a wide range of contexts, including staff training, staff selection, planning meetings, committees and other consultations. One example is the commissioning in 1990, through People First London, of two people with learning difficulties, assisted by advisers, to evaluate community residential services in the London Borough of Hillingdon.

Summary

We have tried in this postscript to give a brief account of the very successful and encouraging development of self-advocacy by people with learning difficulties during the 1980s, and to identify some themes in that development that give pointers to the future. Hopefully this complements our original account of the early history of this exciting movement, and the practical suggestions that we included.

Paul Williams
Bonnie Shoultz
September 1991